Food and Nutrition in the Early Years

Carolyn Childs

Hodder & Stoughton

A MEMBER OF THE HODDER HEADLINE GROUP

Orders: please contact Bookpoint Ltd, 78 Milton Park, Abingdon, Oxon OX14 4TD. Telephone: (44) 01235 827720, Fax: (44) 01235 400454. Lines are open from 9.00–6.00, Monday to Saturday, with a 24-hour message answering service. Email address: orders@bookpoint.co.uk

British Library Cataloguing in Publication Data
A catalogue record for this title is available from The British Library

ISBN 0 340 772 697

First published 2001
Impression number   10 9 8 7 6 5 4 3 2 1
Year   2005 2004 2003 2002 2001

Copyright © 2001 Carolyn Childs

Cover illustration by Debbie Tonge
Typeset by Multiplex Techniques, St Mary Cray, Kent
Printed in Great Britain for Hodder & Stoughton Educational, a division of Hodder Headline Plc, 338 Euston Road, London NW1 3BH by Martins the Printers Ltd., Spittal, Berwick upon Tweed.

Contents

Foreword   iv
Acknowledgements   v

Chapter 1: Thinking About Food   1

Chapter 2: Food, Nutrition and How the Body Works   22

Chapter 3: The Seven Essential Nutrients   36

Chapter 4: Nutritional Needs: Making Sense of the   66
Five Food Groups

Chapter 5: Providing a Healthy Start in Life   84

Chapter 6: Weaning: from Milk to Food in Easy Stages!   112

Chapter 7: Life After Weaning: or Not Biting Off   138
More Than You Can Chew

Chapter 8: Social Factors and Children's Eating   158

Chapter 9: Understanding and Supporting Special   180
Requirements

Chapter 10: Food, Health, Safety and Hygiene   211

Chapter 11: Eating and Dental Health   237

Chapter 12: Children, Food and Education   254

Practical Teaching Resources   286
Addresses for Resources   289
Food and Nutrition Contact Addresses   291
Contacts for Information on Pregnancy and Babies   292
Organisations   293
References   294
Index   296

Foreword

As well as being fundamental to living, eating is also associated with strong feelings and patterns of behaviour. These feelings start from birth and continue to develop throughout childhood. They can have an effect on the way we live the rest of our lives.

As a General Practitioner, I deal directly with the effects of diet and health. Obesity and eating disorders are now more common than health problems associated with deficiency. A great deal of my work is trying to put right illness and disease brought on by eating the wrong sorts of food over a period of time. How and what we eat is possibly the major factor in determining our overall health and well-being. Very simply, the better your diet, the better chance you have of living a long, healthy life.

What is a healthy diet? How do you advise children, and assess their diets? How can good eating habits be encouraged? Which media headlines are based on reliable and well-researched information, and which are mis-information, rumours, myths or scares? Knowing what to believe and how to interpret important issues into good practice for ourselves and our children is very difficult. This minefield is navigated daily by parents and professionals involved in childcare.

Carolyn Childs' book is an excellent and comprehensive volume which will prove invaluable for surviving this minefield. Her years of experience in the childcare field has helped her to provide common sense information, and a down to earth picture of what works with children. The book not only deals with the content of children's diets, but also the context – a subject rarely tackled. I hope it might help reduce the epidemic of eating disorders and obesity I will see in the future. A thoroughly recommended book, for parents and childcare professionals alike.

Dr Peter Campbell
MA (Cantab) MBBS (London) DCH DRCOG MRCGP

Acknowledgements

Elizabeth Tribe (Editorial Director: Hodder and Stoughton Educational): for asking me to write this book and for persevering in her request until I agreed to do so, for her generous support and invaluable expertise, and for maintaining her sense of humour whilst sustaining mine throughout the project.

Audrey Wright BSc Dip Ed: for her patience, sensitivity and sheer creative and technical brilliance in providing the best photographs I could have wished for.

Sarah-Louise Childs; Gill Taylor BSc Hons (Health Studies). RGN. RHV. Cert Ed; and Scott Marsden BSc SRD: for generously giving vast amounts of their time, energy and expertise to advise and support me throughout the writing of the book; and for their wisdom, clarity of thought and unerring abilities to communicate pertinent criticism in a good humoured and positive manner!

John Gregg BA Hons: for helping to bring 'Flossie', her quirky thoughts and everyday problems to life through his wonderful illustrations.

Dr Peter Campbell MA (Cantab). MBBS (London). DCH. DRCOG. MRCGP: for his expert advice, unstinting friendship, love of good food, and for writing the Foreword.

My very grateful thanks go to: **Gordon, Felix & Oscar; Caroline & Stephen; Becky, Jenny & Ben; Helen, Neil, Callum & Chloe; Morgan, Carole & Audrey; Georgia; Carolyne, Nicole & Jennifer; Philip & Sarah; Ross & Anna; Edward & Eveline Gay of Riddlecombe Manor Farm; and the staff & children of Byron Nursery, Infant & Junior Schools, Thornton Heath Early Years Centre and St Piers School** for their help with the photographs, and for agreeing to allow me to include them in the book. *Every effort has been made to seek permission appertaining to the photographs. For the very few parents with whom I and the schools have been unable to make direct contact, I hope they are as delighted as I am with the images shown and the value they add to the text. Any ensuing enquiries will be willingly addressed by the publishers.*

For help during my researching I am grateful to:

Clare Ingram (Croydon College), **Peter Winder** (Wolsey Junior School), and **Alison Worwood** (Croydon Community Dietitian), and to **Michael Leach** (Chairman FAIA). And also to: **Maggie Anderson** & **Cathy Payne** (Byron Infant School), **Christine Heasman** (Kingsley Primary School), **Chris Lawrence** (Thornton Heath Early Years Centre): for generously allowing me to tap their vast collective expertise about parents, staff and young children, and for remaining my good friends whilst I made a great nuisance of myself!

Finally my thanks and love go to **Paul** especially for those days when writing a book on nutrition has meant my producing chapters rather than meals; to **Sarah** and **David**, on whom throughout their lives I have shamelessly trialled all my theories and who thankfully appear to the naked eye to have survived unscathed; and above all to **Margaret** and **John**, for their child care expertise and nurturing, and without whom this book would not have been written.

1
Thinking about Food

Aims of the Chapter

To enable you to understand:

- the definition of health and links between health and diet
- how children develop healthy eating habits and attitudes
- what is meant by 'a healthy diet'
- misunderstandings about eating and what to believe about eating well
- some common food myths, fallacies and old wives' tales.

As Flossie's food and nutrition course had emphasised the need to combine regular eating with daily exercise, she now watched her aerobics video twice during dinner.

The definition of health and links between health and diet

It is the right of every child to be well cared for with love and understanding, to be helped to develop and grow and to enjoy good health.

Being healthy is much more than the opposite of being ill. It is a positive and active state.

The World Health Organisation's definition of health is that it is:

'a state of complete social, mental and physical well-being and not merely the absence of disease or infirmity'.

Being healthy means that the likelihood of imminent or future ill health is minimised and there is a state of mental and physical fitness. Eating the right diet is vital for achieving good health.

Happiness and health go together.

Adults need to understand what constitutes a health-promoting diet. With this knowledge they can eat for their own health, feed their children well and also teach them good eating habits for life.

How children develop healthy eating habits and attitudes

Early influences and eating

As with every other aspect of bringing up children, understanding about healthy eating is best learned from adults who actually practise what they preach. Children will not be readily convinced to try a new food or recipe by an adult who is very reticent themselves or who provides a poor role model.

As a professional working with young children it is therefore very important to consider your own attitudes to food and to eating.

Although we may develop different tastes and preferences as we grow older, our fundamental attitudes to food and to eating are formed in childhood. Consequently the experiences and messages that early years professional workers give to children are very likely to affect them for life. Obviously you want to ensure you provide the children in your care with the best opportunities to learn to eat for good health.

Before considering the specialist knowledge and professional skills you need to do this successfully, it may be useful to think back to your own upbringing and childhood experiences, and to look at your present views of food, diet and eating.

ACTIVITY

1. Try to recollect some experiences from your childhood, linked with food. Discuss your memories with a colleague.

▶ Can you remember your favourite foods? Did you have them frequently or only as treats? Are they still your favourites today?
▶ What can you remember about other members of your family and eating? Was anyone ever 'on a diet'?
▶ Were there times you all had a meal sitting together? Did everyone eat the same food at mealtimes? Was there much conversation?
▶ What were mealtimes like for you as a child?
▶ Did any of your friends come to eat at your house? Did you visit friends for meals?
▶ As a young child were you ever involved in choosing menus, shopping, setting the table, cooking or washing up?
▶ What happened when you or a brother or sister did not want to eat some foods?
▶ What is the happiest memory you have that involves something to do with food?

2. Looking back now, how do you view your own preferences and behaviour, and the actions and ideas of the adults who were involved?

3. What views do you now have about 'children' and 'eating'?

Adult behaviours and expectations, such as strictness and sanctions at mealtimes can affect children's attitudes for life. Children are easily influenced by eating attitudes, preferences or food fads of adults close to them. Moreover aspects of eating disorders and poor nutritional practices can be readily picked up and copied, even by young children.

⚠️ **ALERT**

It is important for your own health and for the health and education of the children in your professional care, that you are honest with yourself about your own eating habits.

These days more and more people seem to spend their lives 'being on a diet' or in 'yo-yo' dieting. 'Diets' as such do not effectively bring about a maintained improvement in health, body weight or shape. Any physical changes are usually short term and do not promote good health. (What is more, research shows that bouts of restricted dieting interspersed with returning to previous eating habits actually cause decline in both the proportion of lean body tissue and in overall health.) A long-term commitment to bettering what and how you eat can certainly go a long way towards changing how you look and feel. Eating healthily and taking regular exercise can make you feel good and maintain your health.

ACTIVITY

Consider as honestly as you can some of your own attitudes to eating and food.

▶ Do you regularly try to lose weight?
▶ Do you usually eat with other people or alone?
▶ Do you eat breakfast?
▶ Do you have snacks between meals?
▶ Do you eat regular meals?
▶ Do you feel it is very wrong to eat 'junk food'?
▶ Do you often eat or drink when you are not really hungry, perhaps for comfort or when bored?
▶ Do you eat and then wish you had not?
▶ Are you happy with your eating, your attitudes to food and yourself?

- - - - - - -*Good professional practice*- - - - - - -

If you think you would like some personal nutritional advice or a personal health check your doctor or practice nurse can help. If you wish further guidance you can request your doctor refers you to a dietician. By taking this step to help yourself, you may be significantly helping the many young children that you will care for and influence.

What is meant by a 'healthy diet'?

It might seem from all the frequent and conflicting reports in the press and media about eating, health and food that there is no solid, reliable information. Experts constantly seem to disagree and we feel unsure of who or what to believe.

Food safety issues affect everyone. Some foods are said to be 'good' and then designated 'bad'. Media headlines are designed to make an impact, to sell newspapers but not primarily to educate. Sensationalised food scares leave people feeling confused, worried or cynical.

In reality however, sound nutritional information is widely available. Understanding of the links between food quality, nutrition, health and disease is now greater than ever before. Causes of eating disorders and food-related diseases are well researched and information is publicly available. There is reliable evidence that proves a person's diet has a significant influence on their health. There is secure agreement worldwide between highly respected, qualified experts as to what actually constitutes a health promoting diet and one which guards against poor health, illness and disease.

A 'healthy diet' can be defined by conforming to two facts.

- It must ensure an adequate provision of energy and essential nutrients to gain and maintain health.
- It must contain the correct balance of nutrients to prevent the occurrence of nutrition related health problems.

It is not helpful to think of different foods as being 'good' or 'bad' for you. Chocolate may be thought to be 'bad' as it usually contains high proportions of fat and sugar, but it is also a source of iron! Burgers contain protein but also a high proportion of fat.

Healthy eating:

- does not mean that some foods are compulsory while others are forbidden
- relies on eating a good range of different foods ('variety is the spice of life!')
- means you eat enough of some foods and not too much of others
- depends on having the right balance of foods in your diet.

The Department of Health has issued eight guidelines for ensuring a healthy diet.

- **If you do drink alcohol, stay within sensible limits.** Adults should be careful about alcohol. Moderate drinking, such as a daily glass or two of red wine, may even be beneficial. But heavy drinking can cause irreversible damage and excessive drinking can be lethal.
- **Do not eat sugary foods too often.** Sugar-rich foods and drinks are fine as a small part of your diet but they provide few nutrients. Eating too many fills you up and so replaces foods which are nutritious and needed by the body.
- **Do not eat too much fat.** Foods that are high in fat or cooked in fat directly increase the risk of heart disease and are a key cause of obesity.
- **Eat fresh foods rich in vitamins and minerals.** Fruit and vegetables contain nutrients which protect against heart disease and many types of cancer. Until recently 'TAKE 5' was the adopted slogan. Now nutritionists are recommending everyone has *at least six portions* each day.
- **Eat plenty of foods rich in fibre and starch.** Foods rich in fibre and in starch contain important nutrients and also help to fill you up without having a high number of calories.
- **Eat the right amount to be healthy.** Eating the right amount helps to keep to a healthy weight, and provides optimum nutrition. Do not eat more than you need as obesity is a major contributor to ill health.

Finally . . .

• **Eat a variety of different foods.** Eating a wide variety of different foods helps to ensure you have a wide range of all the necessary nutrients and guards against dietary imbalance and deficiencies.

And always remember to:

• **Enjoy your food,** it is one of life's pleasures! Enjoy the fact it is giving you energy and making you healthy.

. . . these last two guidelines contain the key to ensuring a healthy diet.

— — — — — — — — — — —*Key point:*— — — — — — — — — — —

Healthy eating means getting the right overall balance of the food you need. Healthy eating means balancing the type, amount and pattern of food consumed over time.

ACTIVITY

1. On a blank piece of paper jot down when and what you ate and drank yesterday and also for today. Think carefully and *include everything that passed your lips.* Do it as accurately and as honestly as you can. It is to give *you* information and is not a test! Remember to put down everything you ate and drank – and remember that enjoying food is one of life's pleasures!

2. Using your notes consider the following:

▶ Look at the times and frequency of your eating.
▶ What is the first thing you had this morning?
▶ What time was this?
▶ How long was it between the last food you ate yesterday and the first you ate today?
▶ Are there some main meals recorded?
▶ What are the shortest and the longest times during the day between food?
▶ How many cups of tea or coffee did you drink?
▶ How many litres of water (or part of a litre) do you estimate you drank yesterday?
▶ Put a star against any times when you ate or drank alone.
▶ Underline any foods or drinks that you think were 'healthy'.
▶ Circle any foods you think were not 'healthy' or that afterwards you wished you had not eaten!

3. Do these notes reflect your usual patterns of eating and drinking or did something extraordinary happen yesterday or today to make it unusual?

4. Do you consider yourself to be on 'a diet' at the moment?

5. Use the list of food, drinks and the times of consumption you have recorded for *yesterday*. Fill in the following chart. Each column relates to a different food group. Each serving or portion of food counts as '1' and should be charted under the appropriate food group heading.

Identifying your dietary balance & patterns of eating by food groups & times					
FOOD GROUPS	Cereal/ Potato	Fruit/Veg/ Salads	Dairy/ Milk	Meat/Fish Alternative	Sugary/ Fat-rich
EXAMPLES of FOODS: remember each serving item or portion eaten scores '1'	Serving of pasta, rice potatoes, cereal slice of bread, etc.	Serving of raw or cooked vegetable, portion of salad, piece of fruit fruit/veg. juice	Pot of yoghurt $\frac{1}{4}$pt milk: as a drink in tea or in coffee/on cereal. Piece of cheese	Portion of meat or fish or chicken. Serving of lentils peas, beans or soya. 1–2 eggs	2–3 biscuits. Bag crisps. Pkt sweets. Bar of chocolate. Piece of cake. Scone & jam
Number of portions/items (each scoring '1') eaten at the following times					
Start of morning					
Breakfast					
Mid-morning					
Lunchtime					
Mid-afternoon					
Evening/ dinner time					
Bedtime					
TOTALS					

6. Compare your chart with the following ideal of the total number of daily portions or servings (from each of the five food groups) which are recommended for a healthy adult diet:

Recommended daily totals for an adult's healthy diet

Food groups:	Number of portions:
Cereals/Potatoes	5–7
Fruit/Vegetables	5–6
Milk/Dairy	3
Meat/Alternatives	2–3
Sugary/Fat-Rich	2

7. Using the completed chart and your notes, consider the pattern of your own eating and timing of meals.

▶ Is your eating: 'regular and planned' or 'variable' or 'erratic'?
▶ Breakfast: do you 'always have it', 'sometimes have it' or 'rarely or never have it'?
▶ Are there long gaps between eating?
▶ Is snacking usual and frequent?
▶ What kinds of snack foods do you eat?

8. Study your notes and answers carefully.

▶ Are there aspects of your eating you would like to change?
▶ Are you content that you eat as well as you can to promote your own health?
▶ Do you think you might like to receive further personal guidance?

9. Find out what nutritional or dietetic support is available locally to anyone who may want advice. Share this information with your group and compare the range and ease of access to the different sources.

Important:
Keep all your notes from this activity for future reference and for use in later activities.

■ ─ ■ ─ ■ ─ ■ ─ ■ ─ ■ ─ *Good professional practice* ■ ─ ■ ─ ■ ─ ■ ─ ■ ─ ■

Professionally it is important:

- to be aware of our own eating trends and habits in order to make healthy personal choices
- to be able to provide sound guidance and be good role models for the children in our care
- to remember that food and its related activities should be a source of pleasure and enjoyment.

Eating habits

Overall our food attitudes, preferences, likes and dislikes, are formed very early in life. The influence of parents and early childhood workers is of particular importance. The foods given in early childhood, the choices and range can affect a child's attitudes to eating.

How food and meals fit into family life is critical in establishing personal eating patterns. Families where members rarely manage to eat together, individually prepare their own meals and where eating is usually rushed, will present different learning opportunities for children than families who regularly sit and eat meals together. Even within a single family different circumstances can prevail. Some meals may involve everyone sitting and talking together at a table, handing round and sharing food. At other times meals may be rushed, eaten standing up or sitting in front of the television.

"Would you like one?"

Nursery and school meals and their arrangements are likely to present a young child with further perspectives of eating. Some school meals, routines and expectations may reflect home circumstances but many will be new. Unfamiliar foods and utensils may be introduced. Not all new intake children will have eaten at a table using a knife and fork. Some may only have eaten from a bowl and not from a plate. Others may be very adept with chopsticks but not with western cutlery.

New social behaviours and personal skills may be expected. Communal eating, particularly in a large hall, can be a very daunting new experience. For many young children mealtimes at nursery and at school are a source of anxiety. In their eyes, too many strange and uncontrollable factors may prevail.

▬ ▬ ▬ ▬ ▬ ▬ *Good professional practice* ▬ ▬ ▬ ▬ ▬ ▬

- An important task is to reassure young children about mealtimes.
- Careful observation will give you insight into a child's concerns.
- Talking with parents about their child and eating is essential.
- Explaining and discussing nursery routines and the help they will have with eating can allay most parents' or children's worries.
- Practical help and sensitive awareness of individual children's skills, understanding and needs are essential.

ACTIVITY

In your early childhood setting placement find out what information is available for parents about food and mealtimes. What are the day-to-day arrangements and routines? Are there guidelines for staff on the role of adults at children's mealtimes? When children do need help and assurance how are they supported? What improvements could you suggest?

Children, food and growth

Healthy eating is essential for all-round development and physical growth.

Individual children grow and develop at different rates. There are bands (*percentiles*) of growth, height and weight within which children may be expected to be measured at different ages. These standardised norms provide sound guidelines for parents, early childhood professionals and other health professionals.

— — — — — — — *Good professional practice* — — — — — — —

As a professional you are in an ideal situation to observe a child's development and growth, and moreover to note any lack of progress. Specific and ongoing observations which are carefully recorded give effective evidence of concerns and provide material for making assessments. Child growth charts (Child Growth Foundation, UK) can be used for monitoring and identifying concerns about growth measurements and patterns.

ALERT:
Any cause for concern must be discussed with the parents and always referred to the health visitor, general practitioner, attached medical officer or paediatrician.

Misunderstandings about eating and what to believe about eating well

There are numerous sayings and ideas concerned with food. Some are old and have been retold by generations. Some are very new. Some are correct. Many are basically wrong but harmless, and often entertaining. However, others do give seriously wrong messages. If believed they can cause anxiety. If followed they could cause nutritional problems.

ACTIVITY

1. It is said that 'eating carrots helps you to see in the dark'. Find out what is the element of nutritional truth which gave rise to this saying. If the lights fail would you supply everyone with a torch to use or a bunch of carrots to eat?

2. Note down as many sayings about food, drink and eating that you can recall. Share these with a colleague. Are any of the sayings new to either of you? Underline any you think may be truthful and have a sound origin. Discuss your reasons for choosing these.

Some food myths, fallacies and old wives' tales

Some of the most common misconceptions about nutrition that you might meet are shown below.

• **Some foods are 'good' for you and some are 'bad'.**
All foods provide some nutrients. The importance is the overall balance of foods that are eaten. Too much of some foods and not enough of others is a poor way to eat. Such a diet will not contain the required mixture of essential nutrients. There will be insufficient nutrients eaten to effectively enable the body to grow and repair, to fight infections and to support a healthy, energetic lifestyle. Healthy eating means getting the right overall balance, not banning or promoting specific foods.

ACTIVITY

Visit your local supermarket and obtain some leaflets about healthy eating. How well do they explain to the public at large how to achieve the right nutritional balance?

- 'Low fat' and 'reduced fat' foods are non-fattening and low in calories.

For adults:

Because of the benefits to health of eating less fat, low fat and reduced fat foods are a better choice than foods which are high fat content. They will contain less fat and fewer calories but they are certainly not calorie free. Although they are healthier they are not necessarily a healthy option.

In fact foods labelled 'reduced fat' can be quite high in calories and also still contain quite a lot of fat. The criterion for this title is for the product's fat content to be reduced by only 25%. Consequently 'reduced fat' foods can still contain a high quantity of fat. The important thing is to read labels carefully to see how much fat is still present in the product.

Even 'low fat' labelled foods need to be managed carefully. The critical matter is the quantity eaten. To take the mistaken view that it is all right to eat abundant quantities of a low fat product in the belief that the fat and calorie contents are inconsequential, may mean that just as many or even more calories are consumed than by eating a full fat variety.

ALERT
Low-fat foods or a reduced fat diet are not advocated for children. Unless specified medically any child under five years old should never be given low-fat products.

ACTIVITY

1. Study the labels on packs of 'full fat' and 'reduced fat' sausages, burgers and chocolate biscuits. How much less fat do the 'reduced fat' varieties contain? Are any of the products really low in fat content? Draw a table showing your findings.

2. Calculate how much fat would be eaten by a child having one sausage and one burger if they were (a) both 'full fat' products and (b) both 'reduced fat' products.

- Margarine is less fattening than butter.

This idea is not true! Both margarine and butter have the same fat and calorific values. Each has about 80% fat content. Products labelled 'spreads' contain added water and are slightly lower in fat and calories. However, they are still comprised of around 70% fat, which remains a significant amount. Spreads which are labelled 'reduced fat' contain notably less fat and calories, and 'low fat' products are the lowest in fat and energy content.

ACTIVITY

Compare the fat and calorie contents for a standard serving of each of the following: butter, margarine, 'reduced fat' spread, 'low fat' spread and 'extra light low fat' spread. What would the differences be in fat and calorie intake between your spreading a helping of butter on a slice of toast and your spreading on twice that quantity of 'low fat' spread instead?

- **Eating fresh grapefruit burns fat.**
Although eating fresh fruit is to be encouraged, there is absolutely no evidence that any food accelerates metabolism. Eating fresh grapefruit may make you less likely to crave sweet foods and so cut down intake of calories, but basically the statement is erroneous.

- **Protein and carbohydrates should not be eaten at the same meal (the 'food-combining diet').**
Eating protein and starchy foods together overstresses the digestive system is the inaccurate thinking behind this idea. This theory has no scientific foundation. The human digestive system is well equipped to deal with both food groups at the same time (see Chapter 3).

Where weight loss has been achieved by following this pattern of eating, it is likely to have occurred because the individual took extra care about their fat and calorie intake, and the types of food and total quantities eaten. Dangers (with and without weight loss) can arise when the diet is unbalanced and becomes nutritionally inadequate. This form of eating should never be followed by children and preferably neither by adults.

- **Brown eggs are better for you than white eggs.**
The nutrient content of an egg is totally unaffected by the colour of the shell.

- **Eating eggs makes you constipated.**
Eggs are sometimes used in cooking to bind ingredients together but this is not the effect they have on other foods in the digestive tract. Eggs are broken down and the nutrients absorbed into the body as part of the normal digestive process.

- **Potatoes, pasta and bread are fattening.**

All these foods are rich sources of carbohydrate and are low in fat. They are low in the quickly absorbed types of sugars (having a low *glycaemic index*) and so provide sources of slower-releasing, longer lasting energy. They are nutritious, relatively cheap and filling foods, and importantly should form the main part of any meal (see Chapter 2).

Pasta is a popular and nutritious food.

When fats or fat-rich foods are spread, mixed with or poured over these carbohydrate-rich staple foods it obviously increases fat intake and the number of calories eaten. A slice of bread contains about 90 calories, but when thickly buttered it can provide at least 175 calories. A portion of boiled potatoes yields around 120 calories, but the same amount of potatoes sliced and deep-fat fried produces a serving of chips with at least 400 to 500 calories.

- **Vegetarian foods are better for you.**

As with all diets and food choices a vegetarian diet can be a very healthy way to eat. However, equally as with non-vegetarian diets, the balance and content of food eaten is of paramount importance. Eating convenience foods is fine as long as they do not form the bulk of the diet as many, including those marked vegetarian, are high in fat. Some foods marked vegetarian have no nutritional advantage over similar non-vegetarian items, and in fact some are more unhealthy.

- **Fast foods are junk foods and not good for you.**

As with all food the key importance is balance. Any diet that relies heavily on any one type of food will result in poor nutrition. Fast foods often contain a high proportion of fat. Fish and chips are deep fried, pizza is usually rich in cheese, burgers are high-fat-content foods and French fries have large surface areas which are highly fat-saturated. When eaten infrequently and countered with a wide variety of lower-fat or fat-free foods (such as fruit, vegetables and carbohydrate-rich foods) in the diet, then fast foods can be eaten without real concern. Remember particular foods are never really 'good' or 'bad' as such.

- **Fruit juice and diet drinks are healthy, sugar-free and better for your teeth.**

Sweetened fruit juice has additional sugar added during processing. Even pure, unsweetened fruit juices are naturally high in fruit sugars, generally a mixture of fructose, glucose and sucrose. Sugar interacts with plaque bacteria on the surfaces of teeth and directly causes tooth decay. However, even when a soft or fruit drink is sugar-free or artificially sweetened, the *acidity* of fruit-based drinks, juices and carbonated drinks (especially cola) reacts with tooth enamel, so causing damage and decay to teeth (see Chapter 11 for more information on dental health).

▬ ▬ ▬ ▬ ▬ ▬ ▬ *Good professional practice* ▬ ▬ ▬ ▬ ▬ ▬ ▬

Care should be taken as to whether, how much, how often and when soft drinks are consumed. To offer maximum protection against tooth decay, fruit-based and fizzy drinks should be drunk at mealtimes, and teeth cleaned afterwards.

- **Chicken is healthy but red meat is not.**

This idea stems from the misconception that red meat is high in fat but poultry is not. This is not factually correct. Lean red meat has a very low fat content of around only 3% overall. As with all meats the main fat source comes from the layer of fat to be seen around the lean meat. If this fat layer is trimmed away before cooking and any remainder is drained during cooking then little fat will be eaten. Some meat cuts do have further fat marbled through the leaner meat, but with careful cooking this too can be drained off before serving.

The light breast meat of poultry is slightly lower in fat than the dark leg meat, but overall the fat content of *lean poultry* is virtually the same as for *lean red meat*. Poultry too has a layer of fat over lean meat, lying just below the skin. Goose and duck are particularly fatty meats, but by pricking the skin and flesh very well before cooking, much of the fat will run out of the meat during cooking. As the majority of the fat remaining after cooking lies just below the skin, it is advisable to discard the skin and any remaining visible fat from chicken or other poultry before serving. Cooked carefully and served with the skin and fat removed, lean poultry meat has a fat content of around 3–5%. However, when eaten with the skin and the attached fatty deposits, poultry meat contains about 17% fat.

There is more difficulty in buying leaner meat and trimming off fat when it is pre-minced with the lean and fat mixed together. It is not very easy to determine the proportion of fat in fresh minced meat or meat products as it is not often labelled. However, fat is cheaper than lean meat so the overall product price should reflect this. Consequently price is a fair indication of nutritional quality. The more expensive the product the more likely it is to have a lower fat content.

━ ━ ━ ━ ━ ━ ━ *Good professional practice* ━ ━ ━ ━ ━ ━ ━

It is usually healthier to buy a smaller quantity of higher-quality, leaner meat and meat products and make it feed more people by adding soya, pulses or vegetables, than to buy a larger amount of cheaper, fattier meat. When minced meat is cooking it is good practice to skim off any layers of fat which come to the surface. Trim all visible fat from cuts of meat before cooking. Whenever possible check labels for fat content.

• **Low-fat or skimmed milk contains as much calcium as full-fat milk.** This is true. Only fat is removed from the whole milk. All other nutrients, such as calcium remain. However, the general rule of thumb to choose low-fat over full-fat products needs to be considered carefully when giving milk to young children. Vitamins such as A and D are fat-soluble. The removal of milk fats consequently diminishes the amount of these vitamins in the milk. For most adults this presents no problems but children, with their high nutritional needs should be given full-fat milk.

ALERT
Children should be given full-fat milk, and not skimmed or semi-skimmed as these are slightly lower in nutritional content.

Children need the nutritional content of full fat milk.

• **Eating fat makes you fat.**
When more fat is consumed than the body needs, the excess calories are laid down as fat in the human body. Eating too much fat causes obesity, a major contributor to heart disease. However, everyone needs some fat in their diet to be healthy (see Chapter 3).

• **Fresh vegetables are better for you than frozen.**
This is not necessarily true. With modern harvesting and fast-freezing immediately after picking, the nutritional quality of frozen vegetables is high. Fresh vegetables should be eaten whenever possible, but if stored incorrectly or for too long their nutritional content diminishes considerably. How vegetables, whether frozen or fresh, are cooked has the most bearing on their nutritional value. Many raw vegetables are sources of good nutrition.

• **A little of what you fancy does you good.**
Definitely true!

Quick quiz

Find the answers in the chapter

1. What is the World Health Organisation's definition of health?

2. What information should be sought from parents about their young child's eating before beginning nursery?

3. Why should children not be given skimmed milk to drink?

4. What explanation would you give to a parent who asked you if chocolate is 'bad' for their child?

5. The Department of Health has issued guidelines for ensuring a healthy diet. How many guidelines are there?

6. What do you understand by 'balance' when applied to food and diet?

7. A quarter of a pint of milk is accepted as 'one serving' within the 'dairy/milk' food group. What is the metric equivalent of this quantity?

8. Is it healthier to eat chicken or red meat?

9. What percentage of fat increase occurs when potatoes are deep fried rather than jacket-baked or boiled?

10. Why is it not healthy to try to lose weight by only eating a very limited range of foods?

Summary

Now you have read this chapter you should understand:

- Good health means much more than not being ill.
- Health is 'the state of complete social, mental and physical well-being and not merely the absence of disease or infirmity' (World Health Organisation).
- The links between good health and diet are clearly and indisputably established.
- Children develop good, healthy eating habits and attitudes from well-informed adults, who are good role models and practitioners of what they preach.

- The role of the early years professional worker is critical in helping to guide healthy eating attitudes and habits in children.
- There are many misunderstandings about food, diet and nutrition. Even where there may be an element of truth in a popular saying, it is important to understand the principles of good nutrition and what healthy eating is.
- Early years workers need to understand what is factually correct in order to analyse nutritional information appropriately, apply it appropriately and so work most effectively with parents and children.

2
Food, Nutrition and How the Body Works

Aims of the chapter

To enable you to understand:

- some nutritional terms and definitions
- a simple overview of digestion and absorption and how the body converts food into energy
- excretion: how the body deals with waste materials to prevent a build up of toxins
- the body's life-maintaining needs and functions that all require energy
- how the essential nutrients and water provide the body with energy.

Flossie felt so sorry for the solitary chocolate setting out alone on its long journey along the gastro-intestinal tract that she immediately decided to eat the rest to keep it company.

Some nutritional terms and definitions

It is important that a shared understanding of words and terms is established to enable clear communication. Some of the most frequently used terminology of the subject are outlined below. Return to these definitions as you work your way through the book to re-establish your accuracy and knowledge.

Nutrition or dietetics

- *Nutrition* (or dietetics) is the term used for the science or study of food and how the body uses the constituents of food.

Nutrients

- *Nutrients* are collections of the components that occur in food which are necessary to sustain life, growth and health.

Metabolism

- *Metabolism* is the term used to define chemical reactions carried out by the body.
- In metabolism food is broken down and the resulting products or *metabolites* are used to form further compounds which are necessary for the body to function.
- The *metabolic rate* is the pace at which the body carries out metabolism.

Food

- *Food* covers virtually all substances that we eat (or drink) and can include both solids and fluids.
- The term *food* may include nutritional supplements (such as vitamin drops) taken to enhance nutritional intake from food.
- *Food* does not include illegal or legal drugs or medication which may in some way be considered to be 'eaten' or 'drunk'.
- Most food eaten provides nourishment for the body enabling it to function, such as to grow, maintain its temperature, repair and renew tissues, and to prevent and fight infection.
- The wide variety of food originates from either vegetation or animal sources.
- It can be eaten raw, cooked, on its own or along with other foods.

Diet

- *Diet* is the term which covers the overall content and pattern of eating for an individual or group.
- Different types of diet are predominantly influenced by cultural food choices, sometimes by other factors affecting choice, and can also be determined on the basis of medical needs.
- *Diet* does not simply refer to an eating pattern designed for weight loss. It means the overall content and pattern of eating.

Food products

- *Food products* is the term generally given to a commercially manufactured or processed combination of substances (such as canned soups, sauces, bought meat pies, milkshake mixes, and so on). Unlike home-cooked dishes these products usually contain commercially used binding, emulsifying or preservative substances.
- The term *food products* may also be used for a type of food which is manufactured or produced from another (such as cheese or butter from milk, or flour from wheat).

Food Choices

- *Food choices* are the decisions made regarding what a person eats.
- Food choices may be made by individuals on behalf of themselves or on behalf of others.
- They may be made by selecting from a range available, or by having to select only what is available.
- Food choices are determined by a complex range of influences.
- Several of these determining factors usually work together to determine food choice.

DETERMINING FACTORS OF FOOD CHOICES

There are four different broad categories of influence that determine how *food choices* are made:

- geographical, climatic and seasonal;
- social, cultural, religious and emotional;
- economic and political;
- educational, medical and physical.

For example, *geographical, climatic and seasonal influences* that have *negative* effects on food choices, could mean that people living in very remote parts of the country have few shops or sources of provision, and in winter have particularly difficult road or sea access to collect goods, and shops have fewer deliveries. This results in a limited range of foods being stocked in the shops. Moreover people are often unable to travel to obtain supplies in bad weather.

A positive example of this category affecting food choices could be that people living in a fertile valley, with an equable climate for growing various crops of fruit and vegetables throughout the year, have the opportunity for making food choices from a wide variety of fresh seasonal produce.

A simple overview of digestion and absorption: how the body converts food into energy

Food provides the body with the energy sources it needs to grow, repair itself and work. However, none of these can take place until the nutrients in food have been broken down into forms that the body can effectively absorb and use. The process of the physical and chemical breakdown of food is called *digestion*.

Absorption is the process by which the digested products are taken into the body (via the bloodstream or lymph system) from the gastro-intestinal tract. Most of the *absorption* of the digested food occurs through the walls of the gastro-intestinal tract. This is in effect a long continuous tube starting at the mouth and going through the body to the anus. In an adult the gastro-intestinal tract is about 9 metres long.

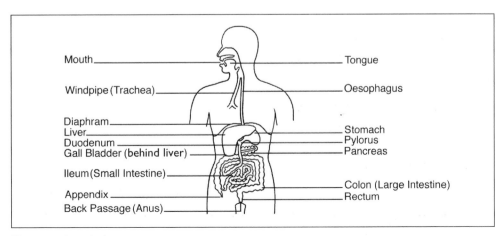

The gastro-intestinal tract.

The journey of food through the body: the route, digestion and absorption

1. Eating, drinking, chewing and swallowing

The digestive system starts in the mouth. Food is mechanically cut up by the *teeth*, crushed and chewed. The action of the tongue helps to mix the food with *saliva* containing *enzymes* which begin to chemically break down the carbohydrates in the food. A *bolus* or ball of softened food is finally formed and swallowed. It passes down the *oesophagus* and into the *stomach*. At the entrance to the stomach is the gastric sphincter; a ring of muscle which opens to allow the bolus of food into the stomach. The digested food is moved along the alimentary canal by a wave-like muscle action. This process, called *peristalsis*, is caused by muscles in the walls of the oesophagus and intestine contracting and relaxing in sequence.

2. What happens in the stomach

- Muscles in the stomach wall relax and contract in waves to churn the food, mixing it with *gastric juice* (composed of mucus, enzymes and hydrochloric acid) to form a semi-liquid smooth pulp called *chyme*.
- The stomach acts as a temporary store.
- It has an *acidic* environment which:
- helps to destroy any bacteria present in the food
- enables the enzyme *pepsin* to effectively begin to break down *proteins*.

3. Leaving the stomach

The chyme is secreted from the stomach, a small amount at a time, through the *pyloric sphincter*. This ring of muscle, which guards the exit from the stomach is usually tightly closed but it opens periodically to allow the chyme to move into the small intestine or *duodenum*.

4. Into the duodenum.

The *duodenum* is the first 30 centimetres of the small intestine. It is here, where most of the digestion and absorption take place. Enzymes from the pancreas and bile from the gall bladder are secreted into the duodenum. These juices break down the acidic chyme into a more alkali and absorbable form for the body to use.

- Proteins are split into *amino acids*★
- Complex sugars such as *glycerols*★, known as *polysaccharides*★ are split into simple sugars, such as *glucose* and *fructose*.
- Fats are turned into *fatty acids*★. (★See Chapter 3 for information).

These end products are collectively termed *metabolites*.

Most of the metabolites are then *absorbed* through the walls of the *ileum* (the remaining part of the small intestine).

- Amino acids, glucose and fructose are absorbed into the bloodstream and carried to the *liver* where they are further processed and stored. The liver also breaks down many toxins and drugs rendering them less harmful to the body. (Some drugs must undergo this process to be absorbed by the body.) The liver's functions are a vital part of digestion.
- Fatty acids are absorbed into the *lymphatic system* and enter the bloodstream later.

5. Onwards, down and out

The semi-liquid unabsorbed and undigested food stuff which remains is now moved on from the small intestine into the large intestine or *colon*.

Travelling through the large intestine some of the few remaining nutrients are fermented by bacteria present in the colon. Most of the water content and any residual nutrients are finally drawn out and readily absorbed through the intestinal walls and into the bloodstream.

The digestive process has now removed as many nutrients and as much water from the food as possible. It has enabled the body to absorb these during their passage through the whole length of the gastro-intestinal tract.

The semi-solid material that remains is made up of dead cells, bacteria and fibre. Dietary fibre is important for ensuring the efficient removal of waste products from the alimentary canal (see Chapter 3). *Peristalsis* continues to move the semi-solid material along the large intestine, aided by the secretion of mucus, into the *rectum* where the waste faecal matter is stored until expelled from the body through the *anus*.

ALERT

The absorption of water at this stage is important in guarding against dehydration. Babies and young children are particularly susceptible to serious illness arising from dehydration. With diarrhoea the effective absorption of water does not take place in the large intestine so great care must be taken to ensure fluid intake is high. If diarrhoea persists in a baby or young child, especially if accompanied by vomiting, medical advice should be urgently sought. In babies these conditions can quickly become life-threatening.

Excretion: how the body deals with waste material to prevent the build up of toxins (poisons)

Bio-chemical reactions that take place in the body produce compounds that enter the bloodstream. These interactions and reactions produce waste materials which also enter the bloodstream. If left to circulate and accumulate in the body, these would cause poisoning or toxicity. Blood must therefore be filtered and thus cleaned, so that the toxic waste can be excreted. This purification of the blood takes place in the kidneys.

- The blood passing through the kidneys is filtered.
- The nutrients in the blood, such as glucose, amino acids and mineral salts, plus most of the water are reabsorbed by the kidneys and passed back into the bloodstream.
- Urea and other waste products pass through the kidneys unabsorbed. The waste liquid is carried by a tube from the kidneys to the bladder and is excreted as urine.

The role of the digestive system in guarding against infections

The digestive system also acts as a chemical barrier. It helps to prevent infections by acting on germs which enter the body particularly through the mouth. Gastric juices will kill most viruses and bacteria but some do survive and attack the body, causing gastric and intestinal upsets and sometimes affecting other body systems.

- - - - - - - *Good professional practice* - - - - - - -

Good hygiene and food safety in storing and handling foods are essential. Freshness, cleanliness and careful preparation and cooking are vital to prevent illness. Safe food practice is absolutely essential when dealing with babies and young children (see Chapter 10).

The body's life-maintaining needs and functions that all require energy

Different foods contain different nutrients which support the whole range of bodily processes. It is therefore essential that each person eats a balanced diet made up of optimum proportions of a wide variety of foods.

- - - - - - - - - - - - *Key point* - - - - - - - - - -

The body needs an adequate, essential and balanced intake of energy and nutrients to maintain health and to prevent nutrition-related health problems. Food provides energy.

Energy

The body needs energy to allow it to:

- grow and to develop
- reproduce
- move
- maintain necessary body temperature
- repair and replace damaged body tissues
- recover after injury or illness
- eliminate and excrete waste products.

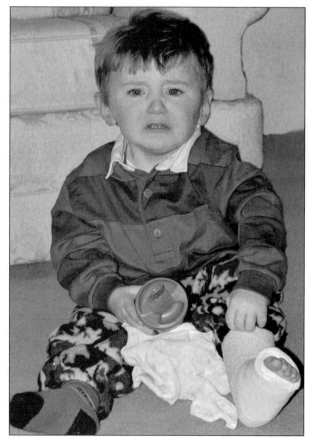

Energy is needed for healing and repair.

Energy is needed for playing.

Energy is needed for solving problems.

Energy is needed for serious partying.

How the essential nutrients and water provide the body with energy

Macronutrients and micronutrients

The body requires some nutrients in large quantities and some, although vital, only in minute amounts.

Proteins, carbohydrates and fats all have different functions but they are all sources of energy for the body. They make up a relatively large part of our diet and so are measured in grams. Collectively they are known as *macronutrients*.

Vitamins and minerals do not directly supply energy but are needed to enable the body to function, that is, for *metabolism* to take place. They are required in relatively small amounts, often just as trace elements or in minute quantities. They are measured in micrograms or milligrams. Collectively they are known as *micronutrients*.

The body also needs *water* and *fibre*, which with *proteins*, *carbohydrates*, *fats*, *vitamins* and *minerals* make up the *seven essential nutrients*.

The seven essential nutrients and their roles: an introduction and overview.

What are they?	Why are they essential?	Sources?
Carbohydrates	– main providers of energy for growth, body maintenance and all movement – energy created is needed for sustaining all metabolic and physical functions vital for life	Bread, cereal, pasta, potatoes, pulses, rice, grains, flours, sugar, syrup, honey, milk, fruit, plantain
Proteins	– are a source of energy. – have a vital function for the growth and repair of body tissues.	Meat, poultry, fish, cheese, milk, milk products, nuts, seeds, soya, pulses, cereals, cereal products
Fats	– provide energy – maintenance of body temperature – contain essential vitamins	Butter, cheese, margarine, lard, meat, poultry, nuts, fish, fish oils, vegetable oils

What are they?	Why are they essential?	Sources?
Minerals	– vital for body function and metabolism – growth of skeletal system, bone strength, nerve regulation and control – enable energy production	In varying quantities in nearly all foods. Some foods naturally richer in specific minerals than others (e.g. salt, bread, meat, fish are high in sodium.)
Vitamins	– support and regulate cellular processes, important in body structure and cell function – growth, prevention of disease, repair, health and function of senses and systems	Fat-soluble: (Vits. A, D, K & E) in green vegetables, carrots, tomatoes, yolk, liver, cheese, butter, oily fish. Water-soluble: (Vits. C & B group) in meat, leaf vegetables, fruits, fruit juices, eggs, beans
Dietary fibre/ Roughage.	– (a general name for food residues which the body needs but does not absorb) – gastro-intestinal function and number of other health benefits	Wholegrain cereals and flours, bran, beans, most fruits and vegetables
Water	– not strictly a 'nutrient' but absolutely essential for life – necessary for cellular function – prevents dehydration and the onset of systemic problems such as kidney disorder and constipation – (acute dehydration, particularly in the very young or very old, can kill swiftly)	Present in all drinks and in almost all food, except dehydrated foods

ALERT

Young children generally obtain sufficient dietary fibre by eating a balanced diet. They should not be given extra fibre or regularly fed many very high-fibre foods as fibre can prevent efficient absorption of essential iron and calcium, and may cause stomach cramps. High-fibre foods are 'filling' and if eaten in significant quantities, may prevent children from eating other much more nutritionally rich foods.

– – – – – – – – – – –*Key point*– – – – – – – – – – – –

Eating the full range of nutrients, found in a wide variety of foods, produces a good fuel source which provides the body with the energy needed for all its different functions and purposes.

Finally, *a handy hint*! Remembering 'Mr Green' may help you to recall the body's needs and functions:

M	movement
R	respiration
G	growth
R	reproduction
E	excretion
E	elimination
N	nutrition

END OF CHAPTER ACTIVITY

1. From memory draw an outline of the digestive tract and label each of the following: 'oesophagus, stomach, gastric sphincter, pancreas, duodenum, liver, small and large intestine, colon, rectum'.

2. What is meant by the following terms: 'chyme, bolus, peristalsis, enzyme, bile, gastric juices'?

3. On your outline drawing indicate where each of the above terms may be located.

4. Check your answers and your memory!

5. Revise the information about absorption of water from the alimentary canal and why dehydration can be very dangerous for babies and young children.

Quick quiz

Find the answers in the chapter.

1. What is meant by 'metabolic rate'?

2. When studying nutrition, what is meant by the terms *diet* and *food*?

3. What is meant by the terms *digestion* and *absorption*.

4. What is the main purpose of digestion?

5. Name four things that *energy* enables the body to do.

6. What are the seven essential nutrients?

7. Which are the three macronutrients?

8. Which nutrients are sources of energy?

9. Which nutrient is important for the maintenance of body temperature?

10. Why should young children *not* be given a lot of high-fibre foods?

Summary

Now you have read this chapter you should understand:

- some nutritional terms and definitions, such as *diet, nutrition, food, food products, metabolism*
- factors that can influence food choices
- how the human body's gastro-intestinal tract and digestive system function to convert food into compounds and elements

- how the body converts food into energy forms which sustain all bodily processes and support life
- that digested food is absorbed into the body and the body converts it into energy
- how the body deals with waste materials to prevent a build up of toxins (excretion)
- what are the body's life-maintaining needs and functions that all require energy
- how the intake of essential nutrients and water provides the body with the energy it needs.

3

The Seven Essential Nutrients

Aims of the chapter

To enable you to understand:

- nutrients that are essential for life and living
- the Seven Essential Nutrients, their composition, main sources and functions
- some of the most significant effects on children of nutritionally poor diets
- the importance of water in the diet.

Flossie's way of limiting her intake of high fat and sugary food was to eat no more than one chocolate bar a day.

Nutrients that are essential for life and living

The seven essential nutrients

These are:

- carbohydrates
- protein
- fats
- dietary fibre

- water
- vitamins
- minerals.

In this chapter we shall look at each of these nutrients in turn, bearing in mind that our understanding of their sources and their nutritional benefits are important if we are to ensure young children are given the best possible diet to help them grow, develop and fight disease.

Carbohydrates

Carbohydrates are:

- derived from plants
- low in fat
- readily digestible
- composed of many vitamins and minerals

- our single most important source of energy
- suppliers of rapidly available, energy-giving glucose
- divided into two types: *simple* and *complex* carbohydrates.

The structures of carbohydrates are based on a common unit known as a *saccharide*. There are different types of carbohydrate based on the number of saccharide units each one contains.

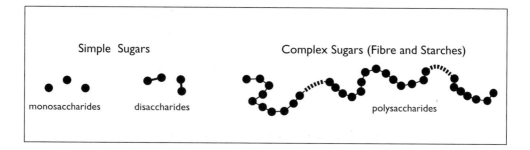

Simple Sugars

monosaccharides   disaccharides

Complex Sugars (Fibre and Starches)

polysaccharides

1. Simple carbohydrates are:

- the *sugars* found in fruits, milk, vegetables, sugar beet, sugar cane and honey
- identifiable by their sweet taste
- short cellular structures made up of single units (*monosaccharides*), and pairs (*disaccharides*).

2. Complex carbohydrates are:

- the *starches* found in tubers (e.g. potatoes), roots (e.g. carrots) and seeds (e.g. legumes, cereal grains: wheat, rice, corn)
- long chain like structures (*polysaccharides*).

The body converts polysaccharides into monosaccharides, such as glucose, which can then be used. Our bodies can only store a small amount of glucose. The remainder is stored as glycogen which is converted into glucose as we need it.

ALERT

- **As young children have high energy requirements they need frequent and regular meals and snacks to ensure both a ready supply of glucose and to prevent their glycogen stores from becoming depleted.**

Satsumas are a source of simple sugars, potassium and vitamin C.

EXTRINSIC AND INTRINSIC SUGARS

Many carbohydrates are naturally rich in vitamins and minerals. However, refined and unrefined extrinsic sugars are processed and extracted forms of carbohydrate (such as table sugar) that do not supply additional nutrients.

Extrinsic sugars are extracted from sugar cane and sugar beet. These are the sugars we use in cooking and add to foods and drinks. They are also used by manufacturers in the processing of many foods, such as sweets, cakes, puddings, soups, and sweet and savoury sauces.

The remaining sugars occur naturally in foods, such as milk, fruits and vegetables. These are known as *intrinsic sugars*.

ALERT

Extrinsic sugar intake should be carefully limited for young children. Sticky, sweet and processed foods containing refined sugars are often effective in satiating hungry appetites but give little or no essential nutrients to meet children's needs. They are also significant contributors to tooth decay. (See Chapter 11.)

Proteins

THE FUNCTION AND IMPORTANCE OF PROTEINS

Protein is a critical nutrient which is involved with every process in the body. Some proteins are needed to build and maintain each cell in the human body. Cells, which themselves are partially composed of proteins, constantly need renewal and repair. Some proteins are needed for the formation, development, growth and repair of body tissues. Hence protein is particularly linked to growth in children. Certain proteins are needed for the production of hormones and enzymes which are the regulators of the body's life processes while other proteins are vital to the function of the immune system. Yet others work as transporters, moving such materials as oxygen, fats and minerals around the body.

If our diet does not contain sufficient carbohydrates and fats to provide energy for other vital body functions (remember '*Mr Green*'?), then proteins may be utilised for these purposes to the detriment of the primary functions of proteins.

WHAT ARE PROTEINS?

Proteins are large complex chemical structures or *molecules* made from building blocks of *amino acids*. Each amino acid has its own name and at

Carbohydrate information

type	Simple carbohydrates						Complex carbohydrates		Results of carbohydrate deficiency
group	Monosaccharides			Disaccharides			Polysaccharides		
name	Glucose	Fructose	Galactose	Sucrose	Lactose	Maltose	Starch	Glycogen	
composition	Single unit	Single unit	Single unit	1 glucose + 1 fructose unit	1 glucose + 1 galactose unit	2 Glucose units	Many units	Many units	
found in	Some fruits, plant saps, honey	Fruit, fruit juices, vegetables, honey	Milk, yoghurt & other milk products	Table sugar, jams, soft drinks, sweets, biscuits, fruits, some vegetables, ice-cream.	Milk & milk products	Some breakfast cereals and bakery goods, malted snacks, beers	Rice, bread, pasta, potatoes, sweetcorn, legumes, breakfast cereals, other cereal products	Animal muscle and liver	Thinness
special notes	*Principal sugar used in the body for energy. *Main source of energy for the brain	*Sweetest sugar, 3.5 times sweeter than glucose	*Released when sugar (lactose) is digested *Important energy source for babies	*Important energy source. *Used as sweetener, flavour enhancer & to improve texture in many foods *Preservative for jams & milk	*Energy source for newborn babies *Broken down in digestion into glucose & galactose	*Produced during malting of grains *Energy source *Main sugar first produced during digestion of starch; broken down into glucose	*Broken down into maltose by enzymes during digestion *Provides around quarter of our energy intake *Starchy foods are bulky & filling so quantity given to young children should be limited *Carry important vitamins & minerals	*Broken down into glucose *Muscle glycogen is the only form of carbohydrate able to be stored in muscle & can only be used by muscles *Liver glycogen provides glucose to help maintain blood sugar levels	Inability to maintain body warmth

Lack of energy |

least 22 amino acids have now been identified. Different protein molecules consist of varying combinations and numbers of these amino acids, resulting in a vast array of proteins.

For children, 10 amino acids are absolutely critical for growth and repair of cells. Adults specifically require eight. However, for good health the human body needs an intake of each of the different amino acids to build all the protein molecules the body needs.

Some amino acids can be synthesised or produced within the body but nine cannot. These nine must be obtained from the protein foods we eat. These are the *essential amino acids*. The remaining amino acids that our bodies *can* synthesise from other amino acids are known as *non-essential amino acids*.

The nutritious quality of proteins varies greatly because protein molecules themselves differ in the amount, type and pattern of amino acids. The closer the sequence and combination of amino acids are in the protein being eaten to that found in the human body, then the higher is the nutritional value of that particular protein.

THE TWO NUTRITIONAL-VALUE TYPES OF PROTEIN

There are two nutritional types or qualities of protein:
- *first class proteins* – also known as *high biological value* (HBV) or *complete proteins*.
  These proteins from animal sources (plus soya beans) contain the whole range of essential amino acids.
- *second class proteins* – also known as *low biological value* (LBV) or *incomplete proteins*.
  Mainly proteins from vegetable sources (except soya beans) containing only small amounts of one or more of the essential amino acids.

Proteins: essential for body growth, development and repair

Type	Contain	Source	Found in
First-class (HBV or complete) proteins	All of the essential amino acids	Animal & soya	Meat, fish, seafood, chicken & other poultry, eggs, cheese, milk & dairy products, soya.
Second class (LBV or incomplete) proteins	Some essential amino acids	Vegetable	Nuts, seeds, pulses (esp. beans, peas & lentils), cereals (rice, barley, cornmeal, oats), cereal products (e.g. pasta, chapatis, breads, breakfast cereals)

Because different plants contain different amino acids, when eaten together they can supplement and complement each other. For example, bread eaten with baked beans provides a mixed vegetarian protein intake which gives a relatively high biological protein value.

The optimum way of serving plant protein is to combine it with animal or soya protein. This means that the deficiencies in amino acids from the plant food are supplemented with all of the essential amino acids from the animal or soya source. The nutritional value of all the foods is then enhanced.

ACTIVITY

1. Fill in the blanks in the following chart so each 'dish' created is a combination of the two types of protein.

Complementary Combinations of the Two Types of Protein.

Second-class Protein Source	First-class protein source	
Plant protein foods	Animal/Soya protein foods	Dish
Pasta	Milk, Cheese	
Bread		Welsh Rarebit
	Milk	Porridge
Rice	Milk	
Potatoes		Tortilla
Breakfast cereal	Soya milk	
	Meat	Chilli con carne
Pasta	Eggs	
Potato		Jacket potato & . . .
Bread		Bread & butter pudding
Bread		Sandwiches
		Beans on toast
Pizza base		
Rice	Meat	

— — — — — — —*Good professional practice*— — — — — — —

When planning vegetarian meals for children it is very important to provide a wide variety of different vegetable foods in the diet in order to provide sufficient quantities of all the essential amino acids. Wherever possible eggs, milk and cheese should be incorporated to provide first class or high-biological value protein foods. Particular care should be taken to regularly use a range of soya products in meals for vegan children (see Chapter 9).

DEVELOPMENTS IN PROTEIN FOODS

During the past two or three decades a range of non-meat protein-rich foods have been developed. The impetus for much of the research came from the need to find cheaper alternatives to meat for people in developing countries, and also to develop foods suitable for preventing protein-based malnutrition in young children and infants. Algae, plankton and other plant materials have been processed and new micro-organisms have all been used to produce new foods. To date these single-cell proteins are low in biological value and mainly used as animal feed, but there has been great success in the development of Quorn for human consumption.

HOW DOES THE BODY USE PROTEIN?

The body cannot directly use the protein from food; changes need to be made to it first. Food proteins supply the building blocks which the body then uses to form its own proteins. When a food is eaten the liver digests the protein contents converting them into amino acids which are absorbed and reformed by the body into particular proteins that are our source of energy for cell formation, growth and repair. If more protein is eaten than the body needs, the excess will be used as k/calories and may be stored as fat.

HOW MUCH PROTEIN DO WE NEED?

Very high protein intakes may relate to renal (kidney) damage. Although slightly high intakes of protein have not been proven to have any harmful side effects, they have not been shown to provide any advantages either.

Figures show that most adults in the UK tend to eat more protein than they actually need and almost two-thirds of this protein comes from animals and animal products.

Breast and formula-fed babies obtain all their nutrition, including protein, from milk but during weaning, with the introduction of different foods, this balance starts to change. Babies have a relatively high protein requirement in relation to their weight, which is usually well met by their diet of breast or formula milks.

Fats

WHY IS DIETARY FAT IMPORTANT?

Fat is an essential nutrient for health and is particularly vital for young children. Fat contributes to the taste and texture of many foods we eat and because it is digested relatively slowly it helps to prevent feelings of hunger.

Fats are a major source of energy for the body, providing a more concentrated form than either carbohydrates or proteins.

The body uses the energy it requires for all its functions, needs and processes and stores any excess in the body in the form of *adipose tissues* or body fat, for any possible future energy requirements.

The body's fat is not only an energy store, it also provides protection, support and cushioning for delicate structures and mechanisms such as the internal organs. Furthermore it forms an insulating layer on the outside of the body to help maintain body temperature against external cold.

Fat also is essential for carrying the fat-soluble vitamins and for helping the body to absorb them.

WHAT IS DIETARY FAT?

Dietary fat is actually a whole range of different types of *fats*. (The term *lipid* is the scientific name often used to describe fatty substances.)

WHAT ARE THE TWO ESSENTIAL FATTY ACIDS?

Essential fatty acids are those needed by the body for good health but which the body cannot make. They **must** be obtained from the food we eat.

There are two nutritionally essential fatty acids: *linoleic acid* (or *omega-6*), and *alpha linolenic acid* (or *omega-3*). Both of these serve as building blocks for other fatty acids. Together these two are vital for the healthy development of every single body cell as well as being absolutely essential for many functions, such as blood pressure regulation and the body's immunity.

Research also indicates they may help prevent blood clots that precede a heart attack or stroke.

These essential fatty acids are found in foods which are high in polyunsaturates, particularly in oily fish, soya beans and sunflower oils.

WHERE ARE DIETARY FATS FOUND?

	Food sources of dietary fats		
	Saturated fats	Unsaturated fats	
	Saturates	Monounsaturates	Polyunsaturates
Foods of animal origin 1	Dairy products (milk, cream, cheese, butter, yoghurt, ghee). Breast milk	Dairy products	
Foods of animal origin 2	Meat, poultry, suet, lard, dripping.	Meat & poultry	Fish oils, oily fish (herring, mackerel, trout, albacore tuna, sardines, salmon) contain omega-3 fatty acids, = very rich sources.
Foods of vegetable origin	Palm oil, coconut oil	Olive oil, peanut oil, rapeseed oil	Mainly derived from seeds and nuts (sunflower oil, corn, soya bean, walnut, cottonseed, safflower oil = very rich sources). Cereal grains (wheat, barley, oats) and some fruits and vegetables = much lesser sources

In general, fats containing a majority of saturated fatty acids tend to be solid at room temperature while those containing mainly unsaturated fatty acids are usually liquid. The exceptions to these include:

- vegetable shortenings or 'spreads' manufactured in solid forms, which can be up to 75% unsaturated

- palm and coconut oils which are liquids but are high in saturated fat.

WHAT'S IN A NAME?

From this table it can be seen that sometimes different types of fats can be obtained from the same food sources. All of the foods containing saturated fats also contain unsaturated fats. For example, almost a third of the fatty acids found in milk, butter and dairy cheese are unsaturates (mainly monounsaturates). However, products like suet and animal meat fat are very low in unsaturates and very high in saturates. Foods are therefore termed to have a generally *low* or *high proportion* of a said type of fat. Thus sardines and sunflower oil are usually termed as being '*high in polyunsaturates*'.

WHAT CAN BE MISLEADING?

Care needs to be taken when buying some products as their origin may indicate they might be expected to be rich in one type of fatty acid but in fact they are not! In some cases the manufacturing processes can radically change the type of fatty acids.

Examples of this are that fats labelled 'blended vegetable oil' or 'cooking oil' (rather than labelled with the actual plant source such as 'sunflower oil'), usually contain a large proportion of saturated fats. This happens because of the chemical changes made to unsaturated fatty acids occurring during processing. Such fats are widely used in commercially processed foods, such as biscuits, cakes, snacks and pastries, making these products high in saturates.

ACTIVITY

Study some food labels, note the fat content of the foods and how they are displayed. On your computer produce a simple spreadsheet with a chart for each group of products. Make a row for each product and columns for the different types of fat (per 100 grams) as shown on the labels.

1. Compare the saturated and unsaturated fat contents (per 100 grams) of a pack of butter, a tub of margarine and a tub of vegetable oil spread labelled 'low fat'. Which product is highest in saturated fats and which in unsaturated fats?

2. Compare the fat contents of three packets of biscuits or crisps. Choose three different types; one pack marked 'reduced fat', one marked 'low fat' and one with no advertised fat-related claims.

CHILDREN, FATS AND HEALTH

Children need a more substantial proportion of fats in their diet than adults do. Fat is an important energy source and children have high energy requirements. Fats are vital for growth and development, physically and mentally. They are nutritionally essential. Different types of fats provide different nutrients, all of which are needed by children.

As with adults, obesity is a serious health problem for many children ,and coronary disease in adult life is often related to obesity. There is general agreement amongst nutritional experts that many people would benefit from reducing their intake of saturated fats and increasing their levels of physical exercise.

Young children should never be placed on a stringent low-fat or fat-free diet without specialised medical consultation. However, limiting the intake of saturated fatty foods to enable a balanced intake of the full range of unsaturated fats is sensible nutritional management. Good childhood nutrition is good prevention against the onset of heart disease. Evidence now shows that heart disease may start as young as 10 or 11 years of age.

‒ ‒ ‒ ‒ ‒ ‒*Good professional practice*‒ ‒ ‒ ‒ ‒ ‒

For overweight children, physical activity and the resultant socialising are often difficult, giving them feelings of failure and rejection. Great care needs to be taken to include and support overweight children in all activities and enable them to feel valued and successful.

ACTIVITY

1. In your work placement obtain a week's menu for children's midday meals. Consider how many of the dishes:

– are likely to contain some kinds of fats
– probably have a high saturated fat content
– contain fats from vegetable, animal and fish sources.

2. Do you think that any children who might rely heavily on the provided midday meal as their main source of daily nutrition are having (a) enough and a wide range of fats and (b) experiences of eating tasty foods which are cooked with unsaturated fats?

3. Ask six children to list their five favourite foods. How many of these are traditionally considered to be high in saturated fats? Select the most popular foods named (which you consider to be high in saturates) and suggest ways you could serve the children their favourites by using a wider range of fats.

Dietary Fibre

WHAT IS DIETARY FIBRE?

Dietary fibre, sometimes called *cellulose* or *roughage*, is the fibrous structure found in the cell walls of plants.

It is composed of carbon, hydrogen and oxygen and is a form of carbohydrate. However, it has a very particular role and different attributes from the other carbohydrates shown above.

There are two types of dietary fibre:

1. INSOLUBLE DIETARY FIBRE (IDF).

This cannot be digested and absorbed by humans, and it does not provide any calories. For these reasons it is termed an *unavailable carbohydrate*.

Functions of IDF.

- It helps movement of food through the digestive system and increases stool bulk.
- It encourages chewing, which for young children is linked to mouth, jaw and vocal control and so to the development of speech.
- It provides little or no energy for the body or other nutrients.
- It helps to make us feel full after eating.

Main sources of IDF

Bran

Wholegrain, cereal and wholemeal products: breads

flours

pasta

rice

whole oats

bran

many breakfast cereals

Cellulose in plants/vegetables.

ALERT

Importantly, although some insoluble dietary fibre must be included in children's diets, its intake should be limited for young children (as it is filling, low in energy and low in nutrients).

2. SOLUBLE DIETARY FIBRE.

This type of fibre is soluble and is absorbed in the intestine.

Functions of SDF

- It helps to control or lower the blood sugar levels in the body (so influencing the glycaemic index).
- It helps to lower cholesterol (or blood lipids).

IMPORTANT SOURCES OF SOLUBLE DIETARY FIBRE:

Fresh fruit (flesh, pips, skin)	apples	oranges	**Dried fruits**	apricots
	apricots	peaches		currants
	bananas	plums		dates
	grapes	raspberries		prunes
	guavas	rhubarb		raisins
	melon	strawberries		sultanas

Vegetables   green leaf – cabbage, broccoli, spinach, lettuce

root – carrots, parsnips, turnip, swede

stalk – celery, spring onion

seed – sweetcorn, peas, beans

pod – mangetout

skin – potato and other root vegetables.

| Pulses | lentils |
| | beans |

Nuts & seeds

Cereal/grain products	breads
	flours
	pasta
	rice
	oats
	many breakfast cereals.

Note: There is virtually *no fibre* in fats, milk and milk products, eggs, sugar.

Apples are a good source of soluble dietary fibre.

Minerals

Minerals are inorganic substances essential for life but only found in tiny amounts in the human body. Some minerals are required in greater quantities (macroelements) than others (trace elements).

Each mineral plays a vital, unique and often complex role in the functioning of the body. Overall some of their main purposes are to release energy from foods, fight infections, transmit nerve impulses, build and maintain teeth and bones, transport oxygen around the body, regulate the balance of water and acids, form and activate essential substances in enzymes and hormones, enable blood clotting, relax and contract muscles, and enable many other functions.

- - - - - - -*Good professional practice*- - - - - - -

Be aware that the increased needs of pregnant and breastfeeding women requires ensuring the diet contains mineral-rich foods. Children are particularly vulnerable to a lack of iron through dietary imbalance and so need carefully planned meals.

The following chart shows some of the most important minerals, foods containing them and why the body needs them. Some practical tips and particular points are included in the last column to help in your overall planning of meals and for discussing children's eating and food choices with parents.

In the chart the non-shaded areas indicate macroelements, more of which are needed than the trace elements, shown in the shaded areas.

ALERT
Mineral supplements should only be given to children on particular medical advice.

Minerals

Mineral	Food sources	Functions and benefits to body	Results of deficiencies or excesses	Serving and cooking tips
Calcium	Milk & milk products, canned small fish with bones, dark green vegetables, dried pulses (especially soya beans), figs, apricots, dates, sesame seeds.	Builds & maintains strong bones & teeth. Enables blood clotting & the transmission of nerve impulses. Enables heart to contract. Needed by breastfeeding women to provide sufficient calcium to growing baby.	Deficiency → stunted growth. Rickets, brittle bones, bones may break easily, osteoporosis. Bone pain. Convulsions.	Include daily: cow's milk, dairy products, e.g. yoghurt, cheese, canned fish, e.g. sardines, pilchards. Fruits in lunch boxes are a good way of giving calcium-rich food to school children.
Chloride	Salt & salty foods.	Helps maintain acid-base balance, used in formation of gastric juice.	Deficiency – virtually unknown. Our bodies lose chloride when sweating heavily & in diarrhoea. Excess intake → vomiting.	Intake of chloride in the diet almost all comes from salt (sodium chloride).
Magnesium	Green vegetables, nuts, whole cereals, wholemeal bread & pasta, soya beans, peas, seafood, dried fruits.	Vital for metabolism. Needed to convert calories in food into body energy. Essential for bone development. Needed for nerve impulse transmission, muscle movement, to repair & maintain healthy body cells.	Deficiency → muscle cramps, tiredness, weakness, vertigo, reduced blood pressure. Excess → vomiting, nausea, hypertension.	Use wholegrain products rather than refined grain products whenever possible. Magnesium can help to relieve migraine & help lower blood pressure.
Phosphorus	Found in calcium-rich foods. Meat, poultry, canned fish, dairy products, dried milk powder, eggs, dried fruits, wholegrain cereal products.	Works together with calcium & magnesium to form & maintain healthy bones & teeth. Aids control of metabolic energy in all body cells.	Deficiency (is rare) → weakness, stiff joints, numbness, mental confusion, demineralisation of bone & loss of calcium. Excess → lowers calcium levels in blood.	Many processed foods & soft drinks have high levels of phosphorus. Grill or roast meats & poultry.

A C T I V I T Y

In your placement find out some foods the children do not like or prefer not to eat. Draw a simple table. In one column show the food the child does not wish to eat. In the next column enter a different food which provides the same mineral content as the 'disliked' food. Use the mineral chart (page 52) to help you.

Vitamins

Vitamins are naturally derived, complex organic compounds in food that have a vital role in establishing our health and well being and fighting disease. To date, 13 vitamins have been identified as being necessary for balanced nutrition. They are so critical that we cannot live without them. They are necessary to every body part and for every function. Although only required in very small quantities (compared to the amounts of the macronutrients we need) each of these micronutrients is absolutely essential.

Vitamins must be taken regularly and in moderation as part of a well-balanced diet. If a vitamin is lacking in the diet, deficiency will cause some degree of poor health, illness or disease.

Vitamins are classified into two groups, *fat-soluble* and *water-soluble*.
- **Fat-soluble vitamins** (A, D, E and K) dissolve in fat. They are stored in the liver, body fat and fatty tissues until needed. If fat-soluble vitamins are taken in excess, the surplus stored in the body's fat can reach toxic levels.
- **Water-soluble vitamins** (C and the B complex group of vitamins) dissolve in water. They are mainly found in watery, sap-filled or juicy foods and associated with the watery tissues in the body. Excess amounts are excreted by the body in urine. As water-soluble vitamins cannot be stored by the body they need to be provided frequently in the diet.

Some vitamins such as D and K can be produced within our bodies, but not in sufficient quantity to meet our needs. By eating a balanced diet made up of healthy and wholesome foods, we can ensure our needs are met.

The following table gives information for each vitamin and its main food sources. The shaded areas indicate vitamins which are fat-soluble and the non-shaded areas show vitamins which are water-soluble.

Vitamin	Food source	Functions and benefits to body	Results of deficiency	Processing and cooking tips
A (retinol)	Butter, cheese, eggs, fish-liver oils, green leafy vegetables, yellow & orange fruits & vegetables, e.g. tomatoes, carrots.	Essential for growth & resistance to infection. Promotes healthy skin, hair & mucous membranes; good vision especially in dim light; bone & tooth growth.	Dry scaly skin & skin infections; problems with vision, night blindness; fatigue; stunted growth in children; poor immunity to infections.	Serve fruit & vegetables raw; store covered in refrigerator. Full-fat milk is high in Vitamin A.
B_1 (thiamin)	Wholegrains/wheat germ, fortified cereals & oatmeals, meat, peas, beans, pasta, rice, yeast, egg yolks, liver.	During metabolism helps body release energy from carbohydrates necessary for growth & healthy muscle tone. Needed for functioning of nervous system.	Nerve disorders, fatigue, mental confusion, heart irregularity. Serious deficiency causes beriberi, with either bloating from fluid retention or excessive weight loss.	Cook pasta & rice in minimal water; do not rinse after cooking. Pasta & rice have B_1 added in production as B_1 is lost in milling.
B_2 (riboflavin)	Milk, cheese, eggs, cereal, meat, green leafy vegetables, yeast & yeast extract, such as Marmite, liver, kidneys.	Enables production of many enzymes. Essential for respiration of body cells.	Anaemia, skin rash, corners of mouth crack, inflammation of tongue & lips.	Store foods in light-proof containers. Cook vegetables in minimal water. Roast or grill meats.
B_3 (niacin)	Milk, cheese, meat, poultry, fish, wholegrains, enriched cereals, peanuts, peas, beans, potatoes, yeast, yeast extracts.	Essential for metabolising carbohydrate, & for functioning of digestive tract & nervous system.	General fatigue, scaly skin, skin disorders, diarrhoea, indigestion, depression.	Cook potatoes in minimal water. Roast or grill meat & poultry.
B_5 (pantothenic acid)	Eggs, wholegrain cereals, lean meat, vegetables, fruit.	Enables use of carbohydrates, fats & amino acids.	Muscle cramps, stomach pains & disorders, vomiting, higher susceptibility to infections, fatigue.	Eat vegetables & fruits raw.
B_6 (pyridoxine)	Meat, liver, fish, poultry, egg yolk, wholegrains/cereals, bananas, avocados, prunes, nuts, seeds, some leafy vegetables, dried beans.	Essential for protein & fat metabolism.	Cracks in skin, dermatitis, anaemia, muscle weakness, convulsions.	Roast or grill meats. Eat fruits raw or minimally cook using little or no water.

Vitamin	Food source	Functions and benefits to body	Results of deficiency	Processing and cooking tips
B$_{12}$ (cobalamin)	Liver, kidney, heart, meat, fish, seafood, milk, cheese, eggs.	Essential for working of the central nervous system, & for maturing of red blood cells in the bone marrow.	Fatigue, nervousness, anaemia.	Roast or grill fish & meats. Non-meats eaters may need to take a supplement.
Biotin	Cereal/grain products, liver, yeast, peas, green beans, egg yolk, artichokes, tomatoes, raspberries.	Involved in metabolism of protein, fats & carbohydrates.	Vomiting & nausea, depression, dry scaly skin, hair loss.	It seems to be unaffected by cooking, storage or processing
Folic acid (folate)	Green leafy vegetables especially spinach & broccoli, offal meats, dried peas, beans, lentils, peanuts.	Vital for promotion of genetic material development. Involved in production of red blood. Pregnant women & premature babies are prone to deficiency in folic acid.	Cracked lips, gastro-intestinal disorders, anaemia.	Store vegetables in refrigerator. Cook by steaming, microwaving or simmering in minimal water.
C (absorbic acid)	Citrus fruits, berries, blackcurrants, green vegetables, potatoes, peppers, liver, kidney.	Essential for red blood cell & antibody formation. Ensures healthy formation & maintenance of bones & connective tissue. Needed for maintenance and strength of blood capillaries. Helps healing, needed for blood clotting. Necessary for many metabolic processes. Uses up potentially damaging excess oxygen in the body (anti-oxidant).	Slow healing of wounds, bleeding gums, fatigue, dizziness, scurvy, depression, poor digestion.	Vitamin C content is diminished or lost by soaking vegetables & fruits in water. Contents in fresh fruit juices is lost after 2–3 days; refrigerate & use quickly after opening.
D	Sunlight, infant formulas, oily fish, fish-liver oils, eggs, fortified dairy products & margarine.	Essential for healthy bone growth as enables absorption of calcium and phosphorus.	Children suffer from bone & growth deformities such as rickets. Adults suffer from calcium loss from bones.	Mainly unaffected by storage, cooking & processing. Sunlight on skin starts production of vitamin D in the body.

Vitamin	Food source	Functions and benefits to body	Results of deficiency	Processing and cooking tips
E	Most vegetable oils, eggs, butter, nuts, seeds, soya beans, green leafy vegetables, fortified & multi-grain cereals.	Protects blood cells, body tissue & essential fatty acids from being destroyed in the body. Uses up potentially damaging oxygen in the body (anti-oxidant).	Anaemia, nerve damage, wasting of muscles, failure of reproductive processes.	Store away from light & keep food in air-tight containers. Some breafast cereals & other cereal products are fortified with vitamin E.
K	Green leafy vegetables, fruit, liver, dairy & grain products. Can be formed in the colon in the human digestive tract.	Essential for blood clotting mechanisms to work.	New-born babies suffer bleeding disorders. People taking medication to thin their blood also suffer from this.	Store away from light in containers. Bacteria in the colon form some vitamin K in the body.

VITAMIN AND MINERAL SUPPLEMENTS.

There are some circumstances where medical advice does advocate the taking of vitamin supplements for children's health. These include:

- women planning a pregnancy: *folic acid (taken pre-conceptually)*
- women in pregnancy, between conception and the twelfth week: *folic acid*
- children from six months to five years: *vitamin A, C, D drops available from health clinics*
- vegan children: *vitamin B$_{12}$, riboflavin with perhaps calcium and iron*
- children with a significant milk or dairy food intolerance: *calcium*
- children on a very restricted diet, such as for food allergy or intolerance.

ALERT:

Vitamin supplements
An excess of vitamins can be dangerous, giving side effects such as nausea, skin rashes, diarrhoea and fatigue. Fat soluble vitamin supplements require particular care. Taking a large excess of water-soluble vitamins can also be very dangerous. *Vitamin supplements should only be given to children or pregnant women on medical advice.*

UNNECESSARY INTAKE OF SUPPLEMENTS

Research shows that many people who regularly take vitamin and mineral supplements are in fact some of the most affluent and well-fed members of the population, and so are the least likely to need them! A well-balanced diet will provide all the essential nutrients that most people will ever need. As a rule it is always better to obtain vitamins and minerals from food than from supplements. Vitamins tend to be absorbed better from food and there is no real risk of overdosing.

There has been a popular trend in taking supplements of *antioxidants*, especially vitamins A, C and E and selenium in response to the information that, by mopping up excess oxygen in the body, they play a protective role against heart disease and some cancers. Research has proven their benefits when absorbed from foods, but evidence is less convincing that they are effective when taken as supplements. People wishing to increase their intake of antioxidants are now advised to do so by increasing the amount of fruit and vegetables they eat to at least six portions a day.

▬ ▬ ▬ ▬ ▬ ▬ ▬*Good professional practice* ▬ ▬ ▬ ▬ ▬ ▬ ▬

Nutritional supplements are an area of nutrition where there is a lot of misinformation, much advertising pressure and media-reported trends. It can be a minefield and an expensive minefield at that! Always seek medical advice before giving any supplements to children. The importance is to **ensure children have a balanced diet and don't rely on supplements.**

ACTIVITY

1. Study a selection of food labels. On the nutritional contents tables find out whether any figures for '% RDA' (recommended daily amounts) are shown for vitamins and minerals.

2. Compare the vitamin and mineral contents of three different types of breakfast cereals. Which would be the best cereal for a child who was anaemic? Why?

The importance of water in the diet

Water is essential to life. A fit healthy adult human can survive for several weeks without food but only a few days without water. Water is found in all parts of our bodies particularly in the cells, tissues and blood. Water makes up around two-thirds of our total body weight.

The body cannot store water and is constantly using and losing it through sweat, urine, faeces and moist exhaled breath. Water in the body needs to be replenished daily. Drinking it regularly and several times a day is optimum.

How much water do we need to drink?

Children with their active lifestyles, hard-working metabolisms and smaller stomach capacities need to drink water more frequently and regularly than adults.

A Guide of daily requirements for water	
Age	Mls of water per kg of body weight
1–3 years	95 mls/kg
4–6 years	85 mls/kg
7–10 years	75 mls/kg
Adults	35 mls/kg

As a rule of thumb, a healthy adult should aim to drink at least 2 litres of water a day.

ACTIVITY

1. Enter the details for five children between the ages of one and eight years old to the following table.

Child's Name	Age	Weight	Mls/kg needed daily (according to above chart)	Estimated total daily water requirement

2. Share your figures with your colleagues and together work out a rough 'rule of thumb' for your own reference which gives a guidance for children's daily water drinking needs for the three age bands shown in the chart above.

Vital functions of water are to:
- enable the formation of cells and tissues
- carry oxygen and carbon-dioxide in the blood
- transport nutrients around the body
- carry the enzymes and support digestion
- allow the excretion of waste products from the body tissues and the elimination of urine from the body
- protect the central nervous system
- regulate body temperature
- form a lubricant for joints and membranes.

- - - - - - - - - - -Key point- - - - - - - - - - - -

Fluid requirements increase greatly when a fever is present and when the external temperature is high. **Dehydration can quickly become serious for small children. Babies are at particular risk in hot weather and when ill.**

Sources of water

Water is mainly obtained from drinking fluids, although many foods have a high water content which also help to meet our needs. Juicy fruits and vegetables as well as more liquid foods, such as jelly, custard, soup, gravy and sauces, all have a high water content which make a contribution to fluid intake.

- - - - - - - -Good professional practice- - - - - - - -

It is good Early Years practice to provide opportunities for young children to pour their own drinks and to offer drinks to others. Children should be encouraged to drink water frequently and manage their drinking sensibly. Fine motor, social and communication skills can all be learnt together with the nutritionally healthy practice of drinking water.

Watch me! . . . Going! . . . Gone! Water is good to drink!

ALERT

Care should be taken in the timing and selection of types of drinks for children as those with high fruit, sugar and acid contents can cause tooth decay. Soft drinks can also provide 'empty calories' which fill children up without providing adequate nutrition.

ACTIVITY

1. Estimate and write down how much water you drink on average each day.

2. Fill plastic bottles with 2 litres of water and refrigerate overnight. During the course of the following day regularly drink water from the bottles.

3. Measure any water remaining before you go to bed and record the quantity drunk. Refill the bottles with fresh water ready for the next day.

4. Repeat the exercise for a week, measuring and recording the amount drunk each day.

5. At the end of the week, with a colleague:
   (a) Look at your quantities of daily intake of water.
   (b) Look at your patterns of daily intake over the week.
   (c) Compare your intakes on day seven with (i) your estimated intakes as in item 1 and (ii) your intakes on day one.

END OF CHAPTER ACTIVITY

You have a secure understanding why children need to drink water frequently. You know that it is good practice to educate young children to drink independently and regularly throughout the day. In your placement: Look at the types of drinks, the children's access to them and the frequency during the day they drink them. Find out:

1. What drinks the children have and how they are organised.

2. What drinking water sources are available for children? Do they have free access to drinking water at all times or only at certain times during the day?

3. Is milk provided? Do children bring in drinks from home? (If so what kind of drinks are they?)

4. Do you think the children have enough to drink, especially in hot weather and following concentrated physical activity? Might it be possible for a child to go all day without having a drink at all?

5. Are the children helped and encouraged to become independent in getting their own drinks? If so, how, when and by whom? Are they always dependent on an adult to provide drinks?

6. What changes could you suggest to improve the existing ideas and systems?

7. What impact would these improvements have on the children?

8. File your notes carefully. You may find them useful for a future campaign!

Quick quiz

Find the answers in the chapter.

1. Why should young children not have a high-fibre diet when adults should?

2. Which vitamin enables good absorption of iron?

3. What is the function of: (a) vitamin C (b) vitamin D (c) calcium? What are the main food sources for each of these micronutrients?

4. Why is it very dangerous for babies and toddlers to have salty food or food with added salt (sodium chloride)?

5. What are the two main types of fats? Which type has been shown to be related to the onset of heart disease?

6. There are two types of protein. What are they and what does each nutritionally provide?

7. What is meant by 'suitable protein combinations' of foods? Give an example of a protein-combination dish suitable for a vegetarian.

8. What is meant by 'intrinsic' and 'extrinsic' sugars?

9. What could cause dehydration in babies and young children?

10. What kind of milk and yoghurts should be given to young children?

Summary

Now you have read this chapter you should understand:

- what are the seven essential nutrients, their composition, main sources and functions
- the key to good health is through eating a well-balanced diet, rich in various fruits, leafy vegetables, cereal products, lean meat and fish
- some important principles of children's nutritional needs and how these differ from adults'

4

Nutritional Needs: Making Sense of the Five Food Groups

Aims of the chapter

To enable you to understand:

- the importance of calories
- some important principles of children's nutritional needs and how these differ from adults'
- the relationship between the seven essential nutrients and the five food groups: the *Balance of Good Health* model
- the five food groups and how they can support the planning of nutritionally balanced eating for children.

Amazed and depressed that the six-day carrot and chocolate diet had not worked, Flossie decided she had to choose another regime.

The importance of calories
Food, energy and energy stores

Food provides the body with energy. Without energy the metabolic and physical bodily functions essential for life cannot be sustained. If the body is denied its essential source of energy, there is a greater susceptibility to infection, healing is poor, growth and development are affected, bodily functions start to fail, tiredness and lethargy set in.

The body protects itself when there is a poor energy intake by using up its energy stores to keep on functioning. The body has various sources of stored energy. It prioritises which of its stores to use in order to maintain essential functions and its major organs. Some stores are more readily accessible for conversion into usable energy than others, and our stored body fat is not the easiest one to use up! (A sad but true fact!)

A cautionary word about energy stores, body fat and 'crash' or 'yo-yo' dieting!

An adult can only burn just under 1 kilogram (2lbs) of stored body fat per week. When the body's energy intake is greatly reduced by limited eating, the primary weight loss is of water and lean body tissue (muscle). This is because muscle is more easily utilised or *metabolised* by the body for energy than its stored fat.

Sudden weight loss resulting from 'crash' diets is not caused by significant reduction in total body fat. The body's capacity to survive provides the reason why someone following a 'crash' or 'starvation' diet in the hope of losing weight quickly, readily puts on weight as soon as they return to their former eating habits. These diets are not successful and not nutritionally sound.

When a 'crash' diet is ended and old eating habits resumed, body weight is not only quickly regained, it often readily increases to a higher fat level than prior to the 'diet'. This occurs because the body has been under threat of starvation and makes contingency plans to store fat against any possible recurrence of famine. Therefore energy from food that is eaten following the starvation period is stored in the form of fat. It is a basic survival mechanism!

This natural response explains why 'serial' or 'yo-yo' dieters usually fail to make permanent positive changes to their lives, energy levels and bodies. This is why a balanced diet and a long term commitment to a healthy lifestyle is the only way to achieving optimum nutrition and well being.

ALERT

Professional medical and specialist dietary advice should be sought for children who are overweight or thought to be obese. Great care must be taken to give correct nutrition and adequate energy intake to growing children. Weight loss diets for children are different from those suitable for adults and should only be followed under medical supervision.

The measurement of energy in food

Most people are very familiar with the term *calories*. Calorie controlled weight-loss diets are popular, being based on the simple fact that if you eat more calories than your body uses up in energy then the excess is stored in your body as fat. Calories are simply a way of measuring the energy value of food.

A single calorie is such a tiny energy measurement in food that the Department of Health uses kilocalories (1000 calories), alongside the internationally accepted *kilojoule* (1000 joules), in its published table of *Estimated Average Requirements*. Most food labelling of nutritional information also uses both these terms.

However often when we use the term calorie we are not being strictly correct, as food energy is usually measured in kilocalories, generally shown as k/cal or kcal. (In general conversation about food, using the word 'calorie' can be seen as a kind of spoken shorthand.)

Felix needs a well balanced healthy diet to maintain his health, growth and energetic lifestyle.

1 kilocalorie (kcal) = 4.2 kilojoules (kJ)

As *calorie* is the long-standing unit which is still mostly used in the UK, it will be used in this book.

- - - - - - -*Good professional practice*- - - - - - -

Start to read food labels regularly. Become aware of similar foods and products which have higher and lower calorific values.

Sources of energy

The body obtains the energy or calories it needs from the energy bearing nutrients in food, and in particular from fats, proteins and carbohydrates.

- *Fat* in the diet provides the most concentrated source of energy, giving 9 k/calories per gram.
- *Protein* provides 4 k/calories per gram.
- *Carbohydrate* provides about 4 k/calories per gram.

ALERT

Choosing foods only by their calorific values is not nutritionally sound practice. The nutritional content of food must be considered in addition to the energy value.

- - - - - - - - - - - *Key point*- - - - - - - - - - -

The golden rule is to eat a balanced and varied diet, made up of a full range and types of foods, *but with a limited intake of highly processed, high-fat and high-sugar foods* (see Chapter 4).

ACTIVITY

Obtain a selection of leaflets on *balanced diets* from some supermarkets and also *The Food Sense Booklet: Healthy Eating* (*published by MAFF*). Compare how the information about the five main food groups is set out.

▶ How do the leaflets try to explain to the reader what makes for balanced eating?
▶ How well are the five food groups explained?

▶ How do the leaflets set out the information about the various quantities and proportions of different food groups that should go to forming a healthy diet?

▶ What warnings or special information are given in the leaflets about the requirements of babies and young children? Is this information clear to find and to understand?

▶ How useful are these leaflets for giving clear guidance for families with young children?

Some important principles of children's nutritional needs and how these differ from adults': young children and healthy eating

Healthy eating is important for children. They do require relatively large proportions of nutrients and calories to meet their high energy needs, for growth, body maintenance, to combat illness and enable a busy and active lifestyle.

'Healthy eating for young children' is not exactly the same as 'healthy eating for adults'. Each group has different needs. Children have smaller stomachs but very high energy expenditure. They must eat smaller amounts but regularly and more often than adults.

If young children regularly fill themselves up with low-nutrient food this can affect their health and development. If they have too much fibre or eat too many foods with a high sugar and fat content, these readily fill their small stomachs and can prevent them from eating more nutritious foods in sufficient and necessary quantities.

Children require concentrated forms of high calorie foods which are also full of necessary nutrients. Young children need the nutrients and calories contained in full-fat milk and dairy products. For young children dairy fats, found especially in full-fat milk products, are important high energy sources.

Three year old Becky has a very active life, is growing fast and proportionally needs to eat many more calories than her grandfather.

	Weight	Daily k/cals needed	Intake of k/cals per kg/ of body weight
Becky	15kg	1500	100
Grandad	83kg	2330	28

- - - - - - - - - - - - Key point - - - - - - - - - - -

Babies and young children, *in relation to their size*, need relatively much higher proportions of calories than adults. Be very careful not to deny children the essential calories they need, especially if the adults around them are restricting their own intake.

Why young children need a high-energy healthy balanced diet

The two main reasons why young children (and adolescents) have a significant energy requirement are because they are usually very active and simultaneously they are growing relatively fast. Many parents of older children will tell you that over the years their children have gone through some very noticeable 'growth spurts', often suddenly increasing in height or shoe size. They will also give testimony to their children's related and sudden increases in appetite, which can be especially challenging when feeding rapidly growing teenagers.

Most children quite naturally will eat what their bodies need for healthy growth and to sustain their busy active lives. Poor eating habits tend to result in a child putting on excess weight rather than gaining insufficient weight for optimum growth. It is comparatively rare to find a young child, who is offered a balanced range of foods, whose overall eating fails to meet their nutritional needs. (See Chapter 7 for information about 'food fads' and 'difficult eaters').

People who are active need much more energy than someone of the same age and gender who leads a more sedentary life.

Helping young children to develop early healthy eating habits and attitudes gives them the greatest chance to continue to eat healthily as they grow up. A healthy diet from an early age reduces their chances of developing coronary and other dietary related diseases later in life.

Getting older does not have to mean giving up enjoyable and healthy activity. Healthy eating and regular exercise enable long, happy and active living.

- - - - - - - - -Key points- - - - - - - - - -

- *In relation to their size*, young children use much more energy than adults, so they need a higher calorie intake.
- They need a balanced diet which includes full-fat milk and dairy products.
- Filling foods with low nutrient contents should be given very sparingly.
- Low fat, skimmed or fat-free products should **not** be given regularly to young children.
- Their intake of high fibre foods should also be limited.

The relationship between the seven essential nutrients and the five food groups

The five food groups

The model was developed using information and guidance arising from the Department of Health Reports and detailed in 1994 in *The National Food Guide: The Balance of Good Health*.

The concept of the Food Groups has been developed to inform people about healthy balanced eating without requiring them to have significant or specialised knowledge about the subject of nutrition. Using this model makes it simpler to plan meals and to keep an eye on eating patterns.

The Balance of Good Health

Types of food are ascribed to each of the *five food groups* according to which of the *seven essential nutrients* they contain, and the nutrition they provide when digested and absorbed by the body.

The foods in each food group contain a range of nutrients but are categorised according to their largest *essential nutrient* constituent.

▬ ▬ ▬ ▬ ▬ ▬ ▬ ▬ ▬ ─ **Key point** ─ ▬ ▬ ▬ ▬ ▬ ▬ ▬ ▬ ▬

> If foods are eaten in the recommended proportions from each food group, the full range of the Seven Essential Nutrients will be provided.

The *Balance of Good Health* is a visual model which has been developed to show the proportions of the different food groups which should be eaten to ensure an optimum diet. Because the model demonstrates the *proportion of foods* in the diet rather than specific quantities, it can be used to plan eating for people with differing energy needs. In other words the plate in the picture can be huge or small according to the needs of the individual but the proportions served on each need to be the same.

The model is based on Five Food Groups which are categorised by their main nutritional content. They are:

Group 1: Bread, Cereal Foods and Potatoes.
Group 2: Fruit and Vegetables.
Group 3: Milk and Dairy Products.
Group 4: Meat, Fish and Alternatives - high protein foods.
Group 5: Fat-rich and Sugar-rich Foods.

▬ ▬ ▬ ▬ ▬ ▬ ▬ ▬ ▬ ─ **Key point** ─ ▬ ▬ ▬ ▬ ▬ ▬ ▬ ▬ ▬

> The Balance of Good Health model shows that around two-thirds of our diet should come from two groups of foods; the Bread and Cereal Group and the Fruit and Vegetables Group. The intake of food from the Meat and Alternatives Group and the Milk and Dairy Group together make up the majority of the rest of the diet, with the final small proportion coming from the Fat-rich and Sugar-rich Food Group.

> **ALERT**
> * The nationally published *Balance of Good Health* model is designed primarily for the adult population. It is this model for adult eating which is reproduced in the MAFF leaflets and in supermarket information materials.
> * Young children need a healthy diet, but for them the guidance given in this model on two aspects, fat restriction and adherence to a high fibre intake, is not really suitable for young children.

Making the food groups model more appropriate for children

The overall messages of the *Balance of Good Health* model are relevant but the proportions of foods (shown for adults) are different from those needed by young children.

▬ ▬ ▬ ▬ ▬ ▬ ▬ ▬ ▬ ▬ ▬ ▬ Key point ▬ ▬ ▬ ▬ ▬ ▬ ▬ ▬ ▬ ▬ ▬ ▬

The Balance of Good Health model shows that around two-thirds of our diet should come from two groups of foods; the Bread and Cereal Group and the Fruit and Vegetables Group. The intake of food from the Meat and Alternatives Group and the Milk and Dairy Group together make up the majority of the rest of the diet, with the final small proportion coming from the Fat-rich and Sugar-rich Food Group.

Small children need less fibre and more fat in their diets than older children and adults. Adults need more fibre and less fat than young children.

Guidelines for a healthy diet for young children are to:
• Eat regular meals and snacks, including breakfast.
• Drink plenty of water.
• Eat the right *balance* of foods, which means eating foods from all of the following five food groups but in appropriate *proportions* and *quantities*.

The five food groups and how they can support the planning of nutritionally balanced eating for children

To ensure a child's diet is healthy and is well balanced, an appropriate *proportion* of foods from *each of the food groups* should be included in what the young child eats. If possible this mix should be present every day for older children too, but realistically most children will thrive on a diet which is regularly balanced over two or three days.

How much food should a child have each day?

CHILDREN'S PORTIONS AND DAILY SERVINGS

Where *recommended daily servings for children* from each of the Food Groups and *suggested portions* are shown below, the actual amount of food will need to vary according to the age and size of the individual child. Between eighteen months and eight years children's appetites, tastes, individual needs and capacities change enormously! Two fish fingers may be plenty Group 3 Food for a hungry three year old's dinner, but are likely to be viewed with dismay and disdain by a ravenous eight year old after swimming!

On the whole children do not naturally overeat. They tend to eat what they need to feel comfortably full. It is therefore crucial that adults provide children with a variety of foods which provide adequate all-round nutrition in the diet, and which do not fill them up without meeting their nutritional needs.

These matters should be taken into account when reading the following information.

Food Group 1: bread, other cereals and potatoes

- This group consists of *carbohydrate-rich* foods, starchy, high energy foods. (see *carbohydrates*, page 37).
- They naturally contain many vitamins and minerals.
- Foods in this group are mainly derived from cereal or grain crops and potatoes.
- These are often termed *staple* foods because they are commonly eaten, should form a significant proportion of each main meal and provide the bulk of our diet.

Examples of Group 1 foods are:

- potatoes
- rice
- pasta
- bread (brown, white, wholemeal, pitta, unleavened, etc.)
- breakfast cereals
- pizza bases
- polenta
- oatmeal
- couscous
- millet or mealie
- semolina
- rice cakes
- oat cakes
- crisp bread.

Children's needs:

- Foods from this group are essential energy providers and should be included in every meal.
- Products manufactured from these foods can make high energy snacks.
- Wholemeal, wholegrains and potato skins are high in fibre. Although they contain some additional nutrients, they are filling and so should be limited for young children.
- **Never** give bran to children as it can hinder calcium and iron absorption which are critical nutrients for young children.

CHILDREN'S DAILY REQUIREMENTS OF GROUP 1 FOODS

Five daily servings are needed from this group.
Examples of 'one serving' of Group 1 Foods:

- Two tablespoons of rice or pasta.
- One small boiled potato.
- One slice of bread.

- Two small oatcakes.
- One bowl of porridge.
- One bowl of semolina pudding.

Group 2: fruit and vegetables

- They are high in vitamins and minerals.
- Many are high in fibre.
- Overall they are low in fat, but some such as avocados, seeds and nuts are a source of nutritionally rich fats.
- Substances, such as gums and pectins, found in the plant sap of many vegetables and fruit have been linked with reducing blood cholesterol level and in managing aspects of diabetes.
- These substances also regulate the digestion of other nutrients in foods, and slow the release of food out of the stomach which help control hunger pangs.

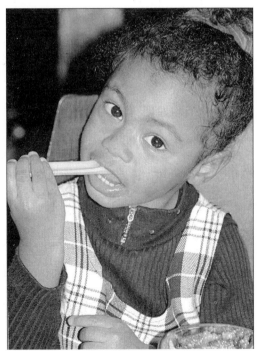

Raw vegetables are great as snacks or with meals.

Children's needs:

- Raw fruit and vegetables are nutritious and often enjoyed by children with meals or as snacks.
- Fruit and vegetable juices are nutrient-rich.
- Frozen vegetables are also nutrient-rich.
- A fruit or vegetable high in vitamin C should be included daily in a child's diet.

CHILDREN'S DAILY REQUIREMENTS OF GROUP 2 FOODS

The slogan for Group 2 foods until recently was 'TAKE FIVE'. The recommendation is now that children need *five or six daily servings* from this group.

Examples of 'one serving' of Group 2 foods:

- one piece of fresh fruit (e.g. an apple or banana), sliced, whole, grated.
- one fruit rich in vitamin C (e.g. a tomato, orange or kiwi fruit.)
- one glass of fruit or vegetable juice.
- one green vegetable(e.g. two tablespoons of peas, grated courgettes, chopped spinach.)
- tablespoon of dried fruit (e.g. raisins, apricots, dates.)
- raw vegetable sticks (e.g. carrot, cucumber, sweet red pepper.)
- bunch of grapes or some stoned cherries.
- two tablespoons of sweet corn.

ALERT:
Processing and cooking can destroy vitamin content of fruit and vegetables. Eating them raw guards against loss of nutrients. Care needs to be taken in cooking.

Group 3: milk and milk/dairy products.

- The group includes cow's, goat's and sheep' milk and products made from milk.
- Breast milk is also included (as a baby's sole source of nutrition and during weaning). (See chapter 5.)
- Milk made from soya beans.
- All of these foods are rich in protein, in saturated and unsaturated fats, calcium and milk sugars.

Examples of Group 3 Foods:

- milk
- milkshakes
- cream
- yoghurt
- fromage frais

- cheese
- cheese spreads
- butter
- creme fraiche
- real dairy or home-made ice cream.

Children's needs:

- Children daily need 1 pint of whole milk or the equivalent in cheese or yoghurt, etc. for their calcium intake requirements.
- Semi-skimmed milk is only ever suitable for children over two years if their daily diet includes sufficient quantities of other full-fat dairy products.
- Reduced dairy fat milks and milk products, such as 'skimmed', 'fat free' or 'reduced fat' are low in energy and they have a low fat-soluble vitamin capacity. They should not be given to children under five.
- Babies under four months should only ever be fed breast or baby formula milks. (See Chapter 5 on feeding young babies and Chapter 6 for weaning.)
- Be aware of 'hidden' non-dairy fats and sugars which may be added to products, such as to some ice creams and processed milk drinks.

CHILDREN'S DAILY REQUIREMENTS OF GROUP 3 FOODS

Children need *three daily servings* from this group.

Examples of 'one serving' of Group 3 Foods are:

- one glass (about a third of a pint) of full fat milk.
- one pot of yoghurt or fromage frais.
- one tablespoon of grated cheese
- a third of a pint of full fat milk on cereal or in a sauce or soup.

Food Group 4: meat, fish and alternatives – high-protein foods

- These are foods which are rich in first class or high nutrient value proteins.
- They are mainly foods from animal sources but also include high nutrient value vegetable foods based on pulses and soya.

Examples of Group 4 foods:

- lean red meat
- **poultry**
- eggs
- fish
- quorn
- tofu
- **pulses** (peas, beans, lentils), seeds, nuts.

Children's needs:

- Foods from animal and vegetable sources as well as combinations of first- and second-class types of protein should be included in a child's diet.

Children's daily requirements of Group 4 foods

Children require *two daily servings* of food from this group.

Examples of 'one serving' from Group 4 foods:

- portion of baked beans
- fish fingers
- small piece of chicken
- portion of savoury minced beef
- portion of chicken nuggets
- bowl of lentil and rice soup

Group 5: fat-rich and sugar-rich foods

These are the foods which ought to form the very smallest proportion of our diet as they are generally filling but low in essential nutrients. Any nutrients they do contain are limited and are more effectively available from the nutritionally richer sources of foods in the other four food groups.

- These foods are all high in energy, i.e. even a low volume has a high energy density.
- They carry few other nutrients.
- They usually contain high levels of refined sugars.
- They are usually highly processed foods, often containing hydrogenated saturated fats.
- They are filling without being rich in a range of nutrients.
- Eating large proportions of these foods can lead to excessive weight gain, obesity and to dental decay.

Examples of Group 5 foods:

- chocolate and other sweet biscuits
- doughnuts
- sausages
- burgers.
- sweets and candies
- ice-cream
- mayonnaise
- crisps.

- shop bought cakes and pastries
- meat pies
- chips and other foods deep fried in fats
- soft drinks
- table sugar

Children's needs:

- Children do need to eat high energy foods. But foods from this group should **not** provide a significant proportion of their energy intake.
- If young children eat and fill up on too many foods from the Fat-rich and sugar-rich Group it will be at the expense of foods from the other four food groups.
- Eating a high proportion of Group 5 foods means the diet will be unbalanced and most critically it will not meet their nutritional needs.

Children may be offered foods containing high levels of fat or sugar but care must be taken to ensure these are not replacing food from the other four food groups.

------------- Key point -----------------

If we **daily** eat a **variety** of foods from each of the **five food groups**, and eat appropriate **proportions** of foods from the groups, we can readily and automatically balance our diet and also ensure that children are healthily and well fed.

The key words for ensuring healthy eating are BALANCE, VARIETY, RANGE and PROPORTION – and don't forget ENJOYMENT!

------- Good professional practice --------

Make a chart for your personal reference of how many portions (or servings) of each of the five food groups that a child should have daily.

END OF CHAPTER ACTIVITY

1. Obtain a range of leaflets on 'healthy eating' which use the Food Groups as the basis for their main messages. What changes would you need to make to one of these pamphlets to make the more information applicable for young children?

2. Draw a poster or a diagram that shows how the Seven Essential Nutrients relate to the Five Food Groups.

Quick quiz

Find the answers in the chapter.

1. Why do young children need a proportionally higher energy giving and a more nutritionally rich diet than adults?

2. How could you ensure a child's *required daily intake* if she did not want to eat fresh fruit?

3. Why should children be given 'full fat' milk every day but not fat-rich doughnuts?

4. How many servings of Group 2 foods should a child have daily?

5. Give four examples of different foods in Food Group 4.

6. Which vitamin, contained in fruit, should you give every child every day?

7. In what food group would you categorise nan bread, spaghetti, mealie and rice?

8. What nutrient in fruit and vegetables can be destroyed during cooking?

9. Which Group 3 food, essential for children, is rich in protein, saturated and unsaturated fats, calcium and sugars.

10. What would you say to a parent who worries about their child eating 'too many' sweets?

Summary

Having studied this chapter you should now understand:

- about calories, energy and food
- how nutritional and energy needs of different people vary according to age, gender, lifestyle and occupation
- some important principles of children's nutritional needs and how these differ from adults'
- the relations between the five food groups and the seven essential nutrients
- how to ensure children's nutritional needs can be met through providing a range and variety of different foods
- what are the five food groups and how they can support the planning of nutritionally balanced eating for children.

5

Providing a Healthy Start in Life

Aims of the chapter

To enable you to understand:

- the importance of good nutrition in pregnancy for the baby's health
- the nutritional needs of the newborn baby and during the first months of life
- choosing between breast or formula feeding
- the nutritional properties of breast milk and how breastfeeding can be effective for babies' growth and development
- advantages, disadvantages, management and good practices of formula feeding.

Flossie found it hard enough to face the day, never mind facing breakfast

The importance of good nutrition in pregnancy for the baby's health

For a healthy baby to have the best start in life she should choose two healthy parents! A planned pregnancy, with good professional support, gives a baby the best chances for good health, growth and development.

Medical care and advice for parents should begin before the baby is conceived. Good *pre-conceptual care* fully involves parents in taking responsibility for themselves and their planned baby. Both need to be as healthy as possible before even starting the pregnancy. This includes giving up smoking, not taking any drugs or medicines

Caroline knows a healthy diet is vital during pregnancy. She needs energy to nourish the developing baby and to cope with her young child.

(unless prescribed by a doctor), and eating well.

Good nutrition in pregnancy

It is *not true* that a pregnant woman needs to eat for two in terms of quantities, as only an extra 200 calories a day are needed to support pregnancy. However, it is *true* in terms of her taking responsibility for her eating needed for the sake of her own health and that of her baby's.

It is very important that she has a balanced diet containing all of the *seven required essential nutrients* for her pregnancy, and that food from each of the *four main food groups* is eaten every day.

A pregnant woman should avoid eating shellfish, raw or undercooked eggs, unpasteurised milk and cheese, and any blue cheeses. These foods are a high risk for carrying listeria, salmonella or other harmful bacteria.

The inclusion of vitamin A in animal feeds as growth promoters for livestock means that most liver now contains too high a level of vitamin A for safety in pregnancy. Too much vitamin A can cause serious birth defects, so a woman should avoid eating liver and liver products, such as pâté and sausage just before and during pregnancy. She will not have a deficiency of vitamin A as the body can turn beta-carotene (found in orange and green fruit and vegetables) into vitamin A as it is needed.

She should eat fresh food whenever possible. Her intake of any alcohol, sugar, saturated (particularly animal) fats, and salt in foods should be minimised.

ALERT
A pregnant woman should avoid eating:

- foods containing raw eggs
- undercooked eggs
- raw or undercooked meat
- unpasteurised milk or cheeses
- blue cheeses and pates
- liver and liver products
- unwashed fruit and vegetables.

Essential supplements and pregnancy

In pregnancy a woman's body has special, additional and particular nutritional needs.

Folic acid, a B group vitamin, is an especially important nutrient. It is vital for foetal cell formation, in particular for the development of the baby's brain and spinal cord. It helps to protect against spina bifida.

Folic acid tablets are an essential supplement to be taken most importantly pre-conceptually, but also during pregnancy and for the first 12 weeks of pregnancy.

Foods rich in folic acid should also be frequently eaten by an expectant mother, especially before she conceives and during the first 12 weeks of pregnancy.

Folic acid is found in:
- wholemeal bread
- fortified breakfast cereals
- green leafy vegetables
- yeast extracts such as Marmite.

- - - - - - - - - - - *Key point* - - - - - - - - - - -

The most critical time in pregnancy is during the first 12 weeks. It is the period of fastest development in the formation of the baby's systems and organs. A healthy lifestyle and the mother's care of her own health and diet are particularly vital in these first months.

Energy intake and needs in pregnancy

Food and drinks taken into the body must be in balance with the energy the body uses up. If the amount eaten provides an energy intake which is more than the body really needs, the body will store the unused excess calories as fat. The average healthy weight gain for a woman of average weight during pregnancy is between 10 and 15 kilograms.

Care is needed to ensure the quantities the mother eats (even of correct healthy food) matches the energy needs of the mother and developing baby. Too little food or the wrong types of low nutrient foods can prevent the baby from growing sufficiently.

In the last three months of pregnancy the mother's need for energy increases. The baby is now growing rapidly. This increase in weight and continuing development must be supported.

ALERT

A poor or unbalanced diet can lead to the mother becoming either underweight or overweight. This situation is very likely to negatively affect the baby's well being and healthy development.

The nutritional needs of the new born baby and during the first months of life

Babies need food for growth and replacement of body tissues, the regulation of their body temperature, the formation of bones, the transmission of nerve impulses and for having enough energy for the body to function and to move.

Babies' growth rates

During the first year of life the baby's growth rate is at its greatest; this is especially so during the first months:

Age in months	Weight gain per week
From 0–6 mths	4–8 ozs
From 6–12 mths	3–5 ozs

A thriving healthy baby will put on between 4 and 8 ounces per week from birth to six months old. From six months to twelve months a baby should gain between 3 and 5 ounces a week. However, it is not only observable weight and height growth that occur. **The most important rate of growth happens with the brain.** It is very important to ensure that a baby receives nutrition which fully meets all her needs.

Successful Feeding

Successful feeding means that the baby thrives and *gains weight* within the norms shown above. The baby needs to take in the optimum quantity of milk and to feel comforted, safe and secure.

ALERT

Feeding is not simply a time for giving the baby nutrition for physical growth and movement. It is an important time for many more reasons.

During feeding the mother and baby develop a shared communication and understanding of each other. Their relationship blossoms and they learn more and more about each other. This *bonding* is essential for the baby's social, emotional and intellectual development. If a baby is bottle fed it enables the father to share these experiences with the baby too. Feeding time should be relaxed, comfortable and enjoyable for both parent and baby. Speaking, making eye contact and listening are all activities for the adult to encourage and share with the baby.

Shared communication between Chloe and her mother at feeding time.

- - - - - - - *Good professional practice* - - - - - -

It is important to understand that at every feed the baby's social, emotional and communication development are all involved and need attention. Feeding time is an important learning time.

Feeding skills, learning and development

Babies are born with many skills and abilities. The newborn baby has an ability to turn towards a touch on her face. This is called the *rooting reflex*. If the baby's face is brushed with the nipple or a bottle teat, the baby turns to it, opens her mouth, curls back her lips and searches for the nipple with her mouth. When the nipple, teat or even a finger enters between her lips she begins to suck. Sucking is also a reflex action in the newly born.

As the baby gets older she begins to recognise earlier signs that food is about to arrive. It may be she sees the bottle or breast before it touches her mouth. It is well known that breastfed babies react strongly to the smell of their mothers' milk before even touching the breast for feeding.

With an older baby yet even earlier clues in the feeding routine are picked up. She may become agitated or excited. She can remember previous feeds, the pattern of events and has learnt to anticipate and predict. She has developed intellectually and is communicating her pleasure and wishes.

1. Observe a young baby being fed. Note her anticipation, vocalisation and physical movements which show how she communicates her hunger, excitement or pleasure. Observe her mouth, eyes, hand and whole body movements during feeding. Do these change during the feed?

2. Observe an older baby noting the same range of movements and behaviours. How does this baby differ from the younger baby? What does this tell you about her learning and development?

Choosing between breast or formula feeding

Decide what your own personal attitudes are to breastfeeding and bottle-feeding formula milk. Note down your main points.

During the *ante-natal* period parents should be given professional advice and information on different feeding methods, their various benefits and babies' needs. The actual choice of methods must always be the parents' own.

For parents the process of deciding how to feed their baby may be complex, difficult and influenced by many factors which may or may not be disclosed to professionals. Cultural, social, medical and personal factors can all play a part in the choice.

– – – – – – –*Good professional practice* – – – – – – –

Remember! The decision whether to breast or formula feed is for *the parents* to make.

Professionals must be sensitive and never jump to any conclusions. A mother may really want to formula feed and, through outside pressure can be made to feel very guilty for not choosing breastfeeding. Similarly a mother who may want to breastfeed, can feel failure and misery when feeding difficulties arise. It can be compounded if she is unsympathetically told to start bottle-feeding immediately by those she looks to for support.

ACTIVITY

Find the most recent article you can on the Internet which addresses this important matter. Make notes which would help you to support a mother faced with an inability to feed her baby in the way she had originally hoped to and had planned.

ALERT

Health professionals, carers or other family members must never coerce or manipulate parents into deciding how to feed their baby. Such external pressure is unhelpful at best and very damaging at worst. It can result in the mother feeding her baby in a way which causes her unhappiness or guilt.

The mother's success and confidence in whichever method she has chosen is the vital factor for ensuring the mother and baby develop the best relationship, and that the baby has the best start in life.

— — — — — — — *Good professional practice* — — — — — —

Ante-natal education should include consideration of the possibility of having to formula feed a baby if the mother is physically unable to produce enough breast milk.

The nutritional properties of breast milk and how breastfeeding can be effective for babies' growth and development

Facts about breastfeeding

There are some aspects of breastfeeding, affecting the baby and the mother, which are different to formula feeding:

- breastfed babies have less gastro-enteritis, tooth decay and fewer respiratory infections than formula-fed babies
- breast milk helps prevent allergies or at least lessens their severity
- breast milk supplies some significant immunity from disease

- breastfed babies are less likely to be overweight
- breastfeeding directly affects the contraction of the mother's womb (uterus) and speeds this process
- breastfeeding uses a large number of the mother's calories, and with healthy eating, can aid the loss of any excess weight gained by the mother during pregnancy
- breastfeeding does not involve sterilisation of equipment or mixing of feeds
- milk is instantly available, convenient and cannot be mixed incorrectly
- it is cost free, which could be particularly important to low income families not qualifying for state benefits
- breastfeeding is an aspect of the ongoing nutritional partnership between the mother and baby, which starts at conception, continues through pregnancy and then after the birth
- no health-related disadvantages have been found for breastfeeding a baby. (The only condition where this is not true is if the mother is HIV positive, when she will need to be given specialised, detailed and careful information about the choices open to her)
- no manufactured formula milks completely match the full nutritional qualities of human breast milk
- breast milk meets *all* of a baby's developing and changing nutritional needs until the start of weaning (See Chapter 6).

▬ ▬ ▬ ▬ ▬ ▬ ▬*Good professional practice* ▬ ▬ ▬ ▬ ▬ ▬

Whatever decision parents make about feeding their baby it is important that child carers and health professionals inform them clearly, support them fully and respect their choices.

ACTIVITY

Suggest some reasons why an expectant mother might decide not to breastfeed her baby after birth. If you personally disagreed with some of her reasons how would you professionally react?

Management of breastfeeding

BREASTS AND BREASTFEEDING

The size and shape of a woman's breasts are not related to her ability to produce breast milk and feed her baby successfully. However, the shape of the nipple is important. It needs to be able to become erect to allow the baby to latch on to the breast, stimulate the flow of milk and suck effectively. Mothers whose nipples do not readily stand out can be helped and encouraged to manage successful breastfeeding by skilled, sensitive professionals, such as midwives and health visitors.

MILK PRODUCTION AND BREASTFEEDING

During the time when a mother is *lactating* (producing breast milk) she has increased needs for her own nutrition. Her energy requirements are greater than normal. The production of high quality breast milk depends on what food the mother eats. At least three nourishing meals a day plus healthy snacks are essential for the breastfeeding mother. She must also drink plenty of liquid, preferably water. These practices will ensure her milk is nutritious and plentiful for the baby, and she herself is healthy.

Insufficient breast milk production can be caused by :

- the mother's poor diet
- the mother drinking insufficient water
- illness of the mother or baby
- exhaustion or anxiety of the mother
- ineffective feeding techniques
- giving supplementary formula feeds.

ALERT

If a breastfed baby is given bottle feeds as a supplement, subsequent breast milk production will be lessened accordingly. If ever breast and formula feeding are combined, great care needs to be taken to ensure both that the baby thrives and the mother is content.

POSITION AND COMFORT

It may take time for a mother to feel comfortable and to establish feeding patterns. She will benefit from practical professional help and clear answers to her questions.

After the birth the baby's sucking encourages hormone release to aid contraction of the uterus. The skin contact of mother and baby helps them to develop a unique loving relationship. The feeding position is important, especially in the first few days when the mother may prefer to lie on her side rather than sit. The feeding chair or pillows in bed must make her relaxed and comfortable with her lower back well supported.

FIXING THE BABY AT THE BREAST

The mother and baby will feel comfortable if the baby is fixed correctly at the breast. A good seal must be formed against the breast by the baby's mouth. The baby's mouth should be wide open and cover the nipple and the aureola. Sucking only the nipple will cause soreness for the mother. Poor fixing can also cause painful blocked breast ducts.

If the baby seems not to be breathing easily whilst feeding, her head can be tipped back slightly to allow a space between her nostrils and the breast. The breast should not be pressed away from the baby's face as this alters the shape of the nipple.

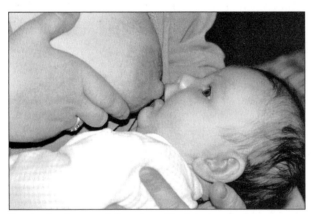 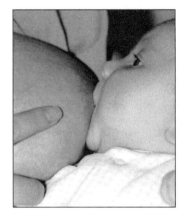

Ready, steady, . . . go! Georgia settles into her feed.

A long time spent at each breastfeed does not always mean milk production is being effectively stimulated. Sometimes the baby spends a long time at the breast without actually feeding well. Inefficient sucking results in a tired, distressed and hungry baby, and consequently in a tired and anxious mother. Helping the mother to fix the baby at the breast can often quickly overcome this problem.

TAKING THE BABY OFF THE BREAST

The baby should feed until she wishes to stop. She should then come off the breast by herself. However, if the mother is uncomfortable and the baby is not correctly fixed at the breast, the mother can gently push a finger under the corner of the baby's lips. This releases the seal. She can then reposition her baby.

HOW MANY FEEDS AND FOR HOW LONG?

Putting the baby to the breast as soon as possible after birth, particularly within the first four hours, helps to establish breastfeeding well. Newborn and small babies need feeding frequently, often every 1 or 2 hours. Feeding on demand means the baby decides the pattern. It also helps breasts from becoming engorged.

The length of feed times will vary from baby to baby. Some feed fully in no more than 5 minutes, others take much longer. The rule is that the baby determines the length of each feed so she can have sufficient quantity of the highly nutritious *hind milk*, which will satisfy her for longer.

It is sensible practice to offer one breast first and one feed and the other first at the next. It is not necessary for the baby to feed from both breasts at every feed.

= = = = = = = = = = = = = — *Key point* = = = = = = = = = = = = =

1. Feeding is for the benefit of the baby and not primarily for the convenience of the adult! The baby's needs should determine the feeding pattern and routine.
2. Breastfeeding works on a demand and supply basis. The more a baby feeds, the more milk is produced.

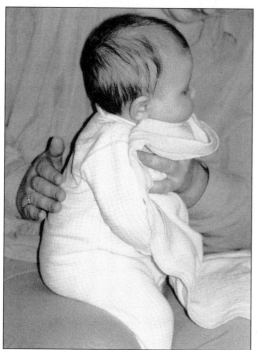

A pause for winding is often necessary to make the baby more comfortable and able to continue feeding effectively.

▬ ▬ ▬ ▬ ▬ ▬ ▬*Good professional practice* ▬ ▬ ▬ ▬ ▬ ▬ ▬

> Further information and specialist help for breastfeeding can be obtained
> from midwives, health visitors or breastfeeding counsellors. Good sources
> of help can also be found through non-professional support such as
> National Childbirth Trust breastfeeding counsellors and La Leche League
> leaders (see appendix for addresses).

Breast milk: its composition and nutritious qualities

Breast milk changes to meet the particular and changing nutritional needs of
the baby. These changing needs can be described as different stages.

Stage 1:

The first type of milk produced is *colostrum*. Most importantly it contains
vital ingredients and properties for the newborn baby's protection and
nutrition.

The breasts start to produce colostrum from around the fifth month of
pregnancy until about the tenth day after the birth. The mother makes all
the colostrum the baby needs. The size of the baby's stomach is roughly the
size of her fist. Colostrum has a tenfold higher carotene content than
mature breast milk. It is this concentration of carotene which gives
colostrum its distinctive yellow colour. It is a rather sticky substance,
somewhat resembling runny honey.

The properties of colostrum:

- It is low in fat and sugars.
- It has much greater protein content than later produced forms of breast
  milk.
- The protein contains many antibodies which after feeding are retained in
  the baby's intestine.
- These antibodies specifically prevent bacteria from entering the baby's
  bloodstream.
- The high concentration of protein in the colostrum means that even a
  baby taking in very small amounts of feed is receiving high levels of
  protein.
- It provides the baby with enough energy between feeds allowing her to
  sleep for comparatively long periods in the first days of life, so conserving
  and effectively using energy for essential growth.

- - - - - - - - - - - Key point - - - - - - - - - - -

Colostrum provides not only for all the nutritional needs of the new baby but gives her first immunisation against infection. There are **no** manufactured formula or artificial feed substitutes for colostrum.

Well ahead of the birth of their baby, mothers should be clearly told about colostrum and its important benefits. But remember the mother's decision on feeding her baby must be fully respected.

Research shows that breastfeeding a baby from soon after birth, even if only for a few days, helps significantly with the emotional *bonding* of the mother and baby. Even if a mother does not intend to continue with breastfeeding, it is very valuable for her baby to be breastfed for the first days of life.

Stage 2:
Milk changes in composition after the first few days. Between the second and the fourth day after birth the breasts start to make milk. This is often referred to as the milk 'coming in'. At this stage the milk is still mixed with colostrum and looks golden and creamy.

Stage 3:
By the tenth day the milk starts to look thinner and much more watery, but its nutrient qualities readily meet the needs of the baby.

Stage 4:
By the end of the fourth week the composition of the milk has changed again. It now contains around a fifth of the protein content of colostrum, but the fat and glucose content have increased.

During the course of each feed the milk now also varies in nutritional content.

- As the baby begins to suck, the *fore milk* is released. It is *low in fat* and so is able to move rapidly through the baby's stomach and duodenum. The fore milk is also high in *lactose* (milk sugar) which gives the baby a concentration of high energy food which is very easily and quickly absorbed into the body.

- The *hind milk* has a much *greater fat* content. It is rich in calories which the baby converts into more slowly released energy for growth.

ALERT
Sucking must be efficient to ensure the baby feeds fully on both types of milk at each feed.

FURTHER NUTRITIONAL QUALITIES OF BREAST MILK

Human breast milk is virtually completely digestible. The liquid component of milk is water. The composition of the proteins in human milk specifically match the baby's digestive system. In the stomach they are readily turned into soft curds which pass effectively into the small intestine.

As with all types of milk, human breast milk is low in *iron*. Babies need iron and nature provides it in a well planned way throughout the time they are fed only on milk.

Whilst in the womb (uterus) the baby's liver lays down a rich store of iron which is sufficient to last the baby for between four and six months. The stored iron is gradually released. Breast milk has high concentrations of lactose and of vitamin C. The presence of these in the milk enables the iron to be absorbed into the baby's body and so used effectively for the baby's growth.

Some breastfeeding problems and solutions

New mothers, although delighted with their newborn babies often feel emotional, nervous, unsure and lacking in skills and knowledge. The first few days after the birth most mothers suffer from what is known as 'the blues'. Hormonal changes following the birth tend to make them feel weepy, weak and often inadequate. 'The blues' even affect confident mothers who have already had children. Many women are still very tired from the birth and their breasts may be swollen and tender.

This physically and emotionally low period coincides with a critical time in establishing breastfeeding. Sensitive and knowledgeable support is needed from professionals in addition to help and understanding from family and friends. The quality of the support given to a breastfeeding mother at this time can often determine its success or failure.

Helping with difficulties in breastfeeding

If any difficulties in feeding do develop the mother's questions need to be answered clearly, concerns discussed and solutions offered. Careful, correct, practical and sympathetic treatment is vital. Accurate advice is essential.

Holding a baby for feeding may be difficult for the mother following a Caesarean birth or for a mother with physical disabilities. Simple help such as strategic placement of pillows and adopting a well supported sitting position can result in feeding being comfortable and successful. Mothers of twins or multiple birth babies will need particular advice, support and practical help in planning and managing feeding. (*See appendix.*)

At all times qualified medical advice must be sought before a breastfeeding mother takes or uses any medication of any type. This includes any herbal or natural remedies as some of these have side effects which could affect the baby.

The use of antibiotics prescribed for the mother need not always result in breastfeeding having to stop, but specific advice should be given in each case.

If breastfeeding is too sore or has to be temporarily halted (if, for example the mother has to take non-compliant prescribed medicine), the expression of breast milk can allow feeding to restart. Breast milk can then be stored in sterile bottles and refrigerated or even frozen for later use.

ALERT
Scrupulous hygiene and the sterilisation of all equipment are essential in expressing, bottling and feeding breast milk.

ACTIVITY

1. (a) List some reasons why expressing milk might be essential or beneficial to the mother and to the baby.
   (b) Compare your list with a colleague's. Into what categories might you put the reasons?

2. Find out which shops and stores in your area provide facilities for breastfeeding mothers. Do they advertise this service well? How good and appropriate are the facilities?

3. Contact one or two of the organisations which offer help and advice to breastfeeding mothers. How helpful do you think their information leaflets are?

Advantages, disadvantages, management and good practices of formula feeding

Making the decision to formula feed

There are many reasons which can influence parents' decisions to *formula* feed their baby. These might be health related, social, economic, practical or psychological. In reality there is often a combination of several reasons.

For most parents the decision to formula feed will be positively made. However, for other mothers formula feeding may be the only option open to them.

Where there is a multiple birth and many babies to be fed, the mother may be physically and practically unable to feed them herself. A mother taking strong medication or receiving radical medical treatment may be unfit or unable to feed as the drugs would pass into her milk. A mother committed in pregnancy to breastfeeding may physically be unable to produce sufficient milk when the baby is born.

▬ ▬ ▬ ▬ ▬ ▬ *Good professional practice* ▬ ▬ ▬ ▬ ▬ ▬

It is important for professionals to realise that some mothers might have liked to breastfeed but are unable to do so. Sensitive support and positive information are particularly required for these women.

ACTIVITY

List some positive points about formula feeding a baby that you might share with a mother needing your support.

Formula milk products

Most infant formula feeds are based on cow's milk which has been radically treated, improved and modified to give as close a resemblance to breast milk as possible. Some formula feeds are based on similarly treated goat's or soya milk. Parents should always be informed of the choices of formula milks available, as sometimes they may have religious or cultural preferences. A vegan mother or a mother of a baby with a cow's-milk intolerance is likely to wish to give their babies a soya or goat's milk based formula.

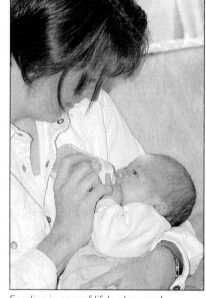
Feeding is one of life's pleasures!

Ordinary cow's milk, goat's milk or evaporated milk **must not** be given to babies as a drink until they are at least one year old. Before these ages their digestive systems cannot cope.

Only formula milk or breast milk is safe for babies as it contains:

- low enough levels of curd protein for the baby to be able to digest
- a low enough salt content to prevent kidney damage
- a low enough proportion of fatty acids in the fat content of the milk, which the baby's body can effectively absorb.

Other forms of milk (only ever suitable for babies over one year) can cause significant problems for 0–1-year-olds because:

- The high levels of curd protein are difficult for the baby to digest.
- The high salt levels are potentially very dangerous for immature kidneys.
- The higher concentrations of fatty acids in the fat contents are hard to absorb and can also badly affect the baby's ability to absorb calcium.

ALERT
Babies can only ever be fed breast or formula milk. No other forms of any milk or milk products should ever be given to babies under six months old. Failure to thrive, severe illnesses and significant allergic responses could result.

Choosing formula feeds

By law the advertising of formula milk in the press, on radio or on television is forbidden. However, at ante-natal clinics or classes and in hospitals new mothers often receive manufacturers' samples and information about baby products. This, combined with the fact that the National Health Service is the largest purchaser of formula milk in the UK, means that mothers are targeted at a time when they are seeking information and support. Mothers starting to formula feed their baby in hospital appear to continue with the same type and brand at home.

In fact it is good practice to keep to one formula to allow the baby's taste and smell to become familiar with it and for her digestive system to settle and adjust. Unless a baby does not tolerate or thrive well on a particular brand or type of formula, there is no reason to change.

Babies have individual nutritional needs and these will change as they grow. Their digestive systems develop and they can cope with less-modified formula milks. The iron store, stockpiled from before birth and gradually released during the first months of life, starts to diminish.

Changing nutritional needs can be met by choosing the appropriate 'stage' and type of formula for the baby's weight, age and maturity, and moving on to the next stage as the baby develops. Health visitor advice about the formula needs of individual babies is essential, but the following information should provide you with an overview to support your work with bottle-fed babies.

Some of the different types of the formula feeds most widely available in the UK are shown in the table below:

Whey (Suitable from birth to six months)	Casein (For 'hungrier babies' from birth to six months)	Follow-on (From six months plus)
SMA Gold	SMA White	SMA Progress
Cow & Gate Premium	Cow & Gate Plus	Cow & Gate Step-up
Farley's First Milk	Farley's Second Milk	Farley's Follow-up Milk
Milupa Aptamil	Milupa Milumil	Follow-up Forward
Boots Infant Milk Formula 1	Boots Infant Milk Formula 2	Boots Follow-on Milk
Sainsbury' First Menu first stage milk	Sainsbury's Second Menu second stage milk	Sainsbury' Follow-on Milk

ACTIVITY

1. Find out what types of formula milk are used for babies in your placement? Add any used and not shown here to the list. Which are the most popular and for what ages? Why do you think this is so?

2. Investigate different bottles available to buy for babies. Are the different styles more useful or appropriate for some babies and mothers than others? What kinds of teats are available? How many bottles might be needed for one baby? How do the costs of bottles and teats vary?

Making up formula feeds

The preparation of equipment and the mixing of powder formula feed must be carried out carefully and to a high standard of accuracy and cleanliness. As a professional working with babies these principles are essential.

Formula feeds must be exactly measured and made up strictly according to the manufacturers' instructions. All packages of formula feed contain a measuring scoop which is especially designed for that and only that particular milk.

ALERT
- Each package of formula feed has its own specially sized measuring scoop.
- Using the wrong scoop can be dangerous.
- Cereals (solids) or sugars should never be added to bottles.

An incorrect mix is dangerous for the baby. *Formula milk which is too strong is very dangerous.* An over-concentration can put a strain on babies' kidneys, leading to kidney failure and excessive, unhealthy weight gain. Too weak a mix produces a hungry distressed baby, poor weight gain, constipation and a failure to thrive.

How much to feed?

There is a standard method of calculating the amount of feed a baby is likely to need.

For every 500g of body weight give 75ml of made-up formula in 24 hours, (or for every lb of body weight give 2.5fl.oz × 24 hours). This total quantity is then divided into the number of bottles the baby is likely to be given over the 24-hour period. A newborn or light for dates baby usually needs more smaller feeds per day (often eight bottles) than an older or larger baby.

ACTIVITY

Two babies are both 14 weeks old. Sarah weighs 5.75 kilos and David weighs 6.25 kilos. Calculate the amount of made-up formula milk you would prepare for each baby's bottle if they each have six feeds each day.

— — — — — —Good professional practice — — — — — —

- Careful observation, including regular weighing of the baby is essential to note any changes of behaviour or needs with feeding.
- Professionals working with babies must know their 'allocated' baby very well and have close daily contact with parents to share observations and information.

Making up and storing feeds

The correct safe storage of made-up feeds is essential. Germs breed fast and live well in warm milk and other foods. Great care must be taken to prevent any chance of contamination of baby feeding equipment, powder or made-up feeds.

— — — — — —Good professional practice — — — — — —

Good personal hygiene is essential. Thorough handwashing with hot water and soap, followed by drying hands on a clean towel must be done frequently and always before handling feeds or feeding equipment.

Sterilisation of feeding equipment

Cleanliness is vital. The four stages of washing, rinsing, sterilising and storing must be rigorously followed to prevent any contamination and consequent danger to the baby.

ALERT

At all times detailed care and attention to detail must be taken at each stage of the procedures. Any lapse in hygiene or routine can easily result in serious harm to the baby.

Washing

- Cloths or brushes used must be clean, washed, disinfected and kept solely for this purpose.
- Work surfaces and utensils must be cleaned with very hot, soapy water.
- Bottles, teats and other equipment must be thoroughly cleaned in hot water with detergent added.
- A bottle brush, kept only for this purpose, must be used for the inside of bottles.
- Teats must be rubbed inside and out, and water squeezed through the feeding hole.

ALERT

Do not rub salt on teats; it perishes the material and does not effectively clean it.

Rinsing

- Everything must be rinsed thoroughly under a running tap.
- All traces of detergent must be removed.

Preparing the steriliser

(a) Chemical method
- Fill the steriliser (container) with clean cold water.
- Following the manufacturers' instructions and dosage, add the chemical sterilising solution. If it is in tablet form, make sure it dissolves completely before continuing.

(b) Boiling method
- If chemical sterilising is not possible or boiling is the chosen method, the container used must be kept only for this purpose. It must be large enough to ensure that all bottles and other equipment can be completely covered with boiling water and remain submerged while being boiled.

(c) Steam method

- Electric steam sterilisers and microwave oven sterilisers are available for home use. They are quick and effective. Instructions are simple and clear and should be carefully followed. You may find that a larger commercial steam steriliser is used in your workplace nursery.

Sterilising the equipment

(a) Chemical steriliser method

- Place all bottles, teats and other equipment into the prepared, filled chemical steriliser.
- Check everything is well submerged, all bottles and containers are fully filled and that there are no bubbles trapped.
- To keep things below the surface of the liquid it may be necessary to weigh them down.
- Leave in the liquid for the time specified in the manufacturer's instructions. Remove items from the solution and rinse carefully with boiled water to remove all traces of the chemicals.

(b) Boiling Method.

- All equipment must be fully covered with boiling water, remain submerged and boiled for 11–12 minutes.

(c) Electrical or microwave steaming methods

- Follow the manufacturers' instructions carefully.

Storing clean equipment

- Bottles and equipment can be stored in the emptied steriliser after it has been rinsed with boiled water.
- Bottles and teats should be drained but not dried inside with a cloth.
- The length of time sterilised equipment may be stored after sterilisation varies according to the type of method used.
- The manufacturers' guidance should be read and followed.

ALERT
Teats should be replaced frequently and always at the earliest sign of any damage or wear.

Storing made-up feeds or bottles of breast milk

Made-up formula feeds or expressed breast milk can only be kept if immediately refrigerated. Bottles can be stored upright, for up to 24 hours in a refrigerator. After this time all unused bottles must be emptied and the milk thrown away. Milk stored for longer than 24 hours carries the risk of being contaminated and is dangerous for the baby. Any milk left over from a feed must always and immediately be thrown away. A bottled feed taken from the refrigerator should be warmed just before feeding and never kept warm or at room temperature for more than a short time.

ALERT

Warm milk is an excellent breeding ground for bacteria, which multiply quickly and are highly virulent. Never feed a baby from an unfinished or previously warmed bottle; it may cause sickness, diarrhoea or serious illness.

A C T I V I T Y

In your placement find out the policy and procedures for making up feeds. Compare the information with your own notes. Make up a batch of bottle feeds for babies in your nursery following strict hygiene and measurement procedures. Log the task and note the important points of each stage.

One benefit of bottle-feeding is that Grandad can help too.

Giving a bottle

The following of procedures develops good professional practice, ensures the baby is well cared for and that routines are well established. Having an agreed routine also means that if different individuals feed the baby they will all follow the same pattern, so giving important continuity and security for the baby.

What to do

- Wash your hands thoroughly.
- Prepare all the items you need for the baby and her feed before picking her up. Collect her bib and tissues. Cover the bottle with a cloth. Stand the bottle in a jug of hot water to keep it warm. Place all items in the feeding area so they are accessible.
- Change the baby's nappy and make her comfortable. Wash your hands.
- Settle yourself comfortably making sure your lower back, shoulders and the arm holding the baby are well supported.
- Hold the baby securely in a cuddle. Spend time talking and responding to the baby. Engage and keep eye-contact with her. Make this time relaxing, calm and enjoyable.
- Talk to and smile at the baby as you proceed with the feeding.
- Lift the bottle from the jug and wipe the outside to prevent drips.
- Check the teat size by inverting the bottle. The milk should freely drip out, a few drops every second.
- Test the milk temperature by dropping a little milk onto the inside of your wrist.
- Touch the baby's lips to stimulate the rooting reflex and as she seeks it place the teat into her mouth over her tongue.
- Keep a gentle tension on the teat to keep the baby sucking.
- During feeding check there is always milk in the teat. An empty teat causes the baby to suck air and become frustrated and tired.
- After about 10 minutes remove the teat and make the baby upright. Gently rub her back or apply very gentle pressure to her stomach. This will help to release any wind trapped in her stomach.
- Finish feeding and let her wind come up again at the end.
- If necessary change her again and settle her comfortably when you are both ready.
- Clear the feeding area. Wash equipment carefully and sterilise it again so it will be ready for giving more formula or cooled boiled water.

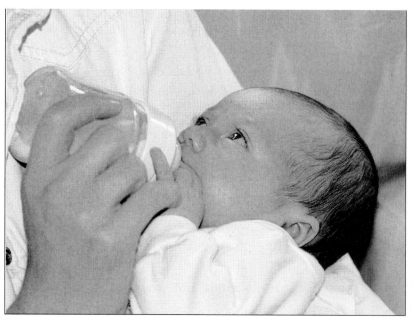

Babies need food, love and security.

▬ ▬ ▬ ▬ ▬ ▬ *Good professional practice* ▬ ▬ ▬ ▬ ▬ ▬

Feeding a baby is much more than just giving a bottle. It offers opportunities for developing relationships. The baby can learn about communicating, listening and expressing herself. There are chances for close physical contact, giving the baby a sense of security and being loved.

ALERT
A baby should never be left alone or propped up with a bottle.

END OF CHAPTER ACTIVITY

1. Draw up a check list for preparing, bottle feeding and settling a baby. Highlight any critically important points.
Give a baby a bottle feed, following your list.
Review your list and add comments noting where aspects went well and what changes you would make to improve things for next time.

2. Obtain some leaflets written for parents that offer information and advice on formula feeding. Study some leaflets on formula milk

products published for professionals. How do these differ? How helpful do you think the information leaflets are?

3. Using ICT software design a handout which clearly presents the most important facts that parents should know about choosing how to feed their baby.

Quick quiz

Find the answers in the chapter.

1. Does a pregnant woman have to think about 'eating for two'?

2. During pregnancy when is the most critical time for the baby's development?

3. What foodstuffs contain folic acid?

4. Why is it important for a newborn baby to have colostrum?

5. Is there a manufactured substitute for colostrum?

6. Give three advantages of breastfeeding (a) for the mother and (b) for the baby.

7. Give three advantages of bottle feeding (a) for the mother and (b) for the baby.

8. What is the expected weekly weight gain for a 6–12-month-old baby?

9. What is the most important role of the professional when a mother has decided how she will feed her young baby?

10. What dangers are there in not exactly following manufacturers' instructions when making up bottles of formula feed?

Summary

Having studied this chapter you should now understand:

- Correct good nutrition in pregnancy is essential for a baby's healthy development.
- Parents need well balanced and accurate information to help them choose the types of feeding best suited to the baby's and mother's needs.
- Colostrum provides the newborn baby with excellent nutrition and protection against allergies and disease.
- The nutritional needs of the baby change from newborn up to one year.
- Nutritional properties of breast milk change as the baby grows.
- Feeding times provide the baby with opportunities for developing awareness of herself and of others, learning physical skills and developing intellectually.
- There are advantages and disadvantages to be considered both with breast and formula feeding.
- Babies are very susceptible to infection from poorly prepared and stored feeds.
- Rigorous hygiene and sterilisation routines must be followed for all baby-feeding equipment and made-up feeds.

6

Weaning: from milk to food in easy stages!

Aims of the chapter

To enable you to understand:

- what is meant by weaning, and when and why it should begin
- what weaning involves for the baby, parents and early years professionals
- the stages of weaning and how to manage the weaning process
- a nutritious diet and an overview feeding plan for weaning a baby
- some of the difficulties that may arise during weaning.

Having spent all morning pureeing carrots Flossie was determined that the baby would love them.

What is meant by weaning, and when and why it should begin

What is meant by weaning?

Weaning is the gradual process of introducing a range of foods into the baby's diet at first to supplement and eventually to replace milk as the sole nutritional source. The process involves moving the baby from a purely liquid diet to one which includes a range of textures and consistencies.

What is the basis for current guidance on weaning?

COMA (The Committee on Medical Aspects of Food Policy) is an independent committee of nutrition and health experts set up by the UK government. Its recommendations are based on widespread scientific research, national monitoring and population investigations. The purpose of COMA is to provide reports and guidance relating to aspects of the health and nutrition of the nation and of sectors of the population.

One of its standing committees, specially briefed to keep children's nutrition under review, is the Panel on Child Nutrition. In 1994 the committee produced a fundamental report on the feeding and nutrition of babies and very young children. Entitled *Weaning and the Weaning Diet*, it also contains vitally important recommendations which now form the basis for all related professional guidance, support and ways of working with parents and their babies.

When and why weaning should begin

At any time **after the age of four months** a baby may be ready to need food from sources other than breast or formula milk. An indication is that when she is taking large quantities of milk and yet appears dissatisfied then weaning might be considered. It is however, important to check that the dissatisfaction really stems from needing further nutritional intake, and that the baby's behaviour is not prompted by boredom or a need for more physical contact and adult attention.

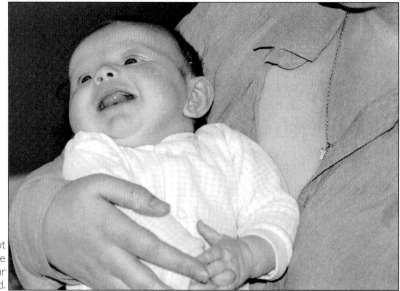

Weaning must not begin before the baby is four months old.

Babies can continue on a milk only diet beyond four months but by six months, milk alone no longer provides enough nutrients. It is nutritionally too late to start weaning at six months unless there are medical reasons for the delay. However, you may come across a baby of six months or older who has not started to be weaned. So although it is 'late' you still have to start the process gradually following the same key principles.

Why should weaning start between four and six months old?

Babies are born with a store of iron which supplies their needs for the first few months of life. During these months the baby's immature digestive system can only cope with milk. The baby's natural iron stores are gradually absorbed into her body and therefore at about five to six months old the baby's iron store begins to deplete. Iron now needs to be supplied from the diet; that is, food is needed in addition to milk. The baby has started to prepare for this development.

Between four and six months of age the baby begins to develop some physical, motor and social skills and capacities which are essential for weaning:

- The digestive system begins to mature.
- The kidneys become able to process small amounts of naturally occurring food salts.

- Digestive enzymes and gastric juices develop further.
- The absorption capacities of the small and large intestine increase.
- Neck and back muscles have developed to allow her to sit up and control her head.
- Her sucking and swallowing is well practised and has enabled some development of mouth, tongue and throat muscles.
- She is interested in mouthing objects as a way of exploring the world and herself.
- She is visually and aurally alert and responsive.
- She responds positively to social attention from care givers enjoying shared vocal and visual communication.
- She is developing an understanding of her own routines and of familiar people.

Physically and physiologically the baby is developing gradually to be able to take some simple and easily digested foods, which will help to meet her increasingly complex nutritional needs. Socially, emotionally and intellectually she is ready for new experiences provided from familiar people in a safe and predictable setting.

▬ ▬ ▬ ▬ ▬ ▬ *Good professional practice* ▬ ▬ ▬ ▬ ▬ ▬

If you come across a baby where weaning has not started by the age of six months, health visitor advice should be sought and the baby's growth and development carefully monitored. If problems persist a referral to a dietitian is recommended.

What weaning involves for the baby, parents and early years professionals

Weaning is a very gradual process. Its progress and establishment are different for every baby. The rate and just how a baby is weaned depend entirely on the baby's own individual timetable.

Weaning is not a race! Parents can readily feel unsure and inadequate when their baby is compared to others or when they are given pressurised 'advice' by well-meaning friends and family. It is not helpful to set expectations for weaning for one child based on the behaviour of another.

Weaning can be a difficult time for the baby, parents and carers. To prevent undue anxiety and worry it is important that the whole process is seen as being slow, gentle, gradual and ongoing. It is a time for adults and the baby to learn together and to enjoy new experiences.

▬ ▬ ▬ ▬ ▬ ▬ *Good professional practice* ▬ ▬ ▬ ▬ ▬ ▬

The important thing is to watch and listen carefully to each individual baby and to feel confident in knowing what you should be doing and why, to meet each baby's needs.

Weaning in a day care placement should always be carried out in full partnership with the parents. The baby's age, maturity and medical condition must always be taken into account. The food and approaches should reflect and complement the baby's culture and always be in line with the family's religious wishes, as well as being nutritionally sound.

▬ ▬ ▬ ▬ ▬ ▬ *Good professional practice* ▬ ▬ ▬ ▬ ▬ ▬

It is important to understand that not all cultures use a spoon when weaning a baby onto solids from milk. Make yourself aware of any families you work with who use other means and discuss with colleagues how you can best work in partnership with the parents for the welfare and security of the child.

The National Children's Bureau gives the following recommendations for working with parents:
Parents should always be consulted about when they wish solids to be introduced and which solids to provide. Parents may wish to provide their own baby foods . . . and it is recommended that the nursery does not disrupt patterns established at home.

ACTIVITY

1. In your day care setting find out about how parents' wishes are discussed, with whom and what framework is used for these meetings. Are the parents asked to give guidance to staff for dealing with a very hungry or upset baby? For example, what happens if a hungry breastfed baby is late being collected? Study some of the written

records noting parental wishes about feeding their child. Summarise the main points they contain.

2. How does the setting ensure the key staff are made aware of the parents' wishes? Does it work in practice? What happens if key staff are absent?

ALERT

Parents have taken legal action against care staff when bottle feeds were given to a baby against the parents' express wishes. Ensure your nursery has means of recording parental wishes and details of agreed discussions about food/milk alternatives which include, for example, dealing with a very hungry or upset baby.

Learning through weaning: supporting the baby's development

When weaning is first introduced it is essentially a learning process for the baby rather than a significant source of nutrition. Up to this point in her life the baby has only had liquids in her mouth and these have been obtained and controlled by her sucking from a nipple or teat.

The transition from milk, to first tastes of smooth purée and onto an ordinary mixed diet demands that the baby will learn to:

- Take food from a spoon – first controlled entirely by the adult but eventually managing the 'spoon to food to mouth' sequence alone.
- Accept a gradually widening range of smells, flavours and tastes.
- Accept food of different temperatures.
- Accept different consistencies and textures of food – (first very sloppy in consistency but eventually incorporating solid lumps and different and stiffer textures).
- Manage to mouth, control and swallow different food textures without choking.
- Gradually reduce the total dependence on milk.
- Drink without relying on sucking – perhaps first using a 'baby trainer' or 'toddler drinking beakers', but eventually from an open cup.
- Take food from and with different members of the family.

The success and management of weaning is in the hands of the baby's primary carers. It should be a time for new learning, development of shared confidence, fun and enjoyment for all concerned! However, it too often is a time of anxiety and worry, especially for first time parents. Calm, friendly and confident support given to parents from early years professionals can be absolutely critical at such times.

Jenny, Becky and Ben are fine examples of successful weaning! Each had their own weaning pattern and timetable.

The stages of weaning and how to manage the weaning process

The first stage: four–six months

Taking the first steps

Anything in life which is new and different can cause us worry and upset if it is handled insensitively, if we are unwell, tired or simply if the timing is wrong. This is just the same for babies. When deciding to start weaning make sure the baby is completely well, not too tired or hungry. The aim is to give the baby the experiences of food from a spoon, a new texture and a new taste. These first little tastes should be offered after part of the milk feed has been taken so the baby is relaxed and comfortable and not ravenously hungry. Remember the baby does not understand that this spoon could provide her with food. Until now she knows she gets food only from the breast or the bottle! Taking the edge off her hunger enables her to be receptive but not so replenished as from a full feed that she may be disinterested and sleepy.

The first tiny taste of warm puréed food should be very liquid, mixed with a little breast milk or formula feed. It should be offered on the very tip of a special softly rounded plastic baby spoon with a flat bowl. This shape allows the baby to suck the food off when the tip is placed between her lips. The spoon must be sterilised.

Decide on one type of food and repeat the 'tiny taste procedure' twice a day for two or three days before introducing a new food. The baby needs very gradual exposure to each weaning food to build up her confidence and understanding. This gentle introductory pattern also allows careful checks to be made on any reaction that might be caused by any particular food. If a food upsets her system it can easily be avoided.

If a baby refuses or spits out a food it does not mean that she dislikes it. It probably means she has not fully developed the knack of sucking the food off the spoon, or that she is reacting to and probably trying to make sense of the whole new experience itself, and maybe having fun too! If a food is refused, stay relaxed, celebrate her interaction with you and the food and try again another time.

What foods to give

First weaning foods should be simple, bland, gluten-free and with nothing added except the baby's usual milk (breast or formula) to improve the consistency.

ALERT

Baby foods should NEVER have salt or sugar added to them.

Sugar is unnecessary, provides 'empty calories' causing obesity and affecting dental health even in very young babies, and unhelpfully encouraging the development of 'a sweet tooth'. Salt is highly dangerous to babies. Their kidneys cannot excrete it, leading to serious illness, kidney damage and even death. Do not give highly spiced food as the baby cannot digest it and it may cause inflammation of the lining of the oesophageal tract (mouth and throat): avoid chilli, cloves and ginger. Cow's milk and goat's milk should not be given as a drink to babies under a year old.

Suitable first weaning foods are:

- Baby rice cereal
- Puréed vegetables
- Puréed (non-citrus) fruits.

ALERT

For babies under six months: citrus and berry fruits are not suitable as they can cause allergic reactions.

Foods containing gluten are not suitable as too early an introduction has been linked to allergies in later life.

— — — — — — *Good professional practice* — — — — — —

It is important to ensure the range of foods (baby rice cereal, vegetables and fruits) is covered as babies often seem to show preference for baby rice cereals over the more distinctive flavours of fruits and vegetables. Feeding baby cereal rice too much and too often can result in babies becoming overweight and puts them at risk of missing out on other essential nutrients.

ALERT

Only specially designated 'baby' rice cereal is suitable for young babies. Similarly textured instant oat breakfast cereals are NOT safe for young babies as their salt content is too high. There have been instances of babies dying from salt overdoses after being fed cereal products designed for older children.

Heartbreak for couple who gave adult food to son of 3 months

BABY KILLED BY TOO MUCH SALT

Developing the pattern over the first few weeks

If the baby has had tastes of a puréed vegetable, such as carrot, for a few days then the next taste could be fruit, such as mashed banana or puréed apple, followed a few days later by tastes of baby rice. Soon the baby will be able to take 1 or 2 teaspoonfuls as part of one feed.

After two or three weeks she will probably be ready to increase her intake by having this amount at two feeds each day. However, it is very important to remember every baby is different and the secret to ensuring the baby's health and happiness is careful observation of her reactions, needs and noting her development and growth. Some babies are bigger and hungrier, needing more solids than a smaller baby of the same age. As a rule most babies are good at making their needs known!

Very gradually the amount given will increase. By the time the baby is around five and a half to six months old she is likely to be having some puréed food three times a day and the overall intake of milk may be gradually reducing. After about five or six weeks from the start of weaning the baby may well be substituting solids for a breast or formula feed at one of the meals. However, for the first year of life milk still remains the baby's most important food.

Summary of the first stage:

• First weaning foods are warm purées of fruit (not citrus), purées of vegetables, dahl or plain baby rice cereal.
• Foods should be softened with boiled water, breast milk or formula feed.
• Breast milk or formula feed continues to be the most important food.

The second stage: after six months

The baby's digestive system and her taste buds have now become used to the limited range of different easily digested foods. Her skills in taking food from a spoon have increased, as has her ability to manage puréed food in her mouth and to swallow it without choking.

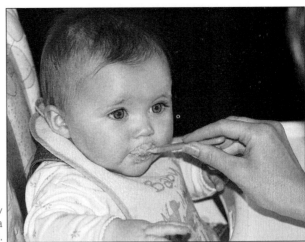

At nearly 8 months, Chloe is now used to taking puréed food from a spoon.

What foods to give

The baby is ready to expand the range and types of foods she can eat, and after having time to get used to these in a puréed form she will be ready to try them with a slightly increased texture.

It is important that the fruits and vegetables introduced at the first stage continue to be offered.

New foods should still be introduced one at a time in order to monitor her tolerance, and breast milk or formula feed still makes up the greatest proportion of her diet.

ALERT
Peanut- and nut-containing foods should be avoided for babies and children up to three years old to lessen chances of developing allergic responses.

Suitable foods which can be gradually introduced are:

chicken	baby cereal foods
lamb	full-fat dairy and milk-containing foods
beef	puréed or mashed 'family foods',
citrus fruits	if they are sugar- and salt-free.

Remember by this age the baby's inherited iron stores may be very low. Foods containing iron should be given. These include:

liver	dahl
beef	fortified breakfast cereals containing iron
lamb	wholemeal bread and pasta
green leafy vegetables	egg yolks.
beans	

ALERT

1. Egg yolks should be introduced carefully and not before six and a half months as some babies develop an allergy to them. Whites are not so readily digestible and so should be introduced about two months later than yolks. All eggs must be cooked until both the yolks and whites are solid to reduce the possibility of salmonella.

2. Cow's and goat's milk should not be offered *as a drink* until the baby is over a year old as they are too indigestible and can provoke allergic reactions.

3. From six months of age babies can have cow's milk as a *food ingredient* (such as in yoghurt, milk puddings or custard).

During this stage the baby will progress from eating only puréed or finely mashed foods to having minced or finely chopped food. By using a blender, family foods can be easily given as long as they contain no added salt or sugar. It is important that babies are introduced to family foods so they experience their own culture and become familiar with their family's dishes.

The baby can now be offered well-diluted unsweetened fresh fruit juice or herbal drinks. These can be given on a spoon, in a small cup or baby training beaker. The increase in solids means the baby will be thirstier than when on a milk only diet. Cooled boiled water should be the choice of drink offered frequently. Only water or milk should be given, as other drinks (with sweet or acidic components, such as fruit juice) can cause dental decay, and can also cause diarrhoea. Preferably, the use of a bottle should be discouraged as soon as other drinking cups can be controlled as these are less harmful to the developing dentition. Dinky or mini feeders are also bad because similarly to bottles, they have a reservoir which holds the fluid in the teat causing the liquid to be in contact with the teeth all the time.

As the number of times per day that solids are offered increases and more solids are consumed, the baby's overall intake of milk will gradually decrease. However, milk is still an extremely important nutrient provider for the baby. It is important to ensure the baby still has about 1 pint of breast milk or formula milk every day in addition to her meals and other drinks. The offering of a breast feed or formula milk from a bottle also provides the baby with a continuing sense of security and comfort.

By this stage the baby should be eating three regular meals a day in addition to having drinks. Progress should continue towards the baby eating normal family foods.

Vitamin drops

Vitamin A, C, D drops should be give to all breastfed babies from six months, and to bottle-fed babies from the time formula milk is discontinued.

Summary of the second stage:

- Food gradually progresses from being puréed to finely chopped or minced.
- Range of suitable foods increase to include many family foods, which can be blended.
- Breast milk or formula intake decreases as more solids are taken.
- Drinks of well diluted pure fruit juice and herbal drinks can be offered in addition to milk and cooled boiled water.

The third stage: 9–12 months

The baby should be eating three regular meals a day in addition to having frequent drinks. Progress should continue towards the baby eating normal family foods. It is important to ensure the baby still has about 1 pint of breast or formula milk every day in addition to her meals and other drinks, as it still provides important nutrients and is readily digestible.

What foods to give

During this stage the variety of food continues to widen and the texture has moved from being mainly puréed, mashed or very finely chopped food to some lumpier foods and finger foods that encourage chewing. Dishes can contain small pieces of bite-sized foods.

To begin with the baby will be given soft finger foods to hold, suck and chew on. A piece of banana, bread or a segment of orange make suitable first finger foods. A little later harder foods such as a piece of toast, slice of apple or carrot can be given. The baby is entering a new period in her development. It is a time of great experimentation, learning and some considerable mess!

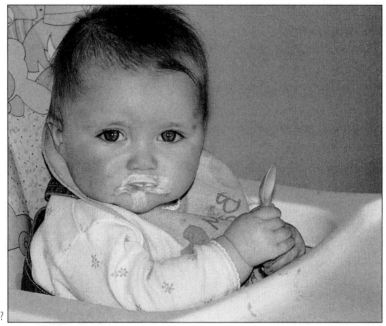

Mess! What mess?

The baby does not need teeth to bite and chew. Her gums are hard and strong, particularly at the back of the mouth, enabling her to manage lumpier food. After a week or two of trying soft finger foods, she will be able to cope with harder finger foods, such as crusts, and pieces of apple or carrot. The eruption of baby teeth will begin at about six months of age which will aid the chewing of these new textures and contribute to the gum strength prior to their eruption.

This is a good time to help the baby develop more independence and mealtimes offer many fun ways to do just this. Encouraging her to hold, control and chew some finger foods is an excellent way of letting her experiment and practise her fine motor skills. Her hand–eye coordination can be practised. She can observe and track movement. Grasping, gripping and aiming for her mouth are all essential developmental skills.

ALERT
Constant supervision is absolutely essential for a baby with any foods. Vigilance is needed for a baby with finger foods to ensure she does not suck off a large lump and choke on it.

The baby is learning more and more about herself and about the environment. She is learning to explore shapes, tastes, smells and textures. She will be experiencing different temperatures and consistencies. Her mouth, lips and tongue will develop new patterns of movement which will not just help her eating skills to progress but which are essential prerequisites for the continuing development of speech and increasingly effective articulation. Mealtimes offer good opportunities for communication and social interaction. A whole range of specific and descriptive language can be introduced, to accompany and enhance the baby's practical experiences.

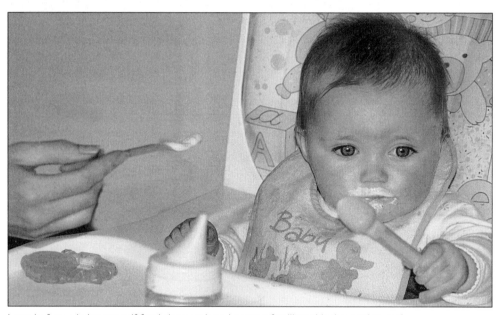

Long before a baby can self-feed she needs to become familiar with the equipment!

ACTIVITY

1. Think of the different aspects of a baby's mealtime, allied to the food, the social setting and the actions of you and the baby. How would you plan to use these to introduce a range of ideas, language and learning experiences to the baby?

2. Make a list of words (under headings such as colour, shape and size, quantity, texture, food type, temperature and so on) which you could use at mealtimes and which could promote early learning in science and mathematics.

3. What opportunities might you be able to give the baby at mealtimes to practise 'predicting' and 'responding'?

SUMMARY OF THE THIRD STAGE

Give lumpier food and finger foods to encourage chewing. Three regular meals are taken plus drinks. Breast milk or formula intake becomes less as more solids are eaten. About 1 pint of breast or formula milk should still be given. Drinking from a cup may be introduced if not already tried.

ALERT

Remember never to give drinks other than milk or water from a bottle. Even well diluted fruit juice (containing naturally occurring sugars and acids) can seriously affect dental health causing tooth decay if allowed to stay in contact with the teeth and gums for too long. This can readily occur when drinking from a baby bottle or teated mini or dinky feeder.

A nutritious diet and an overview feeding plan for weaning a baby

Stage	First stage			Second Stage		Third Stage
Age	4 months	4½ months old	5–6 months old	6–7 months old	7–9 months old	9–12 months old
Consistency/ Texture	Pureed, soft & sloppy, mix with breast/formula milk or water			Puréed food, mixed with finely minced or mashed foods, with added milk or water. Finger foods.	Mashed food mixed with finely chopped and minced food. Finger foods to bite and chew.	Mashed food mixed with well-chopped foods. Wider range of finger foods to bite and chew.
Suitable foods	Baby rice cereal. Some vegetables. Some fruits.	Baby rice cereal. Some vegetables. Some fruits. Lean chicken. White fish. Dahl. Lentils.		Begin to add: increased selection of vegetables, fruits, meat and fish. Wheat products: salt/sugar-free cereals e.g. Weetabix. Bread & toast fingers. Pasta. Citrus & berry fruits. Cooked rice. Egg yolk cooked solid. Small beans (aduki) cooked until soft. Yoghurt. Cheese. Unsalted butter.		Begin to add: Oily fish. Liver. Peanut butter. Large beans cooked until soft. Well cooked egg white. Fromage frais. Overall a wide range of foods with a variety of textures.
Foods UNSUITABLE across this stage	*Some vegetables (spinach, turnip, beetroot). Some fruits (citrus & berry fruits). Wheat cereals and wheat products (e.g. bread, pasta). Nuts or nut-containing foods. Eggs. Dairy products or food containing cow's milk.*			*Egg whites. Nuts or nut-containing products (e.g. peanut butter). Fruit squash or other soft drinks. Tea/coffee/chocolate.*		*Whole nuts (not suitable until 5+ years and then with close supervision). Salty, sugary and fatty foods. Fruit squash, soft or sweetened drinks. Tea/coffee.*
Presentation	On tip of sterilised baby spoon			Baby spoon or fingers. By end of this stage baby will probably start to want her own spoon too! Unless advised otherwise by health visitor, food should start to be offered before the milk, as food starts to provide more nourishment than milk.		Make sure baby has own spoon too when you feed her. Let her pick up her own finger food and experiment with her food. Messy? Yes! But very important for baby's learning, awareness & development, & very important step to feeding herself.
Approximate quantities of 'solids'	1–2 teaspoons once a day	2 teaspoons twice a day	Two, three or four teaspoons 3 times a day	Six to eight teaspoons & some finger food 3 times a day		Gradually increase quantities evenly across all meals to meet the baby's needs.
Suggested timings	Note: the food suggestions below are intended to indicate the type of food which may be suitable at the time shown. Alternatives are suggested to give you further ideas but they are NOT prescriptive. The important fact is to ensure provision of a healthy balance diet and allow the baby to experience a range of suitable foods.					
Early morning	Breast or bottle-feed	Breast or bottle-feed	Breast or bottle-feed	Breast or bottle-feed	Breast or bottle-feed	Breast or bottle-feed if needed

Stage	First stage		Second Stage		Third Stage	
Breakfast	Breast or bottle-feed plus pureed fruit or baby rice or vegetables	Breast or bottle-feed plus pureed food/baby rice.	Cereal mixed with breast or formula milk/soft-cooked fruit; fingers of toast/toast crusts. Drink of milk or water.	Rolled porridge oats/cereal mixed with breast/formula milk: toast fingers & crusts. Drink of milk or water.	Yoghurt & muesli or cereal & milk; fruit; toast fingers/crusts with savoury spread or butter. Drink of milk or very dilute pure fruit juice.	
Mid-morning	Drink of water if required	Drink of water/very dilute non-citrus fruit juice	Drink of water/very dilute juice. Mashed banana/stewed apple: or home-made rusks.		Mashed banana/stewed apple: or mini muffin:	
Midday (Lunch/Dinner)	Breast or bottle-feed	Breast or bottle-feed plus pureed food	Breast or bottle-feed plus savoury food followed by fruit or baby rice or dessert	Mashed or finely minced fish, meat or cheese with mashed vegetables. Soft-cooked fruit, milk pudding or mashed banana. Drink of breast or formula milk or water or very diluted juice.	Minced meat, mashed fish or grated cheese. Finely chopped vegetables. Milk pudding, cooked fruit or fingers of fruit. Drink.	Chopped chicken or grated cheese. Pasta or mashed potatoes. Chopped or mashed vegetables. Bread and butter pudding, semolina & stewed fruit. Drink.
Mid-afternoon	Drink of water if required	Drink of water or very dilute non-citrus juice	Drink of water/very dilute juice. Yoghurt and fruit: or mashed banana: or pieces of tangerine/kiwi/etc.		Drink of water/very dilute juice. Yoghurt and fruit: or mashed banana: or pieces of	
Late afternoon (Dinner/Teatime)	Breast or bottle-feed	Breast or bottle-feed plus pureed fruit or vegetable food	Toast fingers with grated cheese or spread with pureed vegetables. Piece of kiwifruit or pawpaw. Breast or bottle-feed.	Piece of soft banana, red pepper. Bread and unsalted-butter sandwiches, with seedless jam or savoury spread. Home-made rusks, sponge finger or plain biscuit. Drink.	Select a balanced choice from e.g. Home-made rusks, fruit muffin, mashed banana, scrambled egg, chicken soup, chopped tomato, bread, carrot sticks, pieces of fruit. Drink.	
Late evening	Breast or bottle-feed	Breast or bottle-feed as necessary	Breast or bottle-feed as necessary.			
Special Points	*Water used must always be boiled and cooled. Milk used to mix with foods and to drink must be either breast milk or formula (whey or curd-dominant formula before 6 months and 'follow-on' formula for babies over 6 months old).*					
Note	Breast or formula milk still provide all key nutrition		Milk intake is beginning to decrease as solids increase.		Continue to introduce each new food gradually. Give time between new foods to allow for observation of any reaction.	
Alert: NEVER	give any baby under 1 year old: Cow's milk to drink. 'Hot' spices. Salt. Sugar. Fatty or oily foods. It is also safe practice to avoid giving honey, strawberries and nuts, especially peanuts, to any baby if there is any history of allergy in the immediate family.					
Good professional practice	Always consult parents about their wishes about feeding their child. Ensure you are fully aware of and record any allergies, religious guidelines, personal circumstances which may impact on how and what foods you give to the child. Check what a breastfeeding mother wants you to give the child to drink. Try to follow parental wishes; legal action has been taken against child carers who have given bottle feeds against parental instructions.					

Understanding about 'snacks' and 'meals'

Small children have small stomachs and large energy requirements. These simple facts make it essential that their eating is healthy, nutritious, regular and frequent.

As adults we mainly think of 'meals' as being breakfast, lunch or dinner. When we talk of 'snacks' we tend to view them as extras to our basic nutritional requirements, and often if we wish to improve the healthy quality of our diet or strive to follow a weight reducing diet, it is 'snacks' that we seek to cut out. Snacks tend to be such things as buns, crisps, biscuits, cakes, sweets and chocolate products. Therefore for us 'snacks' are often high in fat and sugar or salt. When we state that young children need 'snacks', it does not mean that we have to feed them a diet of such products.

We tend to give babies 'main meals' at the same times as we provide them for ourselves. However, the gaps between these meals are too long for young children. They need to eat between 'meals', for example between breakfast and lunch. We usually refer to eating in these times between main meals as snacks. For children snacks are essentially timed sources of nutrition. It is very important that we plan children's snacks with the same care that we give to planning their main meals. A healthy balanced

Young children need healthy-eating snacks.

diet depends on overall nutritional provision for all eating, and not simply for what adults call main meals.

ACTIVITY

1. With a colleague list 15 foods (cooked or raw, cold or hot, sweet or savoury, home-made or bought, fresh, chilled or preserved) that could be suitable 'snack' foods for a baby under a year old.

2. Next to each food indicate its food group category.

3. Look at the range of food groups you have on your list. Is there an even spread across the four main groups?

4. Share your findings with other colleagues and together compile a guideline list of ideas for suitable, healthy eating snacks from each of the four main food groups, which would be suitable for babies.

Safe practices and weaning

Good food safety and hygiene are absolutely essential when preparing food and feeding babies.

- A baby must NEVER be left unsupervised with any food or drink.
- Food should be checked carefully for potential problems such as fish bones or fruit pips.
- The temperature of the baby's food must be checked using a separate (sterilised) spoon (never by putting your finger into it).
- NEVER cool the baby's food by blowing on it.
- Until the age of nine months the baby's spoons, cups and bowls should be sterilised; after nine months they can be cleaned by thorough washing in hot soapy water in a sink or dishwasher.
- Use a clean bib for each meal, removing it afterwards.
- High-chair trays must be carefully disinfected before and after each meal as babies often pick up food from these surfaces.
- Wash your hands and the baby's before and after each meal or snack.

Home cooking versus commercially prepared baby foods

There are some benefits in using commercial baby foods. They are quick to prepare, safe for babies and are available in a wide range. Commercially produced baby foods are useful when travelling and are good stock cupboard stand-bys. They can be given alone or alongside home-made foods. However, they are often less economical than home prepared foods and they provide less variety of taste, consistency and texture.

ALERT

A consumer organisation report issued in May 2000 highlighted concern that labelling of baby food is often insufficiently clear for parents to make informed choices. The researchers also found that sugar is added by manufacturers to many baby food products which encourages a 'sweet tooth' and goes against sound nutritional guidelines. Baby breakfast cereals are amongst the worst culprits. There is a need to provide young children and babies with a high-energy diet but feeding foods with added sugar is not recommended.

If food is prepared and cooked at home you can control the quality and the ingredients. You will not be adding any preservatives and you will be able to provide a full range of textures and tastes for the baby to exactly match her needs and her stage of development. Home-made foods tend to be cheaper although the time taken to prepare them will be more.

When using commercial baby foods follow these guidelines:

- Labels – check 'stage and age' suitability for the baby.
- Contents boxes on labels – always check these before purchase so you are fully aware of all the contents. Look for 'hidden' sugars or salt. Check for suitability for vegetarian or religious needs.
- Instructions – follow directions for heating and mixing carefully. Stir food thoroughly to dispel any hot spots and test the temperature before serving.
- Containers – food in glass jars can be heated in a pan with boiling water or, if the metal lid is removed, in a microwave oven.
- Partly used containers (1) – if the baby has been fed directly from the container or the spoon used to feed the baby has been put into the food in the container after use, discard any remaining food at the end of the meal.
- Partly used containers (2) – if you plan to only use part of the contents of the container, spoon the required amount out of the container and heat it separately. The remainder can be stored, tightly covered in the refrigerator for up to 48 hours. Food should never be stored in an opened tin or uncovered container.
- Leftover food – unless previously separated before heating, any remaining food must be discarded.

Overcoming some of the difficulties that may arise during weaning

Most difficulties in weaning are caused by adults and not by the baby! Weaning can cause great anxiety for parents concerned about their child's perceived 'slow' progress in eating solids. Remind parents that weaning is a gradual process and every baby takes it at her own pace. There is much learning and shared experiences to enjoy, and the nutritional aspect of early weaning is minimal.

Feeding is a messy business, but the messier and more involved the baby is, the more opportunities she is having for learning. Tight adult control can prevent essential experimentation and exploration. The baby needs to practise. The aim is to produce an independent, skilful eater able to feed herself, controlling her food and the implements used. Feeding herself using fingers and managing cups and spoons takes many hours of trial and error, but she needs to be encouraged and not prevented from doing it.

Remember eating should be pleasurable. Eating a savoury course before a sweet course is simply traditional. There is no real reason why a baby cannot have pudding first, or even alternating spoonfuls from each course throughout her meal. But if the baby enjoys this and eats it, then that's fine.

Babies do not naturally overeat and do not starve themselves either. They will eat or seek food when they are hungry. Do not force a baby to eat and never persist in trying to tempt a baby to eat unless she is keen to do so. If she has finished, remove the food and offer the next course you have planned.

Regular health checks include weighing the baby, so parents can have frequent assurance for any concern they may have about their child not eating enough. Unfortunately being overweight is much more common in children, and carries allied health risks. Consequently good diet and sensible management of eating are vital for laying healthy foundations in the early years.

- - - - - - - *Good professional practice* - - - - - - -

A calm, reassuring, well-informed and understanding professional can make a world of difference to a parent and consequently to the baby too. Parents need to be confident in the support you will give them and to see that your expert knowledge is tempered with a good helping of non-patronising common sense, compassion and good humour.

Specific feeding difficulties and coping with problems

Sometimes health problems related to feeding will arise and it is important that you are aware of possible causes and are clear in the action you should take.

Health related problems and feeding		
Problem	**Signs & Symptoms**	**Care & Management**
Allergic reactions	Diarrhoea, vomiting, skin rashes/eczema, wheezing after eating.	Seek medical advice, seek referral to paediatrician/dietician. Feed breast milk if possible. Medical advice may include: Mother may need to restrict drinking cow's milk if breastfeeding: Determining whether to avoid cow's-milk-based formula products and feed soya based formula to baby: Identifying and avoid giving offending food. NOTE: Any dietary changes for baby or mother should be made under medical supervision.
Colic	Abdominal pain causes baby to draw up legs. Abdomen can be hard and a little distended. Causes great distress, baby not easily comforted. Occurs after feeding and often at same time each day. Usual in early evening.	Check teat size on bottle, ensure steady milk flow. Check feeding technique e.g. give bottle so no air flows through teat. Feed baby. Comfort, cuddle and massage baby. Move baby gently, soft horizontal and vertical rocking. Hold baby upright against your shoulder. Reassure parent/carer that pain is spasmodic and self limiting. Seek advice from health visitor.
Constipation	Stools are hard, small, infrequent. Passing them may cause pain or discomfort.	Increase intake of fluids, especially water and milk. Check correct concentration of formula in feed mix. If weaned, increase fruit and vegetable intake. Check baby is not underfed. NEVER give laxatives or sugar in feeds.

Dental decay	Teeth sticky, plaque coated, discoloured, showing signs of caries and may be broken down. Baby may react because of discomfort or pain in mouth.	Caused by: frequent use of sugary drinks, sticky, sugary foods and sweets. Child left with bottle or mini-feeder to suck. Insufficient oral hygiene, including little regular cleaning of mouth, gums and teeth. Care: improve baby's oral hygiene, restrict sugar intake. Seek dental and health visitor advice.
Diarrhoea	Stools are watery, loose, frequent.	Seek early medical advice. Give plenty of clear fluids to counteract dehydration. Check and if needed increase hygiene provision for baby including feed preparation and feeding.
Overfeeding	Excessive weight gain. Baby is uncomfortable/ unsettled, vomits, passes large stools, sometimes sweaty, sore on buttocks and at top of leg/hip creases.	Check concentration and make-up of formula feeds. Check food solids and milk intake are age appropriate. Seek advice from health visitor.
Possetting	Baby frequently brings up some regurgitated feed. Small amount of vomit but baby gains weight and is content.	Check weight gain is maintained, regular and within norms. Baby usually grows out of this when starts to spend more time upright/ walking.
Underfeeding	Baby wakeful and cries from hunger. Poor weight gain. May vomit from excessive crying and air swallowing. Stools are dark and small.	Check correct constitution of formula feeds. Check teat not blocked & review cleaning procedures. Check technique and mother's diet if baby is breastfed. Increase frequency of feeds, followed if necessary by increasing quantities at each feed. May result from delayed weaning, insufficient milk feed in addition to solids, use of low fat dairy products, diet being too high in fibre, diet being over-restricted for cultural, 'health' or ethical reasons. May indicate child neglect.

ALERT

Note that it is quite normal that the stools of breastfed babies change in appearance once weaning starts. However, if the stools of any baby are over large, dark or black in colour or in any way cause you to be concerned about their comfort or health, never hesitate to seek medical advice.

END OF CHAPTER ACTIVITY

Make three weaning plans for babies which will outline how you plan to meet their needs during the first year of life. Use the framework of meals and snacks as indicated in the centre sections of the weaning chart. Your planning should demonstrate your clear understanding of the baby's developmental pattern in moving from sucking milk to coping with first 'solids' to increased management of textures and food ranges. It should demonstrate both your awareness of the suitability of different foods at different ages and your commitment to providing a healthy balanced diet to continuously meet the baby's changing needs.

(a) A weaning plan for a baby whose parents wish her to be given a meat-free (including no poultry) diet.
(b) A weaning plan for a baby whose parents wish her to be brought up in the traditions of their African-Caribbean family.
(c) A weaning plan for a baby from a family who are Muslims.

This activity will require you to research relevant cultural, dietary and nutritional information for each scenario. Refer back to Chapters 4 and 5 for nutrient information and balancing dietary needs. You will find some religious and cultural guidelines in Chapter 9. You will also need to obtain information from your library, local child health centre or health visitor base, and the community dietician.

Quick quiz

Find the answers in the chapter.

1. Why should weaning not begin before the baby is four months old?

2. What liquids are suitable for softening and mixing with baby cereal and purées for a four-month-old baby?

3. About how much 'solids' and how often each day would you expect a five month old baby to take?

4. Why must cow's or goat's milk not be given as a drink to babies under a year old?

5. What ingredients must be omitted from 'family' foods to make them safe for babies?

6. How much breast or formula milk does a six month old baby still need every day in addition to solids?

7. When purchasing commercially prepared baby foods what particular information should you seek from the labels?

8. If a whole jar or portion of prepared baby food is too much for a single meal, what safe procedures can be taken to store some for later use?

9. What are the likely causes of constipation in a baby? How would you care for and manage a baby suffering from this?

10. Why is diarrhoea potentially very dangerous for a baby? What action would you take for a baby suffering from this? How quickly would you act? How would you work with the parents?

Summary

Having studied this chapter you should now understand that:

- Weaning is essential for the baby's health, should not occur before four months and begin no later than six months old.
- Weaning involves the baby in complex experiences and learning opportunities as well as providing essential nutrition.
- The weaning process is gradual, gently paced and individually matched to each baby's needs.
- Weaning has distinct stages and must be carefully managed.
- It is important to provide a nutritiously correct diet for a baby being weaned, by introducing a safe, balanced range of foods appropriately prepared and presented.

7

Life after Weaning: or Not Biting Off More Than You Can Chew

Aims of the chapter

To enable you to understand:
- the nutritional needs of the young child.
- external influences affecting a young child's eating behaviours and attitudes to food.
- why children may choose not to eat: how to manage food, meals and emotions.

Flossie sometimes worried that he would never eat any food that involved chewing.

Most of us do grow out of our limiting likes and dislikes, even those of us who didn't like chewing food as small children!

The role of the professional: ensuring successful healthy eating and child development

The role of the professional is to know each child extremely well, to plan for and meet their specific needs whilst encouraging them to try new experiences, tastes and skills. Children will only be confident in new situations if they feel secure. This is applicable for all learning, including the vast range of exciting opportunities which are related to food and eating.

It is critical that independence is fostered. We must take time and care to encourage self-help and fine manipulative skills. Even if a one year old only seems interested in opening her mouth for you to spoon food in, it is still important that you place a filled spoon in her hand and let her aim it towards her mouth herself. At least some of the food will go in and meanwhile she will be beginning to realise that she has some control over her eating. This concept may well translate into her feeling a little more confident about putting some new tastes into her mouth and so become more adventurous in her eating.

The nutritional needs of the young child

Young children grow rapidly, greatly increase their range of activities and develop an expanding social circle. The high energy requirements for growth, for rapid development and for the establishment and maintenance of good health come from the food children eat. What, when and how they eat is therefore critical for their well being.

Feeding toddlers: plus one year and counting!

The nutritional principles for meeting the needs of babies over a year or 'toddlers' are exactly the same as for all young children. Their diet should be healthy and balanced, based on the five food groups. Daily servings or age-appropriate proportions of these groups should be given as indicated in Chapter 4. If the quality such as the freshness of food is also assured then the child will have good opportunities to eat healthily.

Children up to five years old need:

- A, D and C vitamin drop supplements
- a pint of whole milk a day.

Alert

Young children should continue to have no added salt and no added sugar.

Foods that can be introduced gradually into the diet *after* the child is one year old include:

- cow's, goat's and sheep's milk to drink
- a wider range of pulses
- more citrus fruits
- a greater variety of all foods, tastes and textures
- some (not very hot) spices
- honey.

– – – – – – –*Good professional practice*– – – – – – –

As with younger babies it is good, safe practice to introduce new foods gradually and one at a time. This enables monitoring for any unwanted reactions and allows the child to confidently acquire new tastes and textures.

Alert

Choking:

Taco shells and corn chips can cause choking and should only be given under strict supervision to children over three years old. Peanuts must not be given to children under seven years as their trachea (windpipe) is narrow and choking is a high risk. Larger whole nuts are also not suitable for under five year olds, and above this age should only be offered with close adult supervision.

Individual needs, preferences and patterns of development

Although developmental sequences can be predicted and observed in children, each individual varies in the rate and pattern of development. A 13-month-old who is already walking will tend to use up more energy than a baby of the same age who is still crawling or bottom shuffling. A child who was born eight weeks prematurely is likely to be physically smaller at

18 months than a full-term baby at the same age. Consequently, as their energy needs will be different, it is reasonable to assume their appetites will also vary.

It is important to offer children appropriate quantities of food. To give too little is obviously a concern as nutritional and energy needs are unlikely to be adequately met. To feed too much may result in the child vomiting or becoming overweight. Giving too much may equally result in the child feeling over-faced and becoming a reluctant or 'difficult' eater.

Around their first birthdays most babies are ready to eat many of the main foods and meals served to their families. Some will be adventurous and keen to try new food experiences, but some will be much more conservative in accepting changes. Others may even be quite disinterested in the whole exciting business! Some will insist on being spoon-fed while others will be so fiercely independent that they demand to manage the whole thing themselves. Many babies will vary between these extremes, and continue to fluctuate according to their mood, the food and the people involved with them. In fact, as young children are no less fickle than adults, we should not be surprised that individual appetites and food preferences vary.

If a one-year-old has rather limited tastes and is reluctant to accept different new foods it is important to proceed slowly. Her confidence needs to be fostered and her palate given time to develop. *It is known that the taste buds of young children are much more sensitive and efficient than adults.* This should be kept in mind particularly if we expect them to eat food which is poorly cooked and of unattractive textures. Lumpy grey mashed potatoes, slushy overcooked greens, cold thick gravy, undercooked pastry are anyone's worst gastronomic nightmare! It is worth asking yourself if you would always be delighted to eat the food served from the nursery kitchen!

A willingness to accept new tastes and try new skills will depend greatly on the child's enjoyment of all aspects of food and eating.

Experiencing new foods and developing eating skills can be a tricky business!

The developing needs of three-year-olds and above: eating to live and living to eat

The speed and extent of learning experienced in the first years of life are never again equalled. By their third birthday children have really established their own identities; they have strong ideas about themselves and their likes and dislikes. They can be single-minded one moment and in need of great reassurance and support the next. They are keen to be independent, but only on their terms. In every aspect of their life they are finding out about themselves, how others impact on them and how they relate to the environment. Young children constantly test and try to discover what control they can exert over other people and their own surroundings. Anyone who has spent any time with a lively three year old will testify to their capacity to 'test the bounds'!

The appetites of children between three and four may fluctuate. Depending on their growth patterns, energy outputs and individual make-up each one will have differing food intake needs. Although quantities may vary from child to child, and even for each individual child from time to time, the balance and healthy quality of their diet remain of paramount importance. Regular health and developmental checks are effective ways of monitoring each child's growth, development and overall health.

It is simpler at home than in a nursery or school to give individual children their favourite foods. Nevertheless, where groups of children eat together, by offering them some choices and by careful serving of food it is possible to meet individuals' needs and tastes at mealtimes.

■ — ■ — ■ — ■ — ■ — ■—*Good professional practice*■ — ■ — ■ — ■ — ■ — ■

Try to find alternatives for unpopular foods and textures – raw rather than cooked peppers; more fruit, fruit juice and vegetable juice instead of vegetables; yoghurt or cheese if drinking milk is a problem; minced poultry, ground red meat or fish if she currently hates chewing. Be calm and be creative!

External influences affecting a young child's eating behaviours and attitudes to food

(A) Adults' knowledge, views and behaviours

Parents of the children we work with, like us, have been moulded by individual experiences, and cultural, social and economic influences. Chapter 1 looked at how our own childhood has influenced how we now behave with children. (Reread this section and your filed Activity notes to remind yourself of the key points.)

We need to be aware of how strongly we influence young children. It is important to remember that very young children readily observe if you are saying one thing but doing another yourself. It is what you do and how you act rather than what you say that has the greatest influence on the child.

Never expect a young child to eat something that personally you would not touch with a bargepole! Why should they? After all, we spend our time encouraging them to be observant, communicative and selective! Consequently we should not only accept but positively encourage these critical processes and skills, even when food is involved!

If parents and carers have a poor understanding of basic nutrition they may unsuspectingly feed their children poorly balanced diets which will not meet their energy requirements and their health and nutritional needs.

However, even a sound understanding of nutritional principles has to be combined with an awareness of the total needs of a young child. For example, parents may be so vigilant about the healthy quality of their child's eating that they may be concerned about accepting party invitations as the food served is likely to be 'unhealthy', containing synthetic colourings, sugar and so on. However, the enjoyment and social advantages of such a special occasion may far outweigh the need for a healthy meal!

▬ ▬ ▬ ▬ ▬ ▬ ▬Good professional practice ▬ ▬ ▬ ▬ ▬ ▬ ▬

Clear, well-presented information, telling parents about how the placement plans for and meets children's nutritional and individual needs, can support a working partnership with parents. It can be an effective means for sharing useful information both about good nutrition and good practice in early years education.

(B) Society's views

In some sectors of society and in some cultures it is highly desirable to have a large, plump baby and to delight in the fact a child 'eats absolutely everything'. Elsewhere the envy of others may be aroused by having a very slender, even underweight child. The customs and preferences of society can greatly influence what and how a child is fed.

(C) Family lifestyles

In the past half century eating patterns and styles have radically changed. The role of women has changed although in the UK women still predominate as the main food shoppers and providers of family meals. More mothers with young children work outside the home. There are more interests and demands on our time outside the household. The number of single-parent households has increased. Although there are more labour saving devices in the home, particularly in the kitchen, overall we have less time to shop, prepare, cook and eat meals together as a family. We eat fewer meals together as a family, and recent reports show that for the first time we now tend to feed children of all ages different foods from ourselves.

Research shows that as a nation we consume too much sugar and fatty foods, mainly eaten from highly processed, 'convenience' sources. We take less exercise than 20 years ago, depending greatly on the car even for short journeys, and tend to be overweight.

(D) Variety and choice of foods

The ranges and types of food available in our shops have increased. Pre-prepared, takeaway and processed foods are now widely obtainable. Modern cultivation, transportation and storage methods enable us to buy most foods at any time of the year and not just seasonally. Increased foreign travel and a growth in the multicultural aspect of society have enabled more people to experience a greater variety of foods and dishes. Opportunity to experience variety is obviously crucial but equally important for successful learning is the sensitivity and attitude of the key adult. How foods are offered to a child may repel or excite and delight her.

(E) The timing and duration of meals

Both the timing of and the time and focus given to eating influence how well children eat. Small and frequent meals are needed by young children who have high energy needs but relatively small stomachs with small capacities. However, constant 'grazing' (in place of meals or planned snacks) is poor practice and promotes poor learned behaviour. Many essential foods cannot be eaten in this way, so the diet will be limited. Moreover the child misses out on the social and self-help skills which can be developed at mealtimes. Eating her 'main meal' at midday, in the midst of her main fuel-burning activity time, helps to meet her energy requirements effectively and guards against her becoming overtired.

If meals are hurried children do not have time to eat properly, chewing and swallowing food efficiently. If rushed or feeling that the faster they eat the sooner they can return to another enjoyable activity, they may not eat enough to meet their physical needs. They will also be learning that meals are not very important times. Moreover the actual opportunities for enjoying and learning from mealtimes will be missed.

— — — — — — — — — — —Key point— — — — — — — — — — — —

Young children need time to explore, experiment and practice new skills and attitudes. This includes mealtime learning.

All the aspects given above can impact on how we plan, provide and organise food for our children. They are therefore some of the key influences affecting a young child's eating behaviours, nutrition and attitudes to food. However, it is important to consider these matters (of eating behaviours, nutrition and attitudes to food) from the child's perspective; in particular where there is a cause for concern.

Jennifer needs time to explore, experiment and practice new skills and attitudes. This includes mealtime learning.

'Do you like it?' A party can be the time to try something new.

Why children may choose not to eat: How to manage food, meals and emotions

Children may not want to eat for a wide variety of reasons which may be broadly categorised into 5 areas. Some examples are outlined opposite.

Why Children May Not Want to Eat

Health & Development	Appetite	Food	Environment	Relationships
Generally feeling unwell	Genuinely not hungry	Genuinely dislikes the particular food (either temporarily or permanently)	Worried about something actual or perceived	Worried about being helped by unfamiliar adult
Suffering from constipation	Going through spell of needing less food than during previous energy or growth spurt	Served at wrong temperature, poorly cooked, poor-quality ingredients	Chair/table at wrong height	Being teased, pinched, etc. by another child
Overtired	Limited, as child is not yet walking, running, climbing etc. so has lower energy needs than peers	Thinks it smells 'funny' or it looks 'peculiar'	Anxious about using unfamiliar utensils	Wanting to sit with someone special & not allowed
Running a high temperature	Over-faced by too large portions	Is different from how same food is cooked/ served at home	Would rather still be involved in previous activity	Being told not to eat something by parents or other adults or children
Teething or toothache	In a 'low' intake period of development; e.g. many 3 & 4 yr olds eat comparatively small amounts	Looks too difficult to eat, chew or cut up	Would rather be involved in the next activity	Seeking adult attention
Suffering from catarrh	Too full from eating or drinking recently	Unfamiliarity or lack of recognition: does not know what the food is	New to the nursery/setting so unsure/ unfamiliar	Testing your reaction
Not able/ experienced e.g. in using utensils or sitting at a table to eat		Does not like the way the food is served . . . already put on plate or chopped up	Worried about events/people at home when she's not there	Thinks refusal 'entertains' other children
		Food smothered or mixed up so cannot see what it is		Feels under pressure to eat

Note: Add further information to these lists as you observe and assess children in your placements.

In your placement, observe the children in the newest intake group:

1. How many of the children are able to feed themselves an appropriate dessert using a spoon without relying on their fingers? How many cannot?

2. How many know how to use a fork to spear food? How many cannot?

3. How many try to cut with a knife and hold it in a conventional way? How many cannot?

4. How do the nursery staff support the children in practising and acquiring these tricky skills?

5. What happens to children whose families use different eating implements, not western knives and forks, at home? How are they supported and what care is taken to celebrate and value their culture?

6. Share your findings with your student colleagues. Discuss resulting implications and note instances of good practice.

Managing food, meals and emotions

Young children need to eat little and often, perhaps five or six times a day. Mealtimes are therefore significant, regular and frequent events. Developmentally young children learn how to make choices, assert themselves and establish themselves both as individuals and as a member of a family. It is hardly surprising therefore that eating provides many opportunities for children to practise their ideas and test out various social situations. Food-related activities and mealtimes can be a hotbed for learning, fun and for stupendous interpersonal crises!

A pause for thought

A child has proclaimed a refusal to eat some vegetables. Her parents have stated they want her, when in your care, to eat vegetables. You spend time carefully producing delicious styles, combinations and presentations to tempt her to eat vegetables. She is not keen, and soon refuses to eat any vegetables. She finds them hidden under the gravy or where you sneakily mix them into the mashed potato. If any do get into her mouth she spits them out. The more ruses you try the more determined she becomes. You perform like a manic clown to take her mind off the contents of the spoon you are wielding. You make food 'face pictures' on the plate, with cabbage as hair and peas as teeth. You demonstrate eating it yourself and go overboard saying how magnificently wonderfully scrummy and delicious it is. You poise a filled spoon before her bemused face and as you coax it gently to her lips she screams, grabs the spoon and hurls it across the room! You are exhausted, the place is a mess, the food is wasted and the child has still not eaten any vegetables. Mealtimes are now fully and emotionally charged. The parents are distraught. The battle lines are drawn and the adults are on the losing side!

Young children and decision making

Young children have little or no control over their lives and to what happens to them. However, there are a few things that they can control totally. No adult can make a child like or willingly eat something. The child decides what goes in, and when and where it comes out! If challenged the young child who is developing an awareness of her own identity, will exert her determination with expertise and single-minded purpose! Even quite young children who feel thwarted can be very skilful in exhibiting oral and anal retention and other anti-social behaviours. Such significant problems will affect not only their present eating, but are likely to lead to the establishment of patterns of negative behaviour and attitudes towards eating which can prevail into adult life.

Remember: Although you are deeply involved with a child in your care you do not have the same all consuming emotional investment in your relationship with her as her parents have. Badly managed mealtimes may frustrate you to your personal and professional limits. However, remember they can be totally devastating for the fervent parents, and the child.

– – – – – – *Good professional practice* – – – – – –

> If parents tell you they are concerned about their child's eating it is most important that you take time to hear them, discuss their feelings, analyse the main areas of difficulty and help them plan simple strategies to de-escalate and positively manage the situation.

Effective management

Adults need to follow guidelines and *not* rigid rules when it comes to managing young children's eating. The only non-negotiable rules are those concerned with safety, health and hygiene. Except for these issues the key word is *flexibility*. This will help to retain your humour and sanity, and consequently allow children to develop happily and steadily.

But what *are* you to do if faced with a toddler who absolutely refuses to look at let alone eat an egg (whether scrambled, boiled, baked or poached)?

The route to self-preservation on your part and sound nutrition on the child's part (an action essential for the resurrection of your relationship) is to remove the offending object without fuss or comment, and to stop presenting eggs as eggs! Simply beat an egg into a custard or some cheese sauce. The nutrients are there; the battle is not. At some future date an egg can be re-presented as a new experience, and just as easily withdrawn again if still disliked.

The management of a non-vegetable or fruit eater probably needs a slightly different approach. Be creative and do not worry or pressurise. Offer raw vegetable sticks or fruit chunks as snacks. Encourage her to try one and if not accepted, take it away and do not offer an alternative. Children seeing others trying and enjoying food are more likely to eat it. Offer a wide range of flavours, colours and textures. Grate or chop raw vegetables and mix with other sandwich fillings.

But what about 'greens'?

ACTIVITY

1. You sit with a two year old child in your care who one day refuses to eat green vegetables.

(a) How would you react to the child when she says she does not want them?

(b) If she does not eat them what would you do and would you tell anyone?

(c) What basic checks would you routinely make on the child?

(d) What do you say to another child at the table who is observing her refusal with great interest?

2. The situation happens again over the following two days. Her parents are concerned as she is now not eating them at home. What advice would you give them to manage their concerns and avoid upsets?

3. The real dislike of green vegetables seems set to continue! What main nutrients do green vegetables provide? What alternative foods could you currently substitute to ensure the essential nutrients and balance in her diet?

4. Is 'not eating cabbage' the end of the world?

– – – – – – –*Good professional practice* – – – – – – –

As an early years child care professional you need to be able to manage and prevent potential child conflicts yourself, and to understand the nutritional principles for children's healthy eating so you can plan their diet effectively. In addition you have to be able to explain these facts and strategies to parents to help prevent upsets and to support them and their child when problems have arisen.

The importance of engaging children's interest in food

Young children have a keen interest in being involved in all kinds of activities, especially those where they can 'help' an adult. Young children are naturally good learners and want to try things for themselves.

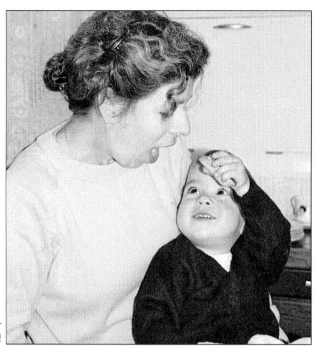

Taking the biscuit . . . But not for
me! . . . It's for my mummy!

As professionals working to support children's learning and all round
development, we need to safely involve children in practical activities.
Those related to food can provide rich learning opportunities. However,
some activities carry too high a risk and are obviously unsuitable for
children. We must identify any possible dangerous elements of a task. If
they cannot be removed or altered sufficiently the child should be told why
she cannot help with it, and that she will be allowed to help as soon as it is
safe. If a child is effectively involved in the shopping and preparation of a
meal she is more likely to be interested in the food and to eat it.

Principles for the positive management of healthy happy eating

How each child will react to new foods, new social situations linked with
eating and new challenges for managing and eating foods will naturally
vary. However, *the principles* for ensuring success and positive attitudes to
healthy eating are clear and consistent for all children.

DO:

- Acknowledge each child is an individual and celebrate the differences
  between the children in your care.

- Understand the nutritional principles which will enable you to provide a healthy balanced diet matched to the child's needs.
- Understand the nutritional principles which will enable you to effectively substitute or alternate foods and so ensure provision of an appropriate and balanced diet.
- Give small tastes of new foods and introduce new flavours, textures and foods gradually.
- Stay calm and positive; provide a secure and relaxed environment.
- Provide appropriate support both to help the child eat and to feed herself.
- Allow plenty of time for meals, for investigating, practising, communicating and enjoying.
- Maintain a sense of fun, interest and enjoyment. Remember, eating is supposed to be one of life's pleasures!

DON'T:

- Don't fight over food. If the child refuses to eat what you offer, remove it quietly without offering an alternative.
- Don't expect a young child to go for more than about two hours without some food. They need smaller and more frequent food intakes than adults.
- Don't rely on biscuits, crisps and cakes for snacks. Yoghurt, fruit, vegetables, toast or a sandwich provide more essential nutrients and longer-lasting forms of energy.
- Don't give sugary foods or drinks very often. Tooth damage, spoilt appetites and mild diarrhoea may result. Milk or water are safer.
- Don't give any peanut-containing foods if there is any history of any family allergy.
- Don't forget dislike of certain food and refusal to try new ones are common in young children.
- Don't let a child's refusal to eat something turn into open conflict.

ABOVE ALL

Never tell a child they must eat something because . . .

- 'It will do you good.'
- 'Other children would really like to be able to have such lovely food.'
- 'I/your mummy/another person will be disappointed/cross if you don't eat it.'
- 'If you don't eat it you will not be allowed to do (something) later.'

- 'It is really delicious and you *will* like it.'
- 'If you don't eat it, I will eat it.'
- 'All the work spent cooking it will have been wasted.'
- 'I say so!'

Negative statements and attitudes are doomed to end in failure and will produce conflict. They can cause long term problems and hang-ups for the child, and possibly for the adult too. An upset or threatened child will not eat well.

■ ■ ■ ■ ■ ■ *Good professional practice* **■ ■ ■ ■ ■ ■**

If a child is not keen to eat we need to search for the underlying causes, try to address them and give her warm gentle support. We would do the same if she was reluctant to listen to stories or finger paint.

END OF CHAPTER ACTIVITY

Consider the following scenario:

Femi is two and a half and attends your nursery two days a week. She is friendly, sociable and generally a very happy child. She usually seems to enjoy mealtimes at nursery. She takes an interest in her food and is managing to eat and drink by herself with reasonable control. She eats most meals without any fuss unless she is unwell. Staff have no concerns. You know Femi's parents are particular about food quality and try to buy as much fresh and organic produce as possible. They take a lot of care over the cooking and preparation of Femi's meals.

This morning her mother asks you about Femi's eating at nursery. The mother says she is feeling exhausted and desperate about Femi and her eating at home. You ask her to talk about it and she explains as follows.

Until a couple of weeks ago all seemed fine, but then Femi has really started to play up and mess about with her food. She used to eat most things happily and without fuss. Now she won't even eat pieces of fresh fruit and refuses to eat all her main course before demanding her dessert. Last night Femi would not eat the lamb and vegetable casserole her mother had spent all afternoon preparing. Femi's grandmother came to stay with the family about 14 days ago to help with the move to their new flat last week. She is kindly staying on for a while and is looking after Femi as her mother has just started a new job. The grandmother has not been very happy with some of the things Femi is usually allowed to do. After last night's tantrums at dinner the grandmother told Femi's parents that they need to act firmly to correct her bad behaviour. Femi's father said that unless she improved he feels they must cancel a visit to his sister's next week. Femi's mother asks you what she can do about Femi's messy eating, limited diet and deliberate naughtiness.

1. Jot down three things 'off the top of your head' that you think you may say in immediate response to the mother's obvious distress.

2. With a colleague reread the account above and note down the key points under the following headings.

'Femi and her eating problems.'

	The situation last month regarding:	The situation now regarding:	Main changes in this time	Possible effect of any of these changes on Femi?
Femi				
Mother				
Father				
Grand-mother				
Other factors				

4. Underline what you both think are some of the most likely causes for Femi's changed behaviour and eating habits.

5. Could each of these causes and their effects have been better managed to minimise their impact on Femi?

6. As the problems have now arisen, decide on the best advice and help you could give to Femi and to her mother to help resolve the situation.

7. Look back together at the answers you each gave to question 1 and discuss them. Can you improve on your initial ideas for the immediate response to Femi's mother?

Quick quiz

Find the answers in the chapter.

1. Why should 'new' foods be introduced one at a time?

2. A child in your care refuses to eat finger wedges of cheese, how could you provide her with cheese in her diet?

3. Why are peanuts dangerous for children under seven years?

4. Why might a child suddenly have a poorer appetite one day?

5. Why might a two year old child refuse to eat a dinner which has already been cut up for her?

6. Why do young children need to eat little and often, perhaps as often as six times a day?

7. What could account for two eighteen-month-old-children having very different sizes of appetite?

8. You plan to encourage a two and a half-year-old to eat a greater range of fruits. How might you do this?

9. Which three vitamins (in the form of drops) should be given to young children?

10. A three-year-old faces her first midday meal in your care. What worries might she have but not be able to verbalise?

Summary

Having studied this chapter you should now understand:

- the nutritional needs of young children after their first birthday; how to support individual needs preferences and patterns of development
- what are the developing needs of three year olds and above
- how external influences affect a young child's eating, behaviours, nutrition and attitudes to food
- why children may choose not to eat
- how to manage food, meals and emotions successfully.

8

Social Factors and Children's Eating

Aims of the chapter

To enable you to understand:

- Effects of low income on food, nutrition and children's health.
- Managing healthy eating on a limited budget.
- School and nursery meals and children's health: quality of nutrition and current regulations.
- The social importance of school and nursery meals.
- Some effects of food and drink advertising on families and young children.

After a week of giving her class bananas for playtime snacks, Flossie thought she could observe a change in the children's behaviour.

The role of the professional

It is important that early years professionals understand the many pressures on families which may affect their ability to provide children with a healthy balanced diet. Factors such as reports in the media, regular food scares, and being bombarded by advertising and by children who themselves are susceptible to strong advertising campaigns and to peer pressure, can all cause problems. Making healthy eating food choices, shopping effectively and cooking well are not simple, particularly when limited by a very low income. In the face of such issues even parents who have sound understanding about children' nutritional needs can find life difficult. Where there is a limited understanding of food values, healthy cooking and nutritional needs, children are less likely to eat a healthy balanced diet. This has a negative affect on every aspect of growth, development and learning.

Help provided in family support units often includes working with parents on planning and providing suitable, affordable and reasonably healthy meals. An early years professional is likely to be on the team when young children are involved. You may not be leading this aspect of the programme but you must be able to understand the issues and offer sensitive guidance.

Effects of low income on food, nutrition and children's health: established links between poverty, diet and health

In 1998 the Department of Health published the *Health Survey of Children and Young People*. The report looked at a wide variety of factors impacting on children's health, including eating habits. For children of ages 2–15 years one of the key findings stated:

Good eating habits, such as eating fruit and vegetables more than once a day, were more likely amongst children in social classes I and II and high income families, while poor dietary habits were more likely amongst children in social classes IV and V and low income families.

Dietary problems shown to be directly related to low income and to poor-quality or overcrowded housing include:

- excessive salt intake (overuse of salt in cooking; heavy intake of convenience/processed/snack foods)
- excessive sugar intake (from snack foods; heavy use of condensed milk)
- excessive fat intake (from frequent eating of fried and processed foods; heavy use of ghee)
- lack of iron (notably from poor vegetarian diets; poor weaning practices)
- lack of folic acid (especially in pregnant vegetarian women)
- lack of vitamin D (insufficient exposure to daylight; supplements of vitamins A, C, D not given to children).

Health problems are linked to the dietary problems above and include:

- anaemia
- obesity
- being underweight
- rickets or poor bone formation
- poor growth rate; decreased stature
- poor dental health; poor formation and development of teeth
- immunodepression: i.e. increased susceptibility to infection and slow recovery from illness and injury
- general weakness; poor muscle formation
- low energy capacity, leading to: increased tiredness, lacking concentration (lessening child's ability to learn), increased irritability (leading to difficulties in tolerating problems and forming relationships).

Poverty and the associated problems of poor housing, inadequate nutrition and ill-health create stressful conditions for parents raising families and can jeopardise children's success in school.

(Learning to Succeed:
Report of National Commission on Education 1993)

As well as the level of income other circumstances affect the availability of a healthy diet:

- quality of housing (including high density of dwellings)
- cooking facilities (quality and access)
- household composition (number, ages and well being of adults and children).

State benefits

Parents with low incomes need up-to-date information about state benefits, claiming for children's free school meals, and receiving welfare milk and vitamins for babies and toddlers. Providing a specialised diet for a chronically ill or disabled child can bring considerable additional expenses, and state financial benefit is available in certain circumstances to support families with disabled members.

Managing healthy eating on a limited budget

It is important that children's diets are as healthy as possible to meet their developmental, lifestyle and energy needs. When money is tight mistakes cannot be afforded. The risk of the family disliking new tastes or being unwilling to sample new foods is likely to outweigh a parent's wish to improve the nutritional content of the diet. Changes in shopping, cooking and eating patterns are likely to take time to establish. This can be difficult to achieve in practice and professionals need to be very sensitive and supportive.

Home-made fruit yoghurt takes time to prepare but is more economical and has no added colourings or sugar.

Without increasing the cost of food shopping it is possible to improve the quality of the diet, by making more nutritious choices. The most nutritious foods do not have to be the most expensive.

By considering each of the five food groups we can consider how high-nutrient foods can be provided at an economical cost.

Some Ways of Managing Healthy Eating on a Budget

Food Group	Servings per Day	Examples of Options Costing More	Examples of Cheaper Healthy Options
1. Cereals, pasta, rice, breads, potatoes	5–7	Sugar, honey or chocolate-covered 'novelty' breakfast cereals Basmati rice Frozen oven chips Branded pastas	Own brand plainer breakfast cereals (served with or without honey, etc.) Plain long grain rice Home cooked thickly cut potato chips Jacket baked potatoes Own-brand and value packs
		Note: Foods in this group are generally good value. They are filling and rich in nutrients. They should form the main constituent of every meal and are suitable foods for snacks.	
2. Fruit & vegetables	5–6	Most vegetables offer good value for money. Some exotic, out of season fruits and vegetables are expensive.	Buy special offers on seasonal produce. Buy from a market rather than supermarket. Tinned or frozen vegetables often are good value and have no wastage.
		Note: 1.Remember reluctant vegetable eaters can be given them as added pizza toppings or cooked into a casserole or pie. 2. Sometimes fruits seem expensive BUT an apple or banana usually costs no more than a bar of chocolate or a bag of crisps.	
3. Milk and dairy products	2–3	Flavoured and fruit desserts. Flavoured milk drinks Pre-packed 'snack cheeses' Cream	Buy or make plain yoghurt and add own stewed fruit, honey, etc. Add cocoa, puréed fruit, etc. to fresh milk. Cut chunks for snacks from a larger block of cheese. Use 'top' of the milk, custard, yoghurt.
		Note: 1. Full-fat milk is a key food for young children. 2. A glass of milk costs no more than a glass of cola.	

Food group	Servings	Examples	Advice
4. Meat, fish, eggs & alternatives (e.g. pulses, peas, lentils.)	2–3	Steaks, chops, cuts for roasting, extra lean cuts	Cuts for slow cooking (& skim any residual fat from surface before serving). Poultry pieces.
		Note: Far healthier to serve small amount of lean meat than larger amount of fattier meat, such as sausages, burgers. Make meals cheaper and healthier and meat go further by cooking it with lots of added root vegetables and/or pulses.	
		Pre-prepared fish products (e.g. in sauces, etc.)	Fresh or frozen fish prepared and cooked at home (served with white sauce or chopped tomatoes).
		Some types of fresh fish.	Fish in season and special offers. (Coley is as nutritious as cod, and sardines as salmon, but much cheaper.)
		Eggs are a good-value, nutrient-rich food.	
		Pulses, lentils, beans, etc. are all good value and highly nutritious foods.	
5a. Fat-rich foods	minimum	Pastries, doughnuts, pies, sausages, crisps, frozen chips.	Choose low-fat options of favourite foods. Do not allow them as substitutes for foods from Groups 1–4.
5b. Sugar-rich foods	minimum	Biscuits, sweets, cakes, chocolate, sugary drinks	Buy fewer of these and substitute dried or fresh fruit for treats and snacks. Bake own lower sugar versions of cakes, buns and biscuits. Offer milk, puréed fruit milkshakes, water, dilute fruit juice as drinks.
			Alert: Overall Group 5 foods are simple to provide and quick to eat; are filling but low in nutrients. Allowing a child to fill up by eating group 5 foods means more nutritiously important foods will not be eaten.

Providing professional support to improve the quality of nutrition within a limited budget

When given sensitive support and clear guidance parents are generally willing to try to make some changes to their diet providing: (a) they understand the benefits for their child, and (b) the changes are not too disruptive.

Where there are stresses on parents to manage tight or inadequate budgets it is crucial that professionals guard against making 'nutrition' another problem. As poverty has proven links with low self-esteem and the incidence of depression where people feel trapped and powerless, it is extremely important that professionals do not appear patronising.

Giving professional support entails helping others to make changes. Success depends on shared understanding and commitment to bringing about change. People need to understand the benefits of long term healthy eating and be helped to achieve it. Being judgemental and making wholesale sweeping demands for significant changes in eating, cooking or style of meals will not prove successful.

— — — — — —*Good professional practice*— — — — — —

If asked to support a family find out what they like and why. Then negotiate one or two specific aspects which could be altered to improve the quality of nutrition. When these are established, negotiate another change. Pace it steadily, set a time frame, give information, encourage discussion and opinions, and ensure practical skills are developed alongside increased understanding.

Remember that:
Effective change takes time and learning (for everyone) has to begin from where the person is!

ACTIVITY

1. Plan a day's healthy, balanced menu suitable for a family on a very limited budget, to feed two parents and three children, who are four, six and eight years old.

2. Discuss your ideas and plans with a colleague, remembering that the purpose of supporting parents (especially those with low income) is:

▶ to promote a healthy balanced diet
▶ to provide as many nutrients as possible in each meal and snack
▶ to keep costs as low as possible; to promote independent thinking and self help skills in children
▶ to enable enjoyment of food and eating.

3. Evaluate your findings against these criteria with your tutor, and file them with any additional comments for future reference.

School and nursery meals and children's health: quality of nutrition and current regulations

In 1994 the Department of Health reported a survey showing that a good diet does not only produce significant long term health benefits but that in childhood it is essential for sustaining mental and physical growth.

Effective education depends greatly upon the child's health, her capacity to concentrate and having sufficient energy to sustain active learning. Thus effective education requires optimum health and consequently, an optimum nutritious diet.

Entitlement to free school meals

Children in full time state school education, who come from families receiving either Income Support or the Job Seekers Allowance are entitled to free school meals in local authority schools. The only other children who can qualify for free school meals are children of asylum seekers who are receiving financial support from the local authority asylum team.

Food eaten in school is only part of the daily intake, but it is important in the overall diet. For children from low-income families, school meals provide a larger percentage of the required daily nutrients than for other children. Therefore it is vital the meal is healthy, balanced and nutritious.

Some schools no longer supply a hot midday meal for pupils. Nevertheless there is still a requirement that food is provided for those pupils entitled to free school meals whose parents claim it.

Poor diet reduces a child's resistance to infection. Deprived children have been shown to be underweight, below average height and suffer an increased rate of anaemia, rickets and tuberculosis.

In recent years there has been an upsurge in cases of TB in children, which experts believe is a sound indicator of declining health and nutritional patterns. TB, which is closely linked to poverty, is now more prevalent in the UK than whooping cough.

Children under seven years receiving free school meals are also entitled to be given free milk. However, the meal and milk come as a single provision and one cannot be claimed without the other.

Now fewer schools than ever supply milk to pupils, and even those children having free meals who are entitled to free milk often do not have it.

ACTIVITY

The National Dairy Council has produced leaflets, 'Nursery Milk' and 'Nursery Milk Guide' which give clear information about the benefits of milk for children. They also outline the Welfare Food Scheme, which provides children under five in approved day care with 200ml of milk a day, free of charge and explains how providers of day care can apply to take part in the scheme.

Obtain copies of these leaflets, and read the guidance and information. If milk is not provided in your placement set up a plan to follow up the suggested stages outlined in the guides. Discuss your plan with your tutor and with the head of your play school, nursery or school.

Legislation and quality of school meals

The free school meal daily allowance for each pupil is limited to a set budget figure which is equivalent to the cost of a set meal as charged to paying pupils. However, where schools operate a full cafeteria system the amount spent can vary from child to child, therefore children having free school meals 'may not always get the same type of meal as those paying in full' (Child Poverty Action Group, 1999).

In December 1999 the Department of Education and Employment published a detailed report on 'School Meals'. As well as reporting concerns the report also describes instances of good practice and improvements made by individual schools.

- - - - - - - - - - -Key point:- - - - - - - - - - - -

Most importantly the report heralds the reintroduction of *nutritional regulations* for school meals and guidelines for the under-fives, although it does not go as far as to specify a minimal nutritional value of the food offered.

The regulations are given in two parts. One for catering professionals and one for parents, carers and other school staff.

- - - - - - - - - - -Key point:- - - - - - - - - - - -

The main proposal of the report is that every day children should be offered food from the four main food groups.

The two following tables summarise the two main proposed food content regulations for school meals for (a) the under-fives and (b) for primary school children. These tables may be used as a checklist to plan meals and menus, and to monitor the food provided.

Nutritional standards and meals for under-fives

Weekly requirements.	Week 1	Week 2	Week 3	Week 4
Chips/fried/roast potatoes NOT MORE THAN 3 times a week. When these are on menu another potato option should be offered.				
Baked beans NOT MORE THAN once a week.				
Cheese (as main alternative to meat/fish) NOT MORE THAN twice a week.				
When beans / pulses form the protein of main course, a vegetable must be served in addition.				
Daily requirements	**EVERYDAY each child must be offered at least one portion of the following foods:**			
Starchy food (e.g. bread, potatoes, rice, pasta)				
Fruit/vegetables/salad				
Milk & dairy foods				
Meat, fish & alternative (non-dairy) sources of protein				

Nutritional Standards and Primary School Meals

Weekly requirements.	Week 1	Week 2	Week 3	Week 4
Chips/fried/roast potatoes NOT MORE THAN 3 times a week maximum. When these are on menu another potato option should be offered.				
Rice at least once a week.				
Pasta at least once a week.				
Baked beans NOT MORE THAN once a week.				
Casseroles, pies etc. must contain at least one portion per serving of vegetables PLUS separate serving of vegetables.				
Fruit must be offered at least twice a week.				
Cheese (as main alternative to meat/fish) NOT MORE THAN twice a week.				
Fish at least once a week.				
Red meat AT LEAST twice a week & NOT MORE THAN 3 times a week.				
Daily requirements	**EVERY PRIMARY SCHOOL MEAL** must include at least one portion of the following foods:			
Starchy food (e.g. bread, potatoes, rice, pasta)				
A fruit dessert (e.g. pie or crumble) must have at least one portion of fruit per serving				
At least one serving from fruit/ vegetables/salad				
Milk & dairy foods				
Meat, fish & alternative (non-dairy) sources of protein				

ACTIVITY

1. Obtain a published menu for a month's school meals in your nursery or primary school placement. Use one of these tables to check how the menu complies with the new regulations.

2. Observe at least two school mealtimes in your placement. Your task is to find out (a) if the menu matches the actual planned provision for the children and (b) how well the portions served meet their appetite and needs. Make notes on your findings and your sources of evidence.

3. Discuss your findings with your colleagues, list any concerns and note suggestions for improving each one.

The social importance of school and nursery meals

Providing a full school meals service has many benefits:

- It addresses children's nutritional and health needs.
- Eating well at midday replenishes energy needs in the middle of the child's most active period.
- Eating well during the day enables better concentration in lessons and promotes better tolerance so helping with social behaviours.
- Mealtimes provide important opportunities for social interactions, development of personal independence and aspects of social and cultural education.
- Food eaten at school can be practically linked to classroom learning about cultural issues, food technology, science, health and well being.
- Nutritious meal provision can enhance a school's reputation, encourage positive attitudes and support its drive to raising standards.

Lunchtimes at school: perceptions and reality

When children start school parents ask: 'Will he have homework?' and 'How soon will she be reading?' When children start school they are concerned about much more significant matters, like being allowed to go to the toilet, changing for PE, finding their coat peg and . . . what happens at lunch time. Lunchtime can be fun or stressful for a child. Sitting with a friend is very important and may well influence whether a child wants to have school dinners or packed lunches, especially if these are seated separately.

When a young child is unfamiliar with dishes on the menu or finds cutlery difficult to manage, kindly help which will also encourage personal skills development is critical.

Young children need kind, understanding support.

- - - - - - - *Good professional practice* - - - - - - -

1. Staff involved with a child at mealtimes, including kitchen staff who serve the children, need to be given relevant information about individual needs so support and teaching can be sensitive, relevant and helpful.
2. Staff must be aware of the many learning opportunities at meal and snack times.
3. Issues of equal opportunity, such as valuing cultural differences and supporting children with communication difficulties must be upheld and understood by every member of staff.
4. All staff must be able to quickly report back observations, successes or concerns to the class teacher or 'key worker' so the child's needs can be addressed and any ongoing or significant issues discussed with parents.

How schools manage the administration of free school meals is very important; children must be able to obtain their entitlement meals with

Staff who know the children well can give them time and help to make appropriate choices.

confidence and with no attached stigma. In some schools pupils purchase dinner bands or tokens before the start of the school day so money is not carried around until lunchtime. Elsewhere children keep their money in purse belts or wrist purses paying the caterers direct as they collect their midday meal. In one school the high number of children entitled to free meals were issued with a small laminated photo-card to show at the canteen till. Far from it causing any problems it proved a source of great pride to those holding the cards and a source of great envy to those without them!

Breakfast clubs

In addition to providing midday meals many schools have now introduced breakfasts.

Breakfast Club Menu

*Pupils are welcome to breakfast in the school dining hall
every morning from 8.15 to 8.45am.*

*For 30p cash they have a drink and something to eat.
They can choose from:*

Drinks

One of: *tea*
              milk
              sugar free fruit squash

AND also have one of the following:

a bowl of cereal with milk   *chipolata in a roll*
2 slices of toast with Marmite/   *muesli bar*
     jam/peanut butter   *baked beans on toast*
yoghurt   *bacon in a roll.*
fresh fruit

This menu seeks to reflect a commitment to healthy eating and provides energy and nutrients to meet children's needs, especially for those children who may otherwise start the day without breakfast. It is also intended to give the day a positive and socially relaxed start, attract poor attenders and help improve punctuality.

ACTIVITY

1. **Why do you think the foods shown in the breakfast menu have been chosen?**

2. **Could a child have a breakfast that is value for money and enjoyable?**

3. **Would it appropriately contain full fat dairy foods, be low in fibre, rich in carbohydrates and give a portion of fruit or vegetables?**

4. **What suggestions would you make to add another option to the menu?**

5. **Do you think the objectives the school has made for the breakfast club are realistic, and are the nutritional claims being met?**

Nursery school meals: a case study

The meals are provided for children in a nursery school. Those arriving at 8am have breakfast and those who stay until 5.45pm have a teatime snack. All children stay for lunch.

The menus seek to reflect the school's commitment to its mixed ethnic intake, multicultural principles and healthy eating policy. They are based on a four-weekly cycle and changed twice a year to offer more seasonal foods.

Organisation and costs prohibit cooking breakfast; foods are chosen for their nutritional content, price and ease of provision.

The cook makes many lunch dishes herself and although frozen products are used, they are carefully selected to be low in saturated fats. Chips are served, but only once a week and are a 'low fat, healthy eating, oven baked' variety. Special diets are catered for. Everyday a cheese-free dish is available, and at least two vegetables are offered.

Morning snacks are available for children to help themselves. Children help to cut up pieces of fruit (offered one week) and vegetables (the next). The wide variety given over time enable rich learning experiences and provide real opportunities for discussion.

Water is always accessible by children, with clean beakers stacked by a low tap in each area. Staff monitor children's drinking and ensure they drink frequently. Milk is available daily for children whose parents purchase it and for those entitled to free milk.

Teatime sandwiches are cut into tiny triangles and fruit and vegetables attractively arranged for serving. Crisps are limited to once a week.

At mealtimes there is a member of staff on every table who eats with the children. An emphasis is placed on food presentation, time to manage and eat the food, and time to develop skills and talk.

ACTIVITY

With a colleague study the following two week menu for a nursery school's meals.

WEEK 1.	Breakfast	AM Snacktime	Lunch	PM Snacktime
Offered everyday:	Drink of milk. Frosties or Rice Crispies & milk	Pieces of seasonal fruits (e.g. apple kiwi melon plum mango berries orange or banana)	Two vegetables to accompany main course	Pieces of fruits (e.g. apple kiwi melon plum mango berries orange or banana)
Monday	**Tuesday**	**Wednesday**	**Thursday**	**Friday**
Lunches:				
Cheese pizza. Sauté potatoes. Angel Delight.	Chicken curry or vegetable Quorn. Rice. Frozen fruit mousse.	Sausage toad-in-the-hole or vegetarian sausage. Mashed potatoes. Gravy. Yoghurt.	Golden whales or vegetable nuggets. Chips. Baked beans. Chocolate sponge & custard.	Lamb hot pot or vegetarian mince. Jelly & ice cream.
Teatimes:				
Butter sandwiches. cucumber sticks. Crisps.	Cheese & Marmite sandwiches. Tomato cubes. Yoghurts.	Honey sandwiches. Fairy Cakes. Carrot sticks.	Jam sandwiches. Yoghurts.	Lemon curd sandwiches. Chocolate biscuits. Shredded lettuce & cabbage.
WEEK 2	**Breakfast**	**AM Snacktime**	**Lunch**	**PM Snacktime**
Offered every day:	Drink of Milk. White & brown toast with various 'spreads'.	Pieces of raw vegetables (e.g. carrot, cucumber, cabbage, sprouts, broccoli, cauliflower).	Two vegetables to accompany main course.	Pieces of raw vegetables (e.g. carrot, cucumber, cabbage, sprouts, broccoli, cauliflower).
Monday	**Tuesday**	**Wednesday**	**Thursday**	**Friday**
Lunches:				
Turkey dinosaurs or veg. grills. Chips. Baked Beans. Semolina & jam.	Shepherds pie or vegetarian mince. Angel Delight.	Chilli con carne or vegetarian variety. Rice. Sponge & custard.	Tuna & pasta bake or veg. pasta. Garlic bread. Ice cream.	Quiche. Jacket potatoes. Coleslaw. Fruit & evaporated milk.
Teatimes:				
Honey sandwiches. Chocolate biscuits. Bananas.	Jam sandwiches. Bread sticks. Raisins & grapes.	Butter sandwiches. Crisps. Oranges.	Lemon curd sandwiches. Yoghurts.	Cheese & Marmite sandwiches. Fairy cakes. Apples.

Note: Water and milk are available everyday throughout the day.

1. How appropriate do you think the breakfast foods are for the children? Do they offer a sound nutritional start to the day for under-fives?

2. Do you think the menu is attractive and suitable?

3. Look at a week's lunch menu. Check your findings against the new weekly and daily regulations for school meals for the under-fives.

4. Add items that a child could choose for breakfast and at teatime to your analysis. Analyse the food groups covered and check the day's food intake against the recommendations given in Chapter 4.

5. Discuss your findings and suggest any changes you would make.

ACTIVITY

Plan a week's packed lunch menu for a three year old and a seven year old from the same family. (Do the foods need to be different for each child?) Indicate quantities for each item for each child. Include drinks.

ALERT
Remember the food will be unrefrigerated in school, so choose foods which will not deteriorate. (See Chapter 10 for information on food storage and safety.)

Some effects of food and drink advertising on families and young children

Food and drink advertising has effects on what parents buy, what children want to eat and thus on their overall diet. Food and drink advertising is very big business. In 1994 advertising budgets for Coca Cola and McDonald's each were £44 million, Rowntree's spent £28 million but the budget in the same year for advertising all fresh fruit and vegetables in the UK was only around £1 million.

Do advertisements inform and educate, or do they simply persuade? The Food Commission surveyed 260 vitamin- and mineral-enriched products, and reported that because these 'health foods' are often high in sugar and saturated fats many are little more than junk foods. In April 2000 the commission also found that 75% of 'children friendly products' (those marketed using cartoon characters and other child-focused devices on packaging and in advertising), had worryingly high levels of saturated fats, sugar and salt. Some food manufacturers were criticised for emphasising that breakfast cereals are 'fortified with vitamins' and fruit sweets contain 'real fruit with vitamin C', whilst not clearly stating that up to *80% of the contents is sugar.*

If advertisers do persuade us to buy, how do they do it so well, especially if we are already aware and forewarned about their persuasive powers? Advertisements are carefully designed to be noticed and to appeal to all our senses. If parents and children are open to strongly focused attractive advertising that they can readily relate to, then they will be influenced.

▬ ▬ ▬ ▬ ▬ ▬ *Good professional practice* ▬ ▬ ▬ ▬ ▬ ▬

Children need to be taught to how to make effective choices and to give reasons for the choices they make. As professionals involved with children, we need to make ourselves very aware of the pressures of advertising and ensure we are able to make effective and healthy decisions about the food we buy.

END OF CHAPTER ACTIVITY

Many school and nursery based initiatives for developing healthy eating have been shown to be successful when children and parents are both involved in appropriate ways. Local health authorities run schemes for awarding 'Healthy School' status when certain criteria have been met.

1. Contact your local community health dietician or visit the appropriate web site. Find out what the criteria are for schools and other establishments being awarded the accolade of healthy provider.

2. Locate a school or nursery near you which has this award or is currently working towards it. Find out and report on:

▶ Why was the scheme started? What prompted the drive for change?
▶ Who are the key people running the scheme?
▶ Has the school had support from outside specialists?
▶ How have the children, the parents and staff been involved?
▶ What areas of change are planned or have occurred?
▶ Does the school operate a tuck shop? What is on sale?
▶ Does what is being taught in the classroom about healthy eating match the nutritional content of school dinners and allied opportunities for learning?
▶ How has the school managed to match children's popular preferences for foods such as chips with the healthy eating policy?
▶ Have the contents of packed lunches improved in quality?
▶ What food choices do the children now make?
▶ What drinks are available to the children at breaks, lunchtime and throughout the day?

Quick quiz

Find the answers in the chapter.

1. What links are there between snack foods children eat and their economic and social background?

2. Why can poor housing affect the ability to provide home cooked meals?

3. List three factors other than poor housing which can make providing healthy fresh food difficult for families on a low income.

4. New regulations are in place regarding school meals: what are two benefits of these for children?

5. List four benefits of school meals.

6. Why might a child not want to eat their school dinner? Give three reasons.

7. What health problems can occur if children do not drink sufficient water during the day?

8. What effect can consuming high sugar snacks and drinks have on children's behaviour and learning?

9. What food groups are absent from a lunch box containing orange squash, crisps, a chocolate biscuit and a jam sandwich?

10. What problems can face a child who has no breakfast before school?

Summary

Having studied this chapter you should now understand:

- there are established links between poverty, diet and health
- some of the complex difficulties facing many families in feeding their children, and the importance of developing sensitive and supportive ways for working with families under pressure
- some effects of low income on food, nutrition and children's health
- how to provide professional support and some practical ways of increasing the quality of nutrition on a low budget
- current regulations regarding nutrition for nursery and school meals, and how to use them in practice
- the importance of school meals for children' health, development and learning
- some effects of food and drink advertising on children and families.

9

Understanding and Supporting Special Requirements

Aims of the chapter

To enable you to understand:

- multicultural and religious aspects of food and eating; respecting and celebrating differences in requirements
- developing independence for children with physical, learning or communication difficulties
- vegetarian and vegan diets for children
- some particular dietary problems that affect young children
- supporting children with food intolerances and allergies, and coping with emergencies.

As Flossie really didn't like pickled eggs and leather soled shoes, she wondered if she could legitimately request the vegetarian option for her in-flight meal?

The early years practitioner: knowing the individual child

We are all individuals. We all have some strong beliefs and values which determine what we do and what we think is important for life. Our role as early years practitioners is to recognise our own strengths, needs and preferences and to work with colleagues and parents to develop understanding and skills so we can encourage children to value diversity and to celebrate differences and achievements.

It is important to remember that children with physical or communication difficulties, digestive problems, illness, food allergies or who follow a particular diet all are first and foremost individuals with talents, likes and dislikes. The skill and professionalism of the practitioner is to know the child individually, develop strong links with her and manage her nutrition and eating within guidelines while actively promoting her learning and independence. It is a complex role but very important and very rewarding.

Multicultural and religious aspects of food and eating

Early years practitioners must not only support a child's own ethnic culture but also confidently introduce a range of customs and lifestyles. We live in a richly diverse, multicultural society; it is vital that children learn about, understand and value these differences, including dietary customs. It is also important to help children and families to be aware of the best nutritional aspects of traditional cuisine, such as the wide use of staple foods like varieties of rice, pulses and more unusual vegetables and fruits.

Our children live in a richly diverse multi-cultural society.

Although many people in ethnic minority groups, particularly the younger generations, have adopted a westernised diet and may not follow any traditional customs, practitioners need to be aware of the main religious and traditional customs which are important in determining the foods some people may eat or choose not to eat.

The following summary gives a broad outline of key dietary patterns. However, it is important to understand this is *very generalised guidance*. Even within a single cultural group eating patterns and types of foods deemed to be acceptable or not, can be very diverse and are a matter for individual choice.

Foods	Muslim	Hindu	Buddhist	Jew	Roman Catholic	Sikh	Rastafarian
Key points	No pork/pork products ever eaten	Many are vegetarians (will not eat foods marked**). The cow is sacred so beef is never eaten.	Religion is against killing, so many are vegetarian although eating meat is not forbidden.	Orthodox Jews need separate cooking equipment for milk & meat; & never eat meat and dairy products in same meal.	*Some choose not to eat meat at all, others do not eat meat on Fridays, & many more do not eat meat during Lent.	Some are vegetarian; others eat mainly mutton or chicken. No or little fish eaten.	Most only eat unprocessed natural/whole/Ital foods. Individuals decide own dietary restrictions except for key forbidden foods.
Beef	Halal	Never	Very unlikely	Kosher	Yes, except*	Never	Some do
Pork	Never	Rarely	Very unlikely	Never	Yes, except*	Rarely	Never
Lamb/mutton	Halal	Some**	Very unlikely	Kosher	Yes, except*	Yes, unless vegetarian	Some do
Chicken	Halal	Some**	Very unlikely	Kosher	Yes, except*	Yes, unless vegetarian	Some do
Fish	Halal	Some scaly fish**	Some	Some scaly fish	Yes, except*	Rarely	Some fish with fins
Shellfish	Halal	Some**	Unlikely	Never	Yes	No	Never
Eggs	Yes	Some**	Some	No blood spots	Yes	Yes	Some do

Foods	Muslim	Hindu	Buddhist	Jew	Roman Catholic	Sikh	Rastafarian
Cheese	Some do	Some**	Unlikely	Not with meat Made only from vegetable rennet	Yes	Yes, especially curd cheese	Some only eat vegetarian cheese, others eat dairy cheese
Milk/Yoghurt	Yes/not with rennet	Yes/not with rennet	Yes	For Orthodox Jews not with meat	Yes	Yes, very important	Some do
Main fats	Ghee & groundnut oil	Ghee & groundnut oil	Vegetable and nut oils	Vegetable and nut oils	All	Vegetable and nut oils	Vegetable and nut oils
Animal fats	Some halal	Some**	No	Kosher. Never eat meat cooked with butter			
Cocoa/tea	Yes	Yes	Yes	Yes	Yes	Yes	Never
Pulses	Important source of protein	Major source of protein	Important source of protein	Yes	Yes	Major source of protein	Important source of protein

Notes:
1. *Ghee* – a form of clarified concentrated butter, made by boiling butter to reduce water content.
   Halal – meat dedicated to God at the killing according to Muslim law.
   Kosher – meat slaughtered and prepared according to Jewish religious rules.
2. *Mormons/Church of the Latter Day Saints*: eat most foods except for cocoa, tea, coffee.
   Seventh Day Adventists: never eat pork, shellfish, animal fats, tea, cocoa, coffee; some are vegetarians and so do not eat beef, lamb, chicken, fish; most do eat eggs, cheese, milk/yoghurt.

The onus is on practitioners to ensure they are clear about parents' wishes and have agreed practices and procedures which include making choices and offering alternatives. For example some Muslim and Jewish parents may ask for their child to be given a vegan diet if no Halal or Kosher meat is available, but details need to be agreed for each individual.

— — — — — — — *Good professional practice* — — — — — — —

It is important to:

- show that you know about some aspects of traditional eating habits and respect families' choices
- be aware of possible cultural or religious dietary requirements but **never** make stereotypical assumptions
- never give any child or family any cause to feel that you may be unsympathetic to their beliefs and customs or to feel you do not understand the importance they hold for the family
- promote open partnership between practitioners and parents to give a ready forum for full discussion about their wishes and their child's needs.

Note: Refer to Chapter 12 for information about 'religious festivals, celebrations and special foods'.

Developing independence for children with physical, learning or communication difficulties

Supporting children who have difficulties in managing and controlling their eating can be challenging but also very rewarding! The key to being confident when you are caring for and teaching a child with disabilities is to work closely with the child's parents, and to work as a member of the child's multidisciplinary professional team.

▬ ▬ ▬ ▬ ▬ ▬ *Essential professional practice* ▬ ▬ ▬ ▬ ▬ ▬ ▬

Before a child's special needs are analysed and a nutrition management plan evolved, it is important to focus on the *child*. All children are individuals with their own needs, strengths and preferences. Children with or without special needs have variations in appetite and have favourite and disliked foods. Considering a difficulty, disability or handicap is secondary to understanding and appreciating the child herself. Interest, commitment, sensitivity and a sense of fun are all essential professional qualities but are particularly important when supporting a child with special needs.

The child's comfort and enjoyment must be ensured just as much as the nutritional aspects of mealtimes. A relaxed and convivial atmosphere, correctly designed seating and table heights, appropriate utensils, attractive environment and good company all are important requisites.

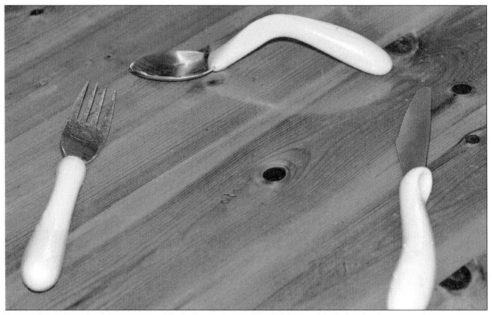

Correctly designed cutlery can enable independence for children with limited grip strength.

Supporting eating for a child with significant physical disabilities

The advice of various professionals involved with the child (such as the speech and language therapist, dietician, physiotherapist and occupational therapist) is needed to effectively and safely support a child with physical disability.

A child who has difficulties with gross motor control (such as occurring with cerebral palsy) will likely need to sit in an individually tailored seat at a correctly positioned table to give her the best chances of controlling her head, mouth and swallowing. If she has difficulties in opening or closing her mouth she may need facial stimulation before eating. If chewing or swallowing is a problem she may require her face and throat to be gently massaged to promote swallowing.

Food consistency and presentation

> **ALERT**
> For any child with chewing or swallowing difficulties, when eating or drinking there is a risk of breathing difficulties or choking. It is absolutely essential that the advice of the speech and language therapist is sought and information on suitable food consistency is given.

Contrary to common perceptions liquid or puréed foods are not the universal answer for children with chewing and swallowing difficulties. Liquids are in fact the most difficult consistency to control. Speech and language therapy advice is essential to agree the optimum approach and to ensure sufficient liquids can be taken.

Some foods may need to be chopped, mashed, or chopped and served with other foods that are sieved. If foods need to be blended components of the meal should be processed individually. It is important that flavours, temperatures and tastes are separated whenever possible to enable stimulation, learning and enjoyment. A blended meal is unappetising and unattractive. Moreover, as it may have to be diluted with water, it may not be as nutritionally sound as a non-blended meal.

■ — ■ — ■ — ■ — ■ — ■ — ■ *Good professional practice* ■ — ■ — ■ — ■ — ■ — ■ — ■

1. Always tell the child what you are offering, describe and talk about the meal and the foods offered.

2. Constant supervision must be given for eating and drinking because of the risk of choking, especially for children with swallowing difficulties. Feed her slowly and carefully. Take the feeding/eating pace from her responses.

3. Take pride and care in food presentation. Serve and arrange food carefully, especially if it is puréed. To the child a small garnish on the food, an attractive plate, a fresh place mat and flowers on the table all give messages of caring, enhance the environment, help to make mealtimes more pleasant and children feel valued.

Planning individual support and recording observations

A child's special requirements must be carefully assessed, planned for and carried out. This is likely to involve several professionals and parents. Individual eating guidelines and a behaviour support or management plan should be documented and made explicit to all relevant staff. It should be regularly reviewed by specialists, such as the speech therapist or dietician, and amended to ensure it meets any change in the child's needs or development. Advice and practical demonstration of the required techniques for each child must be given to practitioners and parents, with a copy of the current plan. Parents should also contribute fully to discussions and reviews.

If a child is not able independently to control and sustain getting food to her mouth, she will need some degree of help. This could be anything from gentle physical or verbal prompts to ensure success, through to an adult feeding her.

How the food is offered to her lips – to the centre or to the side of the mouth – and whereabouts in the mouth, or on the tongue, you place the food are important for a child with motor disabilities.

Keeping daily records of a child's eating and allied behaviours may be required, especially when weight, appetite, patterns or intake of particular foods or fluids are being monitored by a parent, health visitor, paediatrician or dietitian. It is important to agree forms and methods of recording and filing relevant information which can be easily completed and used by all key staff.

ACTIVITY

For your support to be effective you will need both specialist information and guidance from other professionals and parents, and to regularly share your observations and ideas with them.

1. 'You need advice and information about a child who has just come into your care. She has both gross and fine motor difficulties. She appears interested but very shy of new people and situations. You are not certain about her level of understanding language, and her own speech is indistinct.' In your group, discuss:
   (a) How could you find out which professionals are already working with the child, and who might these be?
   (b) What information would you seek from each of them?
   (c) Which adults are always the key experts on any child, her abilities, likes, routines and individual needs?
   (d) List some key national and local organisations which you could contact for further information relevant to any individual child with significant special needs in your care. Keep these on file for future reference.

2. Draw up a chart showing which professionals could provide specific information, resources and advice on issues to support a child and develop her skills at snack and mealtimes. File this for future reference.

Planning for learning: developing independence and decision making

It should be remembered that food and mealtimes give all children rich opportunities for learning and developing ideas, opinions and skills.

Help and activities should be designed to enable children to be as independent as possible. Opportunities can include involvement in preparing food, serving, setting tables and clearing away at the end of a meal.

Sometimes all a child needs to enable them to be independent in their eating is cutlery with an adapted handle, a non-slip place mat, or a plate with a rim. Even the type and size of spoon used may need careful assessment. A double-handled mug, with sufficiently large handles or one with a weighted base may enable a child to manage her own drinking. Other children find controlling and swallowing liquids through a straw to be easier than from a mug or lidded beaker. An occupational therapist will assess individual needs and give advice on these matters.

It is particularly important to engage children in making decisions. Choices about what food they might prefer, how much they would like and what order they wish to eat the food on their plate should all be encouraged. The chance to choose where to sit and with whom is important too.

For children with significant cognitive or communication difficulties enabling choice can prove challenging for staff and parents. Picture and word cards can be specially made. Makaton signing and printed symbols can enable children with limited vocabulary and speech difficulties to make decisions. Specially designed computer overlays for concept keyboards can be used to support decision making.

ACTIVITY

1. Find out what communication support systems or schemes are used in your placement, and also those used in early years settings and schools in your local area. How do staff and parents obtain training?

2. Obtain a 'Makaton' handbook. Look at the range of vocabulary it contains. Find out how it is designed to be used and consider how it could benefit children's communication and learning. Learn the Makaton signs for *hello; more; drink; I've finished; bread; spoon; knife; cup; please; thank you.*

3. Observe meal or snack times where a child has communication difficulties. Note aspects of good practice and any ways in which improvements could be made to promote greater independence, learning and enjoyment for the child.

4. Design an overlay for a computer concept keyboard which could support a child making independent choices about food preferences and help to promote healthy eating.

- - - - - - - - - - -*Key points:* - - - - - - - - - -

Always remember that each child has her own strengths and preferences. Whatever her individual needs may be, she is a child with her own personality and spirit. Every child must be afforded respect and care. It is their right and your responsibility.

Vegetarian and vegan diets for children

The Vegetarian Society defines a vegetarian as 'a person who eats no fish, flesh or fowl'. A vegan is a strict vegetarian who eats no animal or creature-related products. As an early years practitioner it is important to understand that the range of acceptable foods can vary quite considerably according to individuals' different and personal interpretations of vegetarianism.

ALERT

If parents say their child must have a 'vegetarian' diet it is important to discover exactly what *they* mean.

The following table shows the main types of meat and meat-free diets, importantly including the main types of vegetarian diets, but be aware that some vegetarians create their own personal categories.

Vegetarians who:	Risk possible deficiency in:
1. Eat red meat, poultry, fish, dairy products & eggs	Little or no nutrient deficiency is likely
2. Do not eat red meat, but do eat poultry, fish, dairy products & eggs	Iron
3. Do not eat any meat but do eat fish, dairy products & eggs	Iron, zinc (& essential fatty acids if dairy products are fat-free)
4. Do not eat any meat or fish, but do eat eggs & full fat dairy products	Iron, zinc (& essential fatty acids if dairy products are fat-free)
5. Do not eat any meat, fish or eggs, but do eat full fat dairy products	Iron, zinc (& B_{12} & essential fatty acids if dairy products are fat-free)
6. Do not eat any meat, fish, eggs, dairy products, honey or anything derived from living or dead animal sources (strict vegetarians or vegans)	Multiple possible nutrient deficiencies, especially calcium, zinc, B_{12}, iron, essential fatty acids

As animal products can be included in many items care is needed to ensure that flavourings, seasonings, stocks and oils used in cooking and in pre-prepared or processed items are acceptable. Products such as ice cream, jelly, dessert mousses, savoury dips, cakes and biscuits may contain gelatine or fats made from animal products. Labels need to be carefully studied. Many food products have been checked by the Vegetarian Society and carry their symbol.

Remember: The more limited the range of foods eaten increases the chances of becoming deficient in certain nutrients.

A vegetarian diet can be very healthy, but attention is needed to ensure the full range of nutrients available to non-vegetarians from meat, fish and dairy products are provided. In particular iron and protein need careful inclusion. There are vegetarian foods within each of the four main food groups. A balanced nutritional diet can be provided as long as foods from each of the four key groups are **included daily**, *and* as long as vegetarian foods from Group 1 (grains : carbohydrates) and from Group 2 (pulses, nuts and seeds: proteins) are always **combined in a single meal**. This ensures that the full range of amino acids is provided.

Ensuring a nutritious vegetarian diet

- Care must be taken to restrict children's fibre intake for two reasons (a) so they have sufficient appetite to be able to eat nutrient-rich foods and (b) too much fibre prevents absorption of calcium.
- Bread, pasta, cereals such as rice, and potatoes should be a main constituent of every meal. Note: *The use of cereal products fortified with minerals and vitamins is strongly recommended.*
- Fruit and vegetables are vitally important sources of vitamins and minerals. Note: *Vitamin C is particularly important for vegetarians as it enables iron absorption.*
- Meat alternatives must also contain high quantities of vitamins and minerals; e.g. foods such as peas, beans, nuts, soya, lentils, seeds, Quorn.
- Vegetarians who eat dairy products and milk will not need to be overly concerned about lack of protein in the diet. For children full-fat milk and full-fat dairy products are important sources of proteins, vitamins and calcium; non-consumption of these means eating

alternative calcium-rich foods is essential (e.g. bread, green vegetables, sesame seeds, nuts, pulses, tofu, tempeh, soya mince). Note: *Calcium supplements may be very necessary if milk and dairy products are excluded.*

- Over-dependence on cheese as a meat or fish alternative can lead to too high a consumption of animal fat. (Note: peanut butter, vegetarian pâté, eggs, humus, salad and vegetables in sandwiches can provide readily available tasty alternatives to cheese.)
- Processed or manufactured vegetarian 'convenience' foods can be useful but need to be used sparingly. Just as with their non-vegetarian equivalents these are often proportionally very high in fat.
- Regular meals and snacks are very important. Breakfast should include a breakfast cereal fortified with added iron and vitamins; a glass of fruit juice will help iron absorption.
- Fat-rich and sugar-rich foods should be carefully controlled and only form a very minor part of the overall diet. (Beware! Not all vegetarian children like vegetables! Some may eat chips as their only vegetable and consequently chips could regularly be the chief component of their main meal.) Note: Children's fat intake should be carefully monitored.

Not all vegetarians like all vegetables!

1. These following vegetarian dishes, suitable for a vegan, each provide a source of *complete* protein. Why?

- baked beans on toast
- tahini and rice cakes
- bean casserole and bread roll
- rice cereal and soya milk
- mixed beans lasagne
- peanut butter and oat cakes
- humus and pitta bread
- semolina and soya milk pudding

Vegetarians and nutritional risks

An imbalance between the major food groups is often caused by:

	Lack of:	Results in:
1	Meat alternatives (e.g. soya products, beans, lentils, nuts)	LACK of protein, vitamins and minerals (including iron)
2	Range of fruit and vegetables	LACK of vitamins (especially vitamin C essential for iron absorption) and minerals (including iron in green vegetables)
3	Fortified cereal foods	LACK of vitamin D, B vitamins, iron

	Overuse of:	Results in:
1	Cheese and other dairy products (as meat alternatives)	LACK of minerals and vitamins. HIGH INTAKE of fat and thus also of k/calories
2	Fat-rich and sugar-rich foods (e.g. sugary fizzy drinks, chips, fried food, doughnuts, cakes, biscuits and pastries).	LACK of iron & other essential minerals, and vitamins. HIGH INTAKE of fat and sugar, thus also of k/calories

Note: Refer to Chapter 3 for further information about nutrient deficiencies.

The people most at risk from inadequate vegetarian diets are those population groups with the highest nutrient requirements. They are teenagers, pregnant women, toddlers and young children. Children with small appetites are at particular risk (especially with a vegan diet) as it is difficult to eat enough to guard against deficiencies, particularly of vitamins and minerals, e.g. calcium and iron.

The most frequent signs of deficiency arising from poorly planned, unbalanced or inadequate vegetarian diets are anaemia and underweight or unexpected weight loss.

ACTIVITY

1. Contact the Vegetarian Society and the Vegan Society. Find out what sources of information and help they can provide to professionals working with young children and to families. File this information for future reference.

2. Develop your own vegetarian cookery skills. Plan and cook a meal which would be suitable for serving to a vegetarian friend and her two children aged three and six years, who eat dairy foods but no meat, eggs or fish. Use information on food sources from Chapter 3 to ensure you are using ingredients which will provide iron, zinc, essential fatty acids and vitamin B_{12}, as these are the nutrients they are most likely to lack.

Some particular dietary problems which affect young children

It is important that as a professional you are aware of some of the most common problems associated with diet and eating that can affect young children. If you have any concerns these should be discussed with the parents who should be encouraged to consult their health visitor or medical practitioner. If your concerns are significant or if the child continues to appear unwell, lacking in energy or appears to be failing to thrive, medical advice must be sought either with, or if necessary without the parents' cooperation. Your primary care responsibility is to the child.
The table below outlines some of the most frequently encountered problems.

Problem	Likely Dietary Causes	Management
Underweight/Poor Growth/Failure to Thrive	1. Possible medical reason must be considered. 2. Insufficient dietary intake of energy, with associated lack of vitamins and minerals. 3. Diet too high in fibre; or too low in fat. 4. Time in-between meals and snacks is too long.	1. Ensure provision of nutrient-rich foods (e.g. Full-fat milk, fish, meat, eggs, cheese, fruit juice). 2. Increase frequency of eating to give more, small meals.
Overweight/ Obesity	Too many fat-rich and sugar-rich snacks and drinks, especially snacks of biscuits, sweets, crisps, fizzy drinks.	Check balance of diet. Include foods from all major food groups. Provide filling snacks of fruit & sandwiches. Establish regular pattern of meals and snacks to prevent constant 'grazing' throughout the day.
Poor formation and growth of bones and teeth, and dental disease	Lack of calcium and fluoride. Low consumption of milk and dairy products and other calcium rich foods. Sugar and/or acid rich foods and drinks cause dental decay.	Consult dentist and doctor. If milk and dairy foods are excluded from diet seek immediate dietary advice. If milk (as drink) intake is low, add milk to other foods and serve in other forms. Increase intake of calcium-rich foods, e.g. bread, fortified cereals, soya drinks, green leaf vegetables, etc.
Lack of iron/ Anaemia/ Lethargy	Vegetarian or non-red meat eater. Insufficient intake of iron-rich foods. Lack of vitamin C which enables absorption of iron.	If possible increase intake of red meat. Increase intake of foods such as fortified breakfast cereals, tempeh, tofu, fortified soya drinks, pulses, green leaf vegetables. Increase intake of fruit and fruit juice rich in vitamin C.
Constipation	Insufficient natural sugars in diet. Insufficient liquid intake. Insufficient fruit and vegetable intake.	Increase range and quantity of fruit and vegetables in meals and snacks. Increase intake of drinks, especially water and fruit juice.

Problem	Likely Dietary Causes	Management
Mild diarrhoea	When child is otherwise well, often is due to high intake of sugar or fruit juices, as fructose in these is poorly absorbed in young children and can cause diarrhoea.	Limit consumption of sugar drinks and foods. Monitor intake of fruits and high fibre foods. Ensure high intake of water to prevent dehydration.
Food fads/ Food refusal	Dislike of certain foods and refusal to try new foods is usual in young children.	Prevent any form of conflict. Remove offending food without fuss, do not offer alternative to it. Ensure snacks are not low nutrient, high sugar or high fat. Do not allow to fill up on such foods as biscuits, buns, crisps, sweets, etc.

- - - - - - - - - - - - - - - ➔ *Key point:* ➔ - - - - - - - - - - - - - - - - -

Providing children with a healthy balanced diet can be achieved by understanding the principles of nutrition, using good quality foods and providing regular and balanced meals. However, for some children this is not enough to ensure their well being. Sometimes foods which are usually considered to be beneficial to health and development can cause actual physical distress and illness to those with particular medical conditions.

Supporting children with food intolerances and allergies, and coping with emergencies

Definitions:
- *Food intolerance* is a disagreeable, physical or chemical reaction to a specific food or food element which can be reproduced.
- *Food allergy* is a more severe form of food intolerance which produces an abnormal immune response evident in the blood.
- An *exclusion diet* enables foods causing physical problems to be identified by strategically planned elimination of specific foods.
- A balanced *therapeutic diet* allows the child to be well and well nourished, but to deviate from it results in discomfort, illness and often in a failure to thrive.

▬ ▬ ▬ ▬ ▬ ▬ *Good professional practice* ▬ ▬ ▬ ▬ ▬ ▬

> Refer to the guidance in Chapter 6 to remind yourself about food
> introduction and what are unsuitable and 'risky' foods for babies and
> young children.

Although medically substantiated allergies are relatively rare, as an early
years practitioner you will need to be fully aware of any allergies suffered
by children in your care and know how to manage them. It is important to
realise that some negative reactions to foods may be due to strong dislikes
of flavour, smell or texture or to unpleasant associations. Frequent vomiting
can result from viral or physical conditions, such as excessive catarrh,
whooping cough, gastro-enteritis or pyloric stenosis as well as sometimes
being a food intolerance response. Therefore medical advice should always
be urgently sought.

If you or a parent think that by eating certain foods a child is being made
unwell, or asthma or eczema is being triggered, it is important to seek a
formal specialist diagnosis. *You must not embark on dietary experimentation to
test theories.* Limiting a young child's diet can result in nutritional
deficiencies, cause poor overall health and a failure to thrive. A doctor
should be asked to refer the child to a dietician if concerns are significant or
persist.

ALERT

**If a child ever experiences swelling of the lips, mouth and/or throat,
or breathing difficulties medical advice should be sought
immediately. These reactions, as with the appearance of a rash or
severe vomiting, can be as a result of recently eaten food. Parents
must be immediately informed. Urgent contact must be made with a
doctor for treatment and so further investigations can be carried out.**

**Some rare allergies are life-threatening so meticulous care must be
taken for diagnosed children.**

---------------- Key point: -------------

Any restricted diets and limitations on food intake must only be carried out when detailed specialist medical dietary advice has been given. Care details must be always obtained from medical specialists to inform you of the correct support needed for an individual child.

Anaphylactic shock

This is the most extreme allergic response.

Condition: Immediate severe physical reaction to a substance or range
                    of substances.
                    Results in swelling, difficulty in breathing, loss of
                    consciousness, heart failure, can be fatal if not treated
                    promptly.

Diagnosis: Reaction to trigger substance. Most common food causes
                    are nuts, especially peanuts including peanut products
                    (also bee or wasp stings).

Requirements: Total exclusion of offending food from diet and child's
                    environment (even an open jar of peanut butter or a
                    sandwich in the same room can trigger an attack).

                    Knowledge, vigilance of staff and volunteers in setting.

                    Affected children must be helped to understand they do
                    not eat food offered by other children.

                    Unaffected children and parents should be made aware of
                    situation so the trigger food stuff is excluded from the
                    placement and social responsibility and caring are
                    fostered.

EMERGENCY TREATMENT

                    Immediate administration of adrenalin is vital. Staff must
                    be trained in administration (usually by 'Epipen').
                    Medication must be available wherever child goes, which
                    presents implications for access, storage and organisation
                    such as taking the medication everywhere the child goes.

Health disorders and associated dietary needs

Some conditions and disorders cause children to react poorly to some foods. Their bodies cannot fully digest these 'offending' foods, leading to malabsorption of some nutrients. This can result in long term nutritional deficiencies or a toxic response by the body.

When any such condition is formally diagnosed, specialist advice from support organisations and medical professionals can give guidance about management and diet. It is vital for any affected child in your care that you are fully aware of the details and implications of dietary provision, likely reactions and emergency procedures.

Gastro-intestinal disorders

Common disorders such as long term constipation, diarrhoea and irritable bowel syndrome are unpleasant and miserable. They cause discomfort, pain and worry. Some of the symptoms, even of serious disorders such as Crohn's disease, can often be helped by dietary modification. As changes needed to the diet can vary greatly amongst sufferers so expert dietetic advice is essential, especially if food intolerance is suspected. Any modifications to the diet need to be carefully monitored and planned by a dietician to ensure a balanced and adequate nutritional content is maintained for the child' overall health and development.

The following conditions may affect children. Careful management of their food and nutrition is critical to their well being and care.

Coeliac disease

Condition: The lining of the ileum (small intestine) is damaged by gluten, a protein found in wheat, rye, barley and oats.
Damage results in poor absorption of essential nutrients and nutrient deficiency.

Diagnosis: Failure to thrive, muscle wasting of buttocks, distended abdomen, abdominal pain.
Lethargy, irritability, sometimes some developmental delay.
Loose, bulky, foul smelling stools.
In babies diagnosis is usually around three months after weaning onto foods containing gluten.

Can develop in older children and in adults. Often occurs in families.

Even a very small amount of gluten can make a child with CD very ill.

Requirement: Gluten-free diet for life.

Must avoid gluten in any form and any foods containing traces of gluten.

No 'ordinary' flour, bread, cakes, biscuits, semolina, cereals, pasta can be eaten.

Manufactured foods such as sausages, soups, tinned meat cannot be eaten as may contain traces of gluten flour.

Gluten free flour and other labelled 'gluten free' products are available.

Food staples (e.g. flour, bread, biscuits, pasta) are available on prescription.

Sweetcorn, cornflour, corn products, buckwheat flour, rice, soya and potato flour can be eaten.

Fish, meat and poultry are all safe as long as not prepared with flour.

(Note: Coeliac Society print up-to-date product lists.)

Cystic fibrosis

Condition: Most prevalent, inherited, life-threatening disease in the UK.

Blocked pancreatic ducts prevent digestive enzymes from reaching the intestines.

Diagnosis: Poor digestion of nutrients results in failure to thrive.

Requirements: The missing enzyme is manufactured (*pancreatin*) and given in capsule form.

Breast milk is best for babies with cystic fibrosis, but ordinary formula is suitable.

Overall children with cystic fibrosis can eat a normal diet.

But even with oral *pancreatin* absorption of nutrients is not sufficient, so additional supplementary protein and intake of calories are needed.

Regular high-calorie snacks, rich in protein, fats and carbohydrates are essential.

Phenylketonuria (PKU)

Condition: Affects 1:10000 children and is incurable.

Caused by lack of a vital enzyme that digests phenylalanine (an essential amino acid).

If untreated, by special diet, child's development and learning are significantly affected.

Diagnosis: Heel-prick blood test given to all newly born babies.

Requirements: Highly restricted diet.

Babies need a special formula feed.

Most fats, most fruits, some vegetables allowed.

Sugar, boiled sweets, some fruit squashes allowed.

Medically prescribed special low protein foods.

Prescribed phenylalanine-free protein substitute, vitamins, minerals.

Small amounts of milk and cereals *may* be allowed.

Protein-rich foods (eggs, cheese, meat, fish, soya, nuts) *are forbidden.*

Ordinary bread and flour are forbidden.

Products containing aspartame (artificial sweetener) *are forbidden.*

ALERT

Specialist dietary advice from the dietician is essential and must be followed in detail. Liaison with child's parents is absolutely vital.

Diabetes

Condition: Body does not produce adequate supply of insulin so is unable to absorb glucose properly.

Two types: Type 1 (insulin dependent) treated by insulin injections.

Type 2 (non-insulin dependent) treated
(a) by diet, or
(b) by diet and oral hypoglycaemic drugs (insulin).

Diagnosis: Urine and blood tests.

Requirement: Eating must be regular.

Diet is critical, but is equivalent to a *healthy balanced diet* overall.

Daily diet must include healthy balance of foods:

Notably:

Starchy carbohydrate forms major part of every meal and snack.

Fruit and vegetables eaten as snacks and with meals. (Minimum of six daily servings.)

Must ensure low fat intake, so very few fat-rich foods eaten.

Reduced-fat dairy products required, but with fat soluble vitamin supplements.

Lean meat, fish, beans and lentils are main protein sources.

Must avoid sugar-rich foods, drinks and confectionery.⋆ (see note below)

Special diabetic foods are NOT recommended, as are high in calories, expensive and offer no nutritional or medical benefits, but can be given as 'treats', etc.

ALERT

- *Emergency treatment* for each child with diabetes must be individually planned, well documented and resourced. *All staff must be trained in recognising signs of diabetic imbalance.*

- *Hypoglycaemic* ('hypo') attacks (where glucose falls to an unacceptable level) need quick treatment and a sugar rich⋆ product is usually given.

- *Hyperglycaemic* attacks (where there is too much sugar and insufficient insulin in the body) are also potentially very dangerous. The recognition of this condition and the emergency procedures need to be crystal clear.

- *If a child suffers from either of these attacks, emergency treatment without a clear diagnosis is to give a high sugar substance, but medical assistance must be sought immediately.*

Lactose intolerance

Condition: Inability to digest and absorb lactose (a sugar found in milk) as the enzyme lactase is not present in the body. Abdominal bloating, pain and diarrhoea.

Diagnosis: Intolerance tests and medically monitored exclusion diet.

Requirement: Babies may require special formula feed.

Some lactose in milk products (e.g. most cheeses, yoghurt, fromage frais, etc.) is destroyed during processing, making them more digestible and so may be tolerated. (Check for each individual child's diet.)

Soya milk and lactose-free milk can be a suitable alternative.

Must avoid foods containing any kind of milk and milk products.

Must avoid foods containing 'milk solids', 'whey powder', 'lactose'.

Note: Parents of a lactose intolerant child will be able to tell you which foods, products and brands she can eat and will probably have been given a list of 'safe' foods by the child's dietician.

Other food intolerances

Other food intolerances which cause unpleasant reactions include those triggered by:

- Cow's milk – which means avoidance of milk, milk solids, non-fat milk solids, milk powders, cream, yoghurt, butter, some margarines, whey, whey powder, whey protein, casein, lactose.
- Soya – which means avoidance of soya beans, soya curd, soya flour, soya flavourings, soya oil, tofu, hydrolysed vegetable protein, lecithin (E322).
- Eggs – which means avoidance of egg, egg yolk, egg white, egg albumen, egg protein, dried egg, egg lecithin.

Managing a specific product-free diet

Most supermarket chains produce information about product lines that are free from the most frequently occurring high-intolerance ingredients.

Manufacturers' labelling of individual food products and dishes include an ingredients panel which must be checked. However, it is important to note that not every ingredient is always listed. If there is any doubt manufacturers should be contacted for full information about contents before a food is given to a susceptible child.

ALERT

When providing food for a susceptible child always check packaging labels for ingredients, even if it is a regularly used familiar product. Sometimes manufacturers alter recipes although the product name and packet design may not indicate any change.

ACTIVITY

1. Use the Internet to research information produced by the large supermarket chains about 'Food allergies and intolerances'. Which food allergies or intolerances are covered? What general information is given for buying products and foods free from specific ingredients?

2. Obtain some of the leaflets or lists that are advertised on the web-sites as giving more specific details. How useful is this information for parents who wish to shop in one of the stores and have to cater for a child with (a) Coeliac disease, and (b) a child with an inability to tolerate cow's milk and milk products?

3. How could either the website or the printed material be improved to better help and inform parents?

Nutrition and convalescence: illness, recuperation and eating

All children will be ill from time to time during early childhood, catching a cold or a common 'childhood' illness, such as chicken pox. Most will recover quickly and well at home but a few will need hospital care for complications or for more serious conditions. Whatever the extent and severity of the illness, nutrition plays a very important part in recovery.

An ill child often feels listless and disinterested in eating or drinking. If she has a high temperature, upset stomach, swollen glands or a sore throat, then eating may make her feel worse or may be too painful.

As long as liquid intake is kept up then a lack of solid food for a short period, such as a day or two is not a major concern for a normally healthy child.

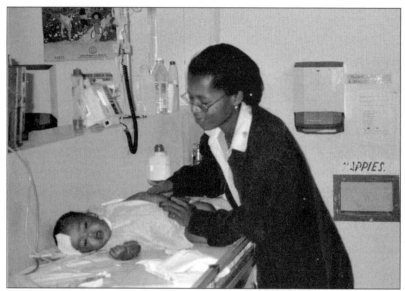

This seriously ill child is unable to eat or drink by mouth. She is being line-fed to prevent dehydration and to ensure the necessary nutrients are given.

Drinks should be fresh and regularly replenished. Water is essential but other liquids can also be given unless there are known contraindications. If a child is not keen to drink then offering diluted fruit juices or squashes could provide a more tempting and tasty alternative. A drink of water offered in a favourite cup or a new beaker or given with a straw can have a similar effect.

ALERT

If heavy catarrh, diarrhoea or gastro-enteritis is present, drinking milk should be avoided for a short time as this can increase catarrh production and, as it is not easily tolerated by an upset digestive tract, can aggravate diarrhoea.

If she has been unable or unwilling to eat for a short time it is important that her well being and recovery are monitored. It is vital that her energy levels are recharged and that she returns to eating a balanced diet as soon as possible.

An ill child or one who is recuperating usually will have little appetite and needs to be tempted by very small amounts. Choosing something which is normally a favourite is often a good starting point as long as it is an easily digestible light food. Dishes such as yoghurt, milk puddings, mashed potato and gravy, poached white fish, ice cream and jelly demand little effort for eating.

When appetite is poor and the child is weak, food presentation and gentle encouragement are particularly important. An unwell child is likely to exhibit rather babyish behaviour, 'asking' for care and attention. Attractive presentation of small portions of lightly cooked foods may prove tempting especially when served with a little bit of 'tender loving care'.

Remember that a small child with vomiting and diarrhoea risks becoming dehydrated very quickly. Powdered supplements (replacement salts) mixed with water-providing minerals and glucose can be given, and are available from pharmacists who will advise the dosage. Drinking water is essential.

ALERT
Medical advice is needed if a child cannot drink little and often, and keep down fluids. If recovery from a childhood illness seems slow, or eating is very poor then medical advice should be sought.

The following conditions may also be helped by sensitive support and well planned menus.

Dry mouth: lack of saliva

- Stimulate saliva flow by offering slices or segments of citrus fruits or mints.
- Offer moistened foods using gravy, savoury sauces, yoghurt, milk or custard.
- Avoid dry, rough foods.

Painful throat or sore mouth

- Offer foods which are soft and moist.
- Use gravy, custard or yoghurt as appropriate to improve food texture.
- Avoid any foods which are:
  - very spicy, acidic, sharp or salty
  - dry and rough in texture (such as toast)
  - very hot or very cold (although ice cream may soothe a sore throat it should be left at room temperature for a few moments before serving).

ACTIVITY

1. Plan a day's meals and snacks for a four year old child just beginning to recover from tonsillitis. Note down what information you would gather in order to make your plan. Ensure the nutritional content is balanced, appropriate and appetising. Make a note about portion sizes. Devise some serving ideas to make the food and drinks as attractive and enticing as possible.

END OF CHAPTER ACTIVITY

1. Design a covering letter and a form for parental use which would give you details of their child's special food and eating requirements. Ensure the form could be used for all children's needs and is a sensitive means of gathering information about religious requirements, food intolerances, physical needs, etc.

2. Prepare a presentation to your student colleagues lasting between 6 and 8 minutes outlining (a) the contents of the letter and the form; (b) how you would follow up the details given in order to ensure all information is clearly and correctly explained to you.

3. Following the presentations from your colleagues, take part in a group discussion about the effectiveness of your proposals and any possible concerns or difficulties you might face.

Quick quiz

Find the answers in the chapter.

1. Would it be appropriate to serve any of the following to Orthodox Jewish children: *smoky bacon crisps, quiche Lorraine, vegetarian sausages, fish fingers, chicken soup, fruit yoghurt, beef stroganoff, chicken in a creamy sauce?* (Give your reasons!)

2. Why are pulses especially important foods for most Buddhists and Muslims?

3. Children following traditional Hindu or Buddhist diets are at risk of low intakes of vitamin D. How could vitamin D intake be increased?

4. What simple equipment could you provide to help a child whose plate slides around as she tries to scoop up food?

5. Why might a child on a vegetarian diet be likely to eat more fibre than a child who eats a wider range of foods? Why could this be a problem?

6. Vegetarians have to ensure the adequate intake of one mineral in particular. What is it? What signs and behaviours might you be able to observe in a child who is lacking in it?

7. Which two food groups must always be served together in a single vegetarian meal?

8. What is it that a small child with diarrhoea and vomiting could quickly develop?

9. What should you do if a child with diabetes is having a 'hypo'?

10. All children need to eat and drink frequently. Why is this *essential* for children with diabetes?

Summary

Having studied this chapter you should now understand:

- It is critical to work closely with parents and with a multidisciplinary professional team.
- It is important to respect and understand the religious, cultural and food related requirements of children and their families.
- All children are individuals in their own right with their own strengths, preferences and personalities.
- No matter what difficulties a child has it is the role of the practitioner, working with colleagues and parents, to devise means of supporting the child's development, including their independence.
- Encouraging enjoyment is a key to developing effective learning and independence for all children.

- Vegetarian diets vary, parental guidance must be clear. Practitioners need to be aware of possible deficiencies which may arise from a poorly planned diet.
- Some of the causes and effects of food intolerances and allergies, and how to manage them.
- Some nutritional disorders and difficulties, their effects on children and their management to limit damage and discomfort.
- Some effects of short term illnesses and infections on appetite, eating and nutrition and how nutrition and convalescence can support a child's recovery from illness.

10

Food, Health, Safety and Hygiene

Aims of the chapter

To enable you to understand:

- Information on food labels: what it means and how to use it
- Food safety and the causes and prevention of food borne illnesses
- Food Safety Regulations and essential professional practice to ensure food safety in the home, nursery and school
- Developments in food production
- The categories and purposes of food additives.

Even Flossie was now beginning to wonder if her good hygiene practices were becoming a little excessive.

Information on food labels: what it means and how to use it

In 1982 a new Committee on Medical Aspects of Food Policy (COMA) panel was set up to further study the relationship between diet and cardiovascular disease. In 1984 it produced a report which recognised the impact of nutrition on heart disease, gave clear quantitative guidelines to the public and called for **better labelling of food** to help people make informed food choices. The main aim was to produce more accessible and accurate lists of ingredients and to date perishable foods.

However, evidence shows that food labels still continue to be ignored, misunderstood and sometimes mislead the population at large.

> **There is much evidence to suggest that the majority of consumers have difficulty understanding current nutrition labels. They are too complicated.**
>
> (IGD: Voluntary Nutritional Labelling Guidelines to Benefit the Consumer, 1998)

It is important that early years practitioners are able to understand information available on food labels and use it wisely to ensure the children in our care are provided with a healthy balanced diet.

Legal requirements and food labelling

The law states that a food label must:

- **Give product information:** Say what it is (e.g. tuna chunks in brine). Country of origin. Address of the main manufacturer or distributor. Net weight or volume of contents.
- **List the ingredients it contains:** Listed in descending order of content quantity.
- **Ensure relevance of any pictures:** Illustrations and product description must reflect actual ingredient content.
- **Give information for safe usage:** How it should be stored. How it should be reconstituted, mixed or cooked. How soon it should be eaten, by showing dates.

Date guidance information on labels

On food labels date guidance is given in different formats. The *'sell by'* date is the last date a shop can legally sell an item. Other dates shown are *'best before'* and *'use by'* dates, which should be carefully observed by the consumer.

It is imperative for food safety that any foods not eaten (or immediately home frozen if suitably labelled) by the *'use-by'* date are thrown away. (See chart on page 217: Types of food poisoning.)

Foods that can safely be stored at home after the *'sell by'* date now also carry a *'best before'* date, which indicates the last date the food will be optimum for eating. If food is kept beyond the *'best before'* date it will begin to deteriorate to some extent, although it is unlikely to present a danger if eaten shortly after this date. To enjoy food at its best and before its nutritional content starts to decrease it should be eaten before the *'best before'* date.

ALERT

Eggs are date stamped and should not be eaten after the *'best before'* date.

▬ ▬ ▬ ▬ ▬ ▬ *Good professional practice* ▬ ▬ ▬ ▬ ▬ ▬

Carefully check all packet dates before purchase and plan your eating of foods to ensure maximum freshness and to limit waste.

Ingredients information on labels

The highest quantity of content is put first on the panel of ingredients listed, and other ingredients follow in descending order. These lists can help to indicate food quality, such as whether a drink has more water than fruit juice, or whether a yoghurt has fruit flavouring or real fruit purée in it. Two equal sized fruit drinks sold as 'high juice' may cost the same, but the ingredients list may reveal that one bottle has much less fruit juice than the other, with water and flavourings making up the total volume.

- - - - - - - - - - - -Key point:- - - - - - - - - - - -

It is important to read food labels for the nutritional information they contain. Foods branded for children in particular may contain very high quantities of sugar or fats.

Reading food ingredients lists can also help you to avoid certain foods. However it is important to understand that this is not a secure way of ensuring any product is totally free of an ingredient. A layered pudding may list 'sponge cake' as an ingredient but without giving the list of items the sponge contains; this could include gluten, nut oil or another food stuff you may need to avoid.

ALERT
Anyone needing a diet totally free from specific food items must receive professional dietetic advice about products to ensure avoidance.

Ingredients listed may be described using terms which are unfamiliar in everyday use. Whey, lactose and curd may not readily appear obvious as being forms of milk. A list may not include the word 'sugar' but remember that fructose, glucose, dextrose, maltose, invert syrup and honey are all forms of sugar!

Food safety and the causes and prevention of food-borne illnesses

Food safety can be ensured, partly by careful adherence to instructions and date guidance on product labels but other factors also have to be taken into account to fully safeguard good health for the young children in our care, colleagues, families and ourselves. Illness from food and food related activities are a major and widespread concern. Good practice and vigilance are essential factors in seeking to minimise food borne illnesses.

The extent of food borne illnesses

The key aim of the government appointed Food Standards Agency is to improve public health. Introducing the establishment of the Agency in 1998, the Minister for Health stated:

Far too many people are being made ill by what they eat. Food poisoning has trebled in the past decade.

In 1997 there were over 100,000 officially reported cases of food poisoning. As it is estimated that only around 10% of all cases are ever reported, the actual annual figure was thought more likely to be about 1,000,000.

Food poisoning

Food poisoning is an infection of the gastro-intestinal tract caused by eating or drinking contaminated food or water. Contamination can be:

Bacterial: bacteria are parasites which infect the body and cause illness.
Toxic: bacteria release toxins or poisons into the body.
Bacterial and Toxic: a combination of both; the body is damaged by the bacteria themselves and by the toxins they release.

Note: Bacteria are micro-organisms. They are so small that millions can be found in an area the size of a pinhead.

Food is contaminated if it contains infectious, harmful:

– bacteria or viruses
– chemicals or metals
– poisonous plants or plant material.

The time between eating infected food and the first signs of food poisoning (the incubation time) can vary according to the level and type of contamination. The greater the number of bacteria, the quicker the onset. Accompanying symptoms vary according to the type of food poisoning. Usually, but not always, they include feeling ill (malaise), diarrhoea, nausea, vomiting, abdominal pain and fever.

The health and age of the individual who is infected can influence their recovery. Usually the illness is short and self-limiting, but some forms of food poisoning can be extremely serious and cause permanent physical damage. Food poisoning resulting in severe dehydration can be life-threatening.

Even the most robust and healthy young child can be at serious risk from food poisoning and dehydration.

ALERT
Babies and young children are a *very* vulnerable group and if food poisoning or dehydration is suspected medical attention must be sought immediately.

■ ■ ■ ■ ■ ■ ■ *Essential professional practice* ■ ■ ■ ■ ■ ■

If *you* contract food poisoning and are only mildly ill drink plenty of fluids, rest and do not eat solid food until you feel ready to do so. Do not prepare food for others if you are suffering from diarrhoea or vomiting. If it is absolutely imperative that you have to, take meticulous care with hand washing.

It is vital that early years practitioners are fully aware of risks associated with various foods, what constitutes essential good practice for managing food safety and how to recognise symptoms of food poisoning.

Food poisoning

Type	Onset after eating contaminated food evident within:	Duration	Symptoms	Most probable causes of contamination	Foods particularly affected	Notes
Staphylococcus aureus	1–18 hours	6–48 hours	Intense vomiting often followed by abdominal cramps & diarrhoea	Coughing or sneezing during handling and preparation of food: food then left at room temperature	Meats, dairy, salads, and bakery products e.g. sandwiches, quiches, sausage rolls.	Now widespread. New form 'Visa' is increasingly resistant to antibiotics
Campylobacter (commonly referred to as 'gastro-enteritis' also nicknamed 'Campy')	2–5 hours, but can take up to 11 days to appear	7–10 days but can last up to 3 weeks. About 25% of cases suffer relapse	Headache, flu-like symptoms, diarrhoea, high fever, abdominal pain	Can be transmitted from pet fur or faeces.	Raw or undercooked chicken, or foods contaminated by raw chicken. Unpasteurised or bird-infected milk. Contaminated water, ice, ice cream, salads washed or watered with contaminated water.	Killed at temperatures above 60°C
Salmonella	Usually 12–36 hours: can be 6–48 hours	1–8 days	Vomiting, mild fever, diarrhoea severe abdominal pain, blood in stools is common	Unwashed hands after visiting toilet. Poorly defrosted frozen food. Cross-contamination from raw meat and poultry to other foods. Poor or no refrigeration of foods.	Found in gut of most animals and birds. Estimated that 80% of chickens are infected. Raw or undercooked ckicken and eggs. Foods contaminated by raw chicken and meats. Home-made dishes containing raw egg yolk or white.	Most common form of food poisoning in the UK. Rampant bacterial growth between 7–45°C. Readily killed and food made safe by thorough cooking. Must ensure poultry and meats are fully cooked through.

Organism	Incubation period	Duration / recovery	Symptoms	Source of contamination	Foods involved	Notes
Clostridium perfrigens	Usually 8–18 hours: can be 8–22 hours	12–24 hours	Profuse diarrhoea, severe abdominal pain, (sometimes vomiting occurs)	Contamination from raw foods to ready-to-eat/cooked foods. Cooked food kept warm or at room temperature.	Meats, meat products, gravy. Warm cooked food such as turkey, casseroles, buffet meat dishes.	Spores in raw food not killed by cooking, but only multiply if food is cooled too slowly or kept warm. Multiply strongly between 15–50°C. Does not grow below 5°C.
Bacillus cereus (two types)	1–7 hours	Under 24 hours	Nausea, vomiting, sometimes diarrhoea depending on the type of infection	Insufficiently cooked foods, foods not rapidly cooled, foods stored at incorrect temperatures, foods incorrectly reheated.	Reheated foods especially rice or pasta. Cold cooked rice. Reconstituted dried foods left at room temperature.	Type one: toxin found in cereal products, potatoes and rice. Organism grows well in soil; in grains can survive processing. Needs heat of 91°C to kill it. Type two: toxin produced in intestine; linked with meats, milk, fish, vegetables.
Escherichia coli (E-coli) (four types)	12–24 hours	1–5 days Symptoms may recur in adults for 3 weeks	Diarrhoea, abdominal pain, nausea. In serious cases, kidney failure.	Sewage infected water or food. Animal faeces on hands. At-risk foods handled by unwashed hands after visiting toilet. Food served in shops with bare hands.	Soft cheeses, cooked meat products, minced beef, chicken. Contaminated water in drinks, on salads, as ice.	Readily killed at temperatures over 55°C. Infants and the elderly are at particular risk. Take care to wash hands thoroughly after handling or stroking pets or farm animals.
Clostridium botulinum (botulism)	Usually 12–18 hours but can be 2 hours to 8 days	Death if antidote not given quickly. Recovery can take months.	Problems in talking, breathing swallowing, vision hearing, headaches, nausea, vomiting.	Poor control over canning production. Damaged tinned foods; tins blown or dented. Under-sterilised foods. Damaged vacuum packed foods. Poor production of raw and smoked fish, and of cooked-chill foods.	Toxin has been found in meat, fish, vegetables and soil. Foods from damaged tins carry a risk.	
Food-borne viruses	12–24 hours	1–3 days	Vomiting, diarrhoea; often violent onset.	Sewage pollution of water. Food handled by person already infected	Shellfish which contain filtered-out viruses from polluted water.	SRSV (Small Round Structured Viruses) are a typical cause of this illness.

- - - - - - - - - - - - - - Key point - - - - - - - - - - - -

If you or your doctor think that a bout of food poisoning is related to a particular place or event (such as a shop, food stall, takeaway outlet, restaurant or school) you must inform the local environmental health officer in order to safeguard other people.

Note: Environmental health officers inspect food premises and ensure regulations regarding food safety are being met. They have powers to insist that sub-standard premises and practices are improved, and can cause a food business to stop trading if concerns are significant. They work closely with public health officers, especially where there are outbreaks of food poisoning linked to food outlets.

Media coverage has reported 'food scares' and raised awareness of possible problems that some foods carry. **However, the greatest risk to causing and suffering from a food borne illness arises from how food is managed, stored and cooked in the home.**

Prevention of food-borne illnesses

Risks of food poisoning can be avoided by:

1. Preventing initial contamination by stopping organisms getting onto food (e.g. by safe food production, transport, storage and handling).

2. Preventing any existing organisms on foods multiplying or spreading to other foods, (e.g. by keeping raw and ready-to-eat foods separated, careful use of utensils and equipment, careful storage).

3. Destroying existing organisms on food before it is eaten (e.g. by thorough cleaning and cooking methods appropriate to the food).

Food safety regulations and essential professional practice to ensure food safety in the home, nursery and school

The wide ranging 1990 Food Safety Act and its reviews in subsequent years reflect government response to the public's burgeoning concern for food safety. The key matters which became law are designed to safeguard public health and give assurances that food bought is safe to eat.

Government regulations affecting producers and food sellers include:

- increased powers for action if food on sale is suspected of being a possible danger to health
- registration and inspection of food premises, with powers both to demand improvements and to force immediate closure if major health risks are identified
- compulsory cool storage to prevent the growth of harmful bacteria on at-risk foods
- compulsory training on hygiene for food handlers
- strict controls on food production and handling
- labelling perishable foods with 'use by' dates, and making it illegal to sell foods after this date.

Although these statutory regulations aim to ensure that what we buy is safe to eat, the consumer also has a great responsibility to adopt safe and rigorous practices when shopping, transporting, storing, preparing and cooking food. Early years professionals must take every precaution to ensure children can eat and drink without risking illness.

ALERT
Smelling and inspecting foods are not reliable ways to determine freshness and safety.

Buying safe food

The following guidelines will help to ensure the food you buy is safe.

- Never buy from counters where raw and cooked meats are not fully separated.
- Assistants must never handle raw and then cooked food without washing hands first.
- Separate serving utensils and scales must be used for raw and cooked foods.
- Do not buy food in damaged packaging if there is the slightest chance of air borne contamination.
- Ensure frozen goods are fully frozen.
- Do not buy from overloaded freezers or chiller cabinets as the stored food may be insufficiently cold.

- Pick up your chilled and frozen foods at the end of your shopping trip.
- Do not buy food where you see insects, flies, animals or other unhygienic incidents.

Getting the food 'home': risks and safe practices

Simple procedures can keep your food safe as you pack it and take it 'home':

- Thoroughly wrap raw foods (like meat, fish or poultry), and bag separately from other foods including pre-cooked meat products, fresh or ready-to-eat foods. Cross-contamination can be very dangerous.
- Pack all chilled and frozen foods together (preferably in an insulated bag) to keep temperatures as low as possible.
- Take food 'home' as quickly as possible after purchase. If this is difficult, any chilled food should be kept in an insulated cold bag or box and packed around with chiller packs, to maintain its temperature.

ALERT

The temperature of chilled or frozen food can rise very quickly. Carrying shopping for an hour may be sufficient time for a significant increase in harmful bacteria, as would keeping it in a car or other non-chilled surroundings.

Unpacking the shopping or storing delivered goods

'Speed and vigilance' are two watchwords for ensuring safe food.

- Remove raw meat, fish, poultry and any defrosting foods from any plastic packaging. They must then be stored in a covered glass or similar container in the bottom of the fridge to prevent any possibility of bacterial contamination.
- Transfer chilled and frozen food to a refrigerator or freezer as quickly as possible after purchase. Chilling food retards the growth speed of most widespread bacteria. Some bacteria but not all are killed by freezing.
- Wash fruit well before putting it in a bowl from where people may help themselves.
- Put newer purchases behind any already in stock for effective usage.

Safe food storage

Storing foods correctly slows deterioration and the growth of bacteria.
Healthy fridge management is crucial.

- Store the most perishable foods in the coldest part of the fridge.
- Carefully read and follow any directions on food pack labels about
  storage, shelf life, environment, temperature and rewrapping of foods for
  home storage.
- Guard against the slightest possibility of any foods dripping onto other
  food in the fridge.
- Keep eggs in the fridge. (The home or nursery kitchen will be subject to
  a range of temperatures; warmth will cause deterioration.)
- Do not keep or use any damaged eggs, as shells harbour bacteria.
- Do not overfill the fridge otherwise a sufficiently low temperature cannot
  be maintained.
- Partly used foods from tins can be stored but only if removed from the
  opened tin, put in a covered dish and kept refrigerated. Use any such
  food within 48 hours.
- Cool food quickly before storing in the fridge.
- Bread should be stored in a bread bin with a tight fitting lid, to retain
  freshness. It will go stale quickly if kept in the fridge, but can be frozen
  for up to three months.
- Keep food covered, free from flies or other insects and away from pets.

Managing food stores

- Foods like cold meats, pie slices or pâté bought from a large pack,
  perhaps from a delicatessen counter, should be eaten within 48 hours of
  purchase.
- Date food put into the fridge or freezer so all staff know its age and can
  discard it if necessary.
- Only open the fridge or freezer door for the shortest possible time to
  conserve the cold.
- Food which has started to thaw must never be refrozen (unless it is
  thawed, cooked and then refrozen).
- Check the star rating on the fridge and freezer; read the handbooks to
  ensure food label instructions for storage are met.
- Install a freezer thermometer to check it remains below –18°C. Check
  temperature daily and ensure that it is working.
- Use a fridge thermometer correctly to check the coldest part of the fridge
  is always between 0 and 5°C.

> **ALERT**
>
> **Harmful microbial growth will occur in foods if the fridge is not cold enough.**

- If the fridge does not have automatic defrost, regular defrosting is needed to maintain low temperatures and make it fuel efficient.
- Remember that frozen, tinned, bottled and dried products have a long but a limited life. At some point they become unfit for consumption.
- Regularly check dates on all stored goods. Dispose of any which are past their 'use by' date.

Safe food preparation

Cleanliness and ensuring the separation of raw and cooked food are of absolute importance. Excellent personal hygiene must be matched by that of work surfaces, utensils, equipment and cooking areas. The points below must be followed to prevent any risk of food contamination to children and staff.

Personal care:

- Tie back hair. Remove any rings or other jewellery. Wear an apron.
- Wash hands thoroughly in hot soapy water before handling food. Dry on a clean towel specially designated for this purpose.
- Wash hands immediately after touching raw foods and before handling ready-to-eat foods.
- Cover any cuts with waterproof plaster dressings. (Caterers usually wear blue ones which can be clearly seen.)
- Never smoke where food is being prepared or served.
- Never touch your face, nose, eyes, mouth, ears, hair when preparing food.
- Never cough or sneeze over food.

Environment care:

- Disinfect work surfaces before (and after) use.
- Keep work surfaces clean during cooking, wiping spillages quickly.
- Wash tops of tins before opening.
- Keep waste bins clean and tightly covered.
- Use differently identified boards and knives for raw meat and poultry, raw fish, vegetables and fruit, and bread etc. to prevent cross-contamination. If the same knife has to be used for different foods it must be thoroughly washed before reuse.

- Wash all chopping boards, knives, utensils and equipment thoroughly in very hot soapy water after use. Rinse in clean water and either leave to air dry or be dried using clean dry tea-towels.
- Ensure a good supply of clean dry towels and cloths. Supply different and identifiable cloths for different purposes.
- Used cloths and towels must be disinfected and washed daily.
- Rinse excess waste from items before loading into dishwasher.
- Set dishwasher to correct programme for the contents.
- Kitchen floor, store cupboard and shelves should be clean and dry.
- Keep animals and insects away from food, food areas, equipment and surfaces.

In November 1998, following the receipt of an expert report on food-borne viral infections, the Departments of Health and of Agriculture issued a joint announcement, which underlined the 'critical importance of paying meticulous attention to good hygiene practice'.

In the late 1990s a survey of consumer awareness and practices showed a high proportion of people questioned regularly bought and used disinfectant sprays. However other parts of the survey found many people showed a lack of understanding about food hygiene resulting in poor practice. There was a significant lack of awareness about the importance of hand washing before and after handling food, about the need to use different chopping boards and clean knives for raw meats and other foods, and about safe storage of food in the refrigerator. To the 'use by' dates on food, 75% paid no attention, 20% of pet owners washed the animals' dishes with the family ones, and 95% used the same dishcloth for more than two days.

A survey linked to outbreaks of food related illness found that a significant proportion of those personally involved, when questioned, felt by using antibacterial cleaning fluids and equipment, things needed much less cleaning.

ALERT
Use of antibacterial impregnated equipment (such as chopping boards) and cleaning agents, demand just as much frequency and rigour in cleaning as when using other products.

Wearing a clean cookery apron is very good practice.

Cooking for safe eating

Depending on the temperature reached, heating foods may either kill harmful bacteria or cause a dramatic and dangerous increase in numbers. Insufficient cooking can result in serious illness.

- It therefore is vital to cook foods appropriately to ensure food safety. Different foods need different cooking times and temperatures. Do not shorten cooking times given in recipes.
- Follow package directions meticulously for defrosting, reheating and cooking foods.
- Know the power rating of your microwave oven and follow the manufacturers' directions.
- When microwaving food ensure heat distribution is even throughout. Stir appropriate foods well at regular intervals during cooking.
- Microwave cooking continues for a short time after the food is removed from the oven. Follow directions for post-cooking, standing times to ensure the food is properly cooked through.
- If a recipe requires a pre-heated oven ensure it is up to temperature before putting food in to cook, otherwise it may not be sufficiently cooked through.
- To kill most harmful bacteria, cook food so that the core or central temperature reaches at least 70°C for at least 2 minutes.
- Ensure large joints of meat are cooked at the centre, check using a meat thermometer.

- Poultry must always be fully defrosted before cooking, and then well cooked through.
- Processed meats such as sausages and burgers must be cooked until the juices are clear and no pink parts remain inside.
- If food is pre-cooked and then reheated, ensure it is fully heated throughout.
- Only ever reheat food once.
- Ensure eggs for children are cooked so whites and yolks are firm and avoid dishes containing uncooked egg.
- If fruit or vegetables are to be eaten raw they need to be carefully washed, and scrubbed or peeled if necessary, to remove soil, surface pesticides and chemical preservatives.

ACTIVITY

1. Find out the main advantages and disadvantages, including nutritional aspects, which microwave cooking has in relation to other conventional cooking methods.

2. What special care needs to be taken when using a microwave oven to:
- reheat baby food?
- cook a chicken?
- boil milk?

3. Why should most foods be covered when being cooked or heated in a microwave oven? Why should the covering be perforated?

Serving and eating food safely

Simple procedures, professional vigilance and common sense can help to prevent accidents and limit the chances of food related illness.

- Discard any chipped or cracked crockery.
- Do not pre-heat plates for young children.
- Before eating wash hands well in hot soapy water and dry on a clean or disposable towel.
- Children should sit at tables of a comfortable height on sturdy chairs, and be able to reach their food easily.
- Cutlery and crockery must be clean and free from any food residues.
- Knives should be appropriate for the children to use safely.

- Food should not be too hot.
- Do not overfill plates and beakers.
- Supervise children at all times.
- Wash all cutlery and crockery immediately after use in hot soapy water.

Keeping cooked food safe for eating later

Food cooked to be eaten later must be covered, cooled as quickly as possible (preferably in under an hour) and then refrigerated at a temperature under 5°C.

Food which is to be eaten cold must be kept refrigerated for as long as possible and be subjected to room temperature for the minimum amount of time.

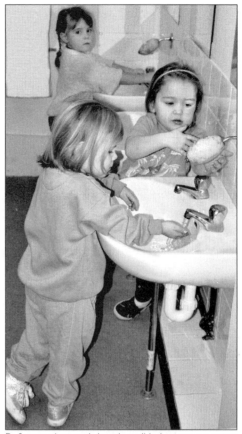

Before eating wash hands well in hot soapy water.

Food pre-cooked and due to be eaten 'hot' later, needs very careful management. Unless food is thoroughly and quickly reheated and then kept 'hot', with a minimum core temperature of 62°C, food poisoning will become a serious risk.

ALERT
Food kept at room temperature is a breeding ground for harmful bacteria, which can double in number in twenty minutes.

The safe way to cook and reheat the same dish:

1. Cook thoroughly.
2. Cover and cool quickly in under an hour.
3. Refrigerate at less than 5°C.
4. Reheat only once to a temperature greater than 62°C.

Packed lunches, school milk and food safety

Although placements encourage children to wash hands before eating, sometimes children become involved in other things between washing and eating. An individually sealed hand wipe, or clean cloth in a plastic bag in the lunch box at least allows the child to wipe her hands immediately before and after eating.

Food for packed lunches needs to be carefully selected, as most schools and nurseries do not have facilities for storing boxes in a chilled or cool environment. When possible an insulated cool box containing a cooling pack should be used. Particular care needs to be taken in warm weather. Food should be refrigerated at home until the latest possible time and cooling packs need to be refrozen daily.

Boxes, containers and drink bottles must be thoroughly washed every day in hot soapy water.

At school or nursery, staff should select the coolest areas in the building for storing lunch boxes and children's milk. Warm cloakrooms and classrooms are unsuitable for safe storage of food. Milk left outside in sunshine or kept in a warm place indoors can quickly deteriorate. The provision of a refrigerator to store children's milk is good practice and should be strongly encouraged.

ACTIVITY

Note: Before beginning this activity, discuss the project with your placement mentor.

1. In your placement check the place where your children store their lunch boxes. Look at the position of heaters, radiators and windows. Check the extent of sunlight on the area on bright days. Research the coolest area of the building and decide if there is a more suitable, safer place for storage.

2. Study the systems and arrangements for milk storage and distribution for the children. Is milk refrigerated immediately on delivery and until the children drink it? If not, for how long is the time between delivery and drinking? Does the milk feel cold when the children drink it? Are special arrangements made for morning deliveries which are consumed in the afternoon? What improvements do you consider could be made to make the milk safer and more palatable?

The following tips summarise some of the main points for food safety.

Ten tips for food safety

- TAKE CHILLED AND FROZEN FOOD HOME QUICKLY – then put it in your fridge or freezer at once.
- PREPARE AND STORE RAW AND COOKED FOOD SEPARATELY. Keep raw meat and fish at the bottom of your fridge.
- KEEP THE COLDEST PART OF YOUR FRIDGE AT 0-5°C. Get a fridge thermometer.
- CHECK 'USE BY 'DATES. Use food within the recommended period.
- KEEP PETS AWAY FROM FOOD and dishes and worktops.
- WASH HANDS THOROUGHLY before preparing food, after going to the toilet or after handling pets.

Wash hands thoroughly after handling pets.

- KEEP YOUR KITCHEN CLEAN. Wash worktops and utensils between handling food which is to be cooked and food which is not.
- DO NOT EAT FOOD CONTAINING UNCOOKED EGGS. Keep eggs in the fridge.
- COOK FOOD WELL. Follow the instructions on the pack. If you reheat make sure it is piping hot.
- KEEP HOT FOOD HOT AND COLD FOOD COLD – don't just leave them standing around.

(Taken from *Food Safety*, a booklet from the *Food Sense* series published by MAFF, 1997.)

Developments in food production

Organic food

It is possible to buy seasonal fresh fruit and vegetables at reasonable prices from some specialist markets, greengrocers, farm shops and farmers markets. But buying 'organic' produce or growing your own food is really the only way to ensure that fruit and vegetables have not been treated either with chemical pesticides or post-harvest chemicals.

Organic crops are grown using environmentally friendly, natural farming methods. Artificial fertilisers, chemical pesticides, insecticides, fungicides, herbicides, waxes or other additives are never used. Soil is enriched and sustained by applying natural waste, such as compost and manure. The same principles underpin meat and poultry production, where animals are raised using non-intensive methods, fed on feed which must be 70% organic, and where routine use of antibiotics and artificial growth enhancers are avoided. (However, if animals are ill they may be treated with veterinary medicines.)

Many people who choose organic food do so for its guaranteed freedom from intensive farming methods and chemicals, the benefits to the countryside, and because they believe the flavours are better. There is no hard scientific evidence to support claims that they are richer in nutrients than conventionally grown foods.

Setting up an organic farm takes several years, food production methods are more labour-intensive and animal feeds are more expensive. Consequently prices are often higher than for conventionally grown foods.

Only foods that are grown in line with the above can be labelled with the word 'organic' as it is a legally defined term. Growers, food packers and any others involved in the production of organic food must be registered and comply with very stringent regulations. Regular monitoring to ensure all requirements are met is carried out by government approved bodies such as the UK Register of Organic Food Standards (UKROFS). Many organic foods are labelled with the UKROFS or Soil Association logo.

Genetically modified food

Scientists are able to identify genes, which are found in virtually every living cell, and are beginning to understand which characteristics of plant or animal growth and development are governed by which gene. More recently the ability to transplant genes between plants or animals (in a way that is not possible through conventional breeding) has been developed. These scientific advances offer both a means of increasing production yields of crops and livestock, and possibilities of increasing their resistance to infection. There is already a genetically modified tomato variety on sale in the USA, which resists softening during ripening so it can remain longer on the plant before picking, giving, it is claimed, a fuller flavour.

There are however, many concerns about the introduction and development of genetic modification. Fears include harm to the environment which could be inadvertently caused by specially resistant plants colonising or breeding with other crops. Insufficient information is yet available to know what the effects might be on humans of eating genetically modified meat, cereals or other plants.

It is recognised there must be important safeguards to the environment and to human health. The UK government only permits the use of genetic modification technology in notified places. There are strict regulations for experimentation and developments and a legal duty of care imposed on all those involved.

Many large supermarket chains and catering suppliers have responded to public concern and have withdrawn foods containing genetically modified ingredients and instructed their suppliers not to use them.

In April 2000 (on the same day as reports from the USA announced that GM growth enhanced salmon could soon be commercially available) the Food Standards Agency announced:

Foods and food ingredients using additives and flavourings which contain GM additives and flavourings will have to be labelled. Additionally, businesses selling foods and catering suppliers will have to label all products containing GM soya and maize.

The agency's chairman announced that these requirements (an EC regulation) are designed to improve consumers' ability to make informed choices. It is therefore up to the individual to be alert to developments in food science and production, and then to make careful decisions.

The categories and purposes of food additives

There has been much press coverage and controversy about the use, necessity and possible physical effects of food additives. Food scares and 'E' numbers cause confusion. To make a carefully judged choice about eating and providing foods containing additives you need to understand some of the main facts.

'Additives' is a widespread term and food additives are used for a wide variety of purposes. However, at a time when public concern about food safety is high, it is important to understand that many additives have an important role to play. Only specified levels of legally permitted additives can be used in food production. The approved list gives the full name of each additive and its assigned number. As these have been approved by the EEC each number is prefixed by the letter 'E'.

Food labels have to show additives in the ingredients list. However, as it is not always easy to recognise an additive by its chemical name or number, the law states that the additive's category must always be given. So it is easy to tell if an additive is a 'colour', 'preservative' or from another category.

ALERT
Some people react to some additives just as some are sensitive to certain foods. Labeled information helps those who need to avoid specific additives.

The categories and purposes of food additives

Colours *are not necessary to keep food safe and do not provide any nutrients.* Legally many foods cannot have colours added, including baby foods, tea, coffee and fresh fruit and vegetables. Colour additives are mainly used either to restore natural food colours lost during processing or to enhance foods to make them look brighter and more appealing, such as making strawberry yoghurt a 'better pink'. Canned fruit and vegetables often have colour added to revive their appearance. Confectionery, cakes and cake decorations, ice lollies, fruit drinks and squashes and many 'flavoured' products often contain colourings. There are about 20 permitted artificial colours (such as E102 tartrazine and E133 brilliant blue); the rest are derived from natural sources (such as E100 turmeric and E162 beetroot red).

Preservatives: without additives which preserve foods during packing, canning, storage and transit until we are ready to eat them, food would deteriorate and quickly become unsafe for consumption. Additives which are preservatives can prolong shelf life, help keep harmful bacteria at bay and so make food safer to eat for longer.

Antioxidants appear on labels of fatty or fruit-based products. They work in the same way as sprinkling lemon juice on sliced apples to stop them turning brown. They stop fat becoming rancid and fruit going brown through oxidation. Vitamin C is a natural antioxidant with the tag, E300.

Emulsifiers, stabilisers and gelling agents act as thickeners, setting or binding agents to improve the consistency and texture of food and to keep it stable. Emulsifiers help foods combine well and prevent separation of oils and water. Lecithin, found in eggs, is a natural emulsifier (E322) as used when making mayonnaise.

Flavourings are not included in the classification system and on labels are simply called 'flavourings'. They are used in small amounts to restore flavour lost in processing or to provide flavour in a product. Look for them in products such as fruit-*flavoured* drinks, chocolate-*flavoured* cake filling, salt and vinegar and barbecue-*flavoured* crisps.

Flavour enhancers bring out the flavour of other ingredients without adding a particular taste of their own. Perhaps the best known of these is monosodium glutamate, which is used widely in Chinese cooking.

Sweeteners mimic the taste of natural sugar and usually have many fewer calories. They are widely used in slimming foods, soft drinks and confectionery.

Other additives include:

Raising agents	help to give baked products a lighter texture.
Anti-caking agents	help powders (e.g. cocoa) and crystals (e.g. salt) to remain free flowing.
Acids	give sharp, sour and tart flavours and help preserve foods.
Flour improvers	improve baking quality (elasticity and strength) of bread dough.

And most importantly:

Nutrients	which replace vitamins and minerals lost during processing and/or enrich legally prescribed foods which may be lacking in essential nutrients.

(Note: Margarine and white bread *must* have nutrients added to enrich them to standards of butter and wholemeal bread.)

A guide to E numbers, categories and additives

Category:	Usually found in E Number band:
Colours	E100s
Preservatives	E200s
Antioxidants	E300s
Emulsifiers & stabilisers	E400s
Flavourings	Not yet classified, just referred to as 'flavourings' on labels
Flavour Enhancers	E620 to E635
Sweeteners	E420 (sorbitol) & E421 (aspartame) are main ones

- - - - - - - *Good professional practice* - - - - - -

- Remember, some additives can provide some important nutrients but others provide none.
- Become familiar with the categories, number bands (and any assigned numbers of food additives which you may wish to avoid or to seek), and read labels closely so you can make informed choices.
- It is important to understand why additives are used and not to be put off a food just because it contains 'additives':
  *a serving of 'water, cellulose, vegetable protein, sucrose, vegetable oil, fructose, glucose, oxalic acid, colours (E140 & E160a), salts and flavouring' does not sound very appetising. However, it **would** do you a lot of good – it is . . . fresh spinach!*
- Remember, E numbers have been given to naturally occurring colours and salts.

END OF CHAPTER ACTIVITY

1. Study the nutrition labels on the following products: cornflakes, 'Readibrek', a can of tomato soup, a packet of ready salted crisps, a can of semolina, baked beans, a can of lemonade, fish fingers, frozen oven ready chips, babies' rusks, long-life organic apple juice, a carton of raspberry yoghurt.

2. Make up a chart listing nutritional contents 'per 100 grams' for each of these products for: carbohydrates, sugar; fat, saturates; fibre, and sodium.

3. Note for each product which categories of additives are used; and in particular where a product contains artificial colourings and flavourings.

Quick quiz

Find the answers in the chapter.

1. What word on food labels gives you indication about the salt content of a product?

2. What type of nutrients are 'maltose', 'sucrose' and 'glucose'?

3. What is meant by 'saturates'?

4. What temperature should a fridge be kept at?

5. What are the rules about cooking and storing raw meat and fish?

6. What is potentially dangerous about eating yoghurt which is past its 'use by' date?

7. What are four of the main signs of food poisoning?

8. If you eat contaminated food are you always immediately ill?

9. What happens to food kept warm at room temperature?

10. What E number band covers 'preservatives'? What nutritional value do they have?

Summary

Having studied this chapter you should now understand:

- food safety needs to be well managed and is of optimum importance to those responsible for feeding young children.
- most food borne illnesses are caused by poor practice in the kitchen and can be largely guarded against by careful food management.
- some of the main issues surrounding current concerns about food quality and production.
- the various categories and purposes of food additives.
- how to use food and product label information to make informed choices and promote healthy, balanced, safe eating.

11

Eating and Dental Health

Aims of the chapter

To enable you to understand:

- the importance of healthy teeth
- the causes of tooth decay and poor oral health
- facts about tooth decay, problems it causes and how foods damage teeth
- how to prevent decay (caries) and encourage healthy teeth.

Although Flossie was feeling rather full, she was determined to safeguard her teeth to the maximum by eating all her sweets in a single sitting.

The importance of healthy teeth
Food, nutrition and dental health

Young children are entirely dependent upon their parents and carers for food and routines which will promote healthy teeth and prevent tooth decay and other oral disease. Foods which are essential for the development and growth of teeth have been fully discussed in earlier chapters. It should be remembered that milk, cheese and other foods high in calcium content are particularly important for the development of strong, healthy teeth.

Children's eating patterns and food choices can have a significant effect on their dental health.

Dental and oral care includes nutrition, feeding patterns and cleaning. Good

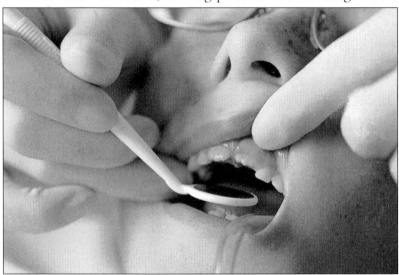

Establishing good dental care from babyhood pays dividends.

dental care practice needs to be established well before the baby's first tooth appears, and continued to protect baby (or deciduous) teeth and later the permanent teeth. Although we only have our baby teeth for a relatively short period of our lives their significance must not be underestimated.

Healthy baby teeth are vital:

– as space holders for the developing permanent teeth.
– as they play a large part in the development of normal speech patterns.
– to give structure to the face and influence the development of facial features.
– for chewing most foods, especially those rich in essential nutrients for growth and good health.

Loss and decay in baby teeth are critical as:

— they can limit access to a full balanced diet.
— they can affect a child's self image and self-esteem.
— tooth decay can cause pain, and severe oral infection can cause facial disfigurement.

The causes of tooth decay and poor oral health

Oral habits: dummies, fingers, bottles and cups

Sucking brings comfort to babies. It is a normal practice for babies and very young children to suck fingers and find pleasure and security in sucking on the nipple or teat. If a dummy is required, advice should be sought from a dentist as some dummies can cause oral problems. Overuse of a dummy often promotes thumb sucking; both of these can displace teeth and interfere with speech development. Crooked or poorly positioned teeth can affect speaking, swallowing, chewing, self-image and self-esteem.

Prolonged thumb or finger sucking, the use of dummies and extended use of bottles or teated feeders can cause significant damage both to erupting baby and permanent teeth, and to established teeth.

ALERT
• **If any such oral habits persist in children of about four years old there is a particular concern. Facial bone structure and the positioning of the permanent teeth can be affected. Dentist and health visitor advice should be sought.**

• Babies should be drinking from a cup and *not* be reliant on a bottle by the time they are 12 months old.

Trainer cup is an appropriate progression from a baby bottle.

The choice of cup is critical for ensuring the development of self-help skills, coordination, oral muscle control and dental health. Using a cup, with or without a perforated drinking lid, means the child has to tip the liquid into her mouth, and learn to coordinate the rate of flow with swallowing.

Drinking from a cup develops coordination and promotes dental health.

ALERT

A trainer cup with a valve mechanism presents the same risk to dental health as a bottle, because the liquid is only released by sucking. As with sucking from a bottle the liquid is held for longer in the mouth, than it is when drunk from a lidded or open cup. Thus valved trainer cups greatly increase the risk of baby tooth decay.

Although these cups have an understandably strong appeal to parents naturally concerned about spillage and keen to safeguard carpets and upholstery, the British Dental Association warns most strongly against the use of valved trainer cups.

ACTIVITY

1. List the reasons, you would explain to a parent, for teaching a baby approaching her first birthday to use a cup and stop depending on a bottle.

2. Research the prices and features of five different trainer beakers available in your local shops. Draw up a chart showing the most to the least expensive, and note particular benefits or drawbacks of each cup. Make a recommendation for your 'best buy' and share your reasons with your colleagues. Compare your findings.

Facts about tooth decay, problems it causes and how foods damage teeth

Poor feeding practices are major causes of 'baby tooth decay'. Prolonged and continuous feeding which allows the baby to continue sucking on a bottle when she is satisfied and no longer swallowing the liquid but holding it in her mouth for longer periods, means the sugars in the milk or diluted juice excessively bathe the teeth. This causes a serious and painful condition sometimes known as 'bottle rot' or 'nursing bottle decay'.

━ ━ ━ ━ ━ ━ *Good professional practice* ━ ━ ━ ━ ━ ━

A baby should never be pacified with a bottle if not hungry or be allowed to fall asleep whilst drinking. Choking and damage to teeth could result. Pure water is the only acceptable liquid which may, under close supervision, be given *if these situations have to occur.*

━ ━ ━ ━ ━ ━ ━ ━ ━ ━*Key point*━ ━ ━ ━ ━ ━ ━ ━ ━ ━

Continued use of a bottle *after the first birthday*, poor feeding and weaning practices and frequent sugar intakes are the main causes of poor dentition and tooth decay in young children.

Children with special needs

Some children have poor oral muscular control and development, and problems with chewing, swallowing and saliva production. Poorly formed or positioned teeth can also make eating difficult. Food may become impacted between or heavily coat the teeth. Cleaning the teeth after eating and drinking and ensuring nutrition supports good oral hygiene are therefore critical. Specialist dental advice to clarify the most suitable and effective methods, equipment and techniques for individual children must be given.

Facts about tooth decay and the problems it causes

Tooth decay is also called 'caries'.

A healthy tooth:

healthy

Plaque, a sticky furry coating which forms on tooth surfaces, is mainly made up of bacteria. When bacteria react with simple carbohydrates (sugars) in the diet they produce acid. Acid causes calcium from the tooth enamel to be removed: this disintegration of the outer tooth layer (enamel) is known as demineralisation:

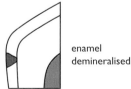

enamel demineralised

If the second layer (dentine) beneath the enamel is also affected by the bacteria a visible hole can be seen in the tooth:

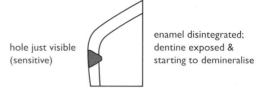

hole just visible (sensitive)

enamel disintegrated; dentine exposed & starting to demineralise

A cavity develops at a demineralised weak spot in the enamel, where both the enamel and the dentine have disintegrated. Frequent and continuing acidic environments

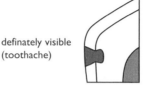

definately visible (toothache)

both enamel & dentine disintegrated

within the mouth cause calcium to be permanently lost from the enamel and subsequently from the dentine:

If left undetected and untreated it will usually result in the softer dentine being exposed and so open to further rapid decay. Toothache begins at this stage and if not treated the tooth may

very large hole (keeping child awake as painful)

pulp infected - tooth likely to die

die and more serious infections can occur. Having the tooth removed may then be the only suitable treatment:

ALERT

Gum disease in children is an indicator of poor cleaning which must be addressed.

Dangers to teeth from the physical content of food

Although various foods cause damage to teeth, the main substance which harms teeth is sugar. However, it is *not* a good idea to attempt to remove from the diet all foods which cause tooth decay.

All sugars affect tooth enamel but some forms of sugars are more harmful than others.

There are three types of sugar:

• **Intrinsic sugars**, which naturally occur in the cells of foods (as found in pasta, bread, rice, potatoes, fresh and dried fruit, vegetables), are *safer for teeth* because the sugars are less readily available, and so can be given as snacks as well as at main meals. However, even these, when broken down into sugars in the mouth, *can* react with plaque on the surface of the teeth to cause decay.

• **Milk sugars** (e.g. lactose) are found naturally in milk, and *rarely* cause tooth decay.

• **Non-milk extrinsic sugars** (as found in table sugar and honey, and added to manufactured foods, drinks and confectionery) pose a *much greater threat* as they can readily be used by the bacteria and damage teeth, *especially if eaten between meals*. Moreover they generally provide few nutrients and can make a child feel less like eating more nutritious food.

> **ALERT**
> **Acidic drinks and foods, carbonated drinks and even unsweetened products (such as sugar-free squash and cola) can readily harm teeth.**

Many foods which contain natural sugars (i.e. intrinsic and milk sugars) also contain essential vitamins and other nutrients vital for children's overall health and for the healthy development of teeth. These must form part of the child's diet.

However, those foods which are both high in non-milk extrinsic sugars *and* low in essential nutrients (such as sweets and soft drinks) can and should be restricted to promote balanced nutrition, to benefit both existing and developing teeth.

Tooth-friendly sweets

A number of sweets are now available which carry a special 'tooth friendly' logo on the wrappers. They have been scientifically tested and passed as safe for teeth by a non-profit international association governed by the dental profession. *However, as their nutrient value is very limited, care must still be taken in their use.*

Ribena Toothkind

The British Dental Association (BDA) has approved 'Ribena Toothkind' as a safe drink for teeth. However, it must be understood that previous tests stating water and milk are the best drinks for healthy teeth are still valid. Ribena Toothkind is suggested by the BDA as a safe alternative to some other drinks, such as squash, fruit juice and fizzy drinks, but it should not be given instead of water and milk.

▬ ▬ ▬ ▬ ▬ ▬ ▬ ▬ ▬ ▬ ▬ ▬**Key point**▬ ▬ ▬ ▬ ▬ ▬ ▬ ▬ ▬ ▬

Remember, a child who *only* drinks Ribena Toothkind will have poorer dental health than another child who drinks water and milk in addition to Ribena Toothkind. However, a child who only drinks Ribena Toothkind will have better dental health than children who drink fizzy or acidic drinks even if they also have water and milk in their diet. Fizzy, sugary and acidic drinks are significant causes of tooth decay.

▬ ▬ ▬ ▬ ▬ ▬ ▬ *Good professional practice* ▬ ▬ ▬ ▬ ▬ ▬

- Read food labels: e.g. some muesli bars, often sold as healthy snacks, are often high in dried fruits, honey, sugar, syrup, treacle and glucose and so are potentially harmful to teeth.
- Be aware of 'hidden' sugars in foods and drinks: e.g. some fruit squashes and yoghurts, many marketed to appeal to young children, are very high in sugar while others are very low or even sugar free.
- Brand names and recipes change. Regularly read labels even of frequently purchased items.
- Ensure you use daily opportunities to teach, model and enforce healthy eating.

ALERT
- **Check the ingredients lists on paediatric medicines. Beware of giving medicines with a high sugar content. They can damage teeth. Ask the pharmacist for a suitable sugar-free alternative; these are readily available.**

How some forms of foods can damage teeth

The following forms of food cause the most dental damage as they readily stick to the enamel surface of teeth:

- Chewy sweets, hard candies and crisps.
- Sticky foods, even healthy ones such as dried fruits.

- Foods which are high in sugar and/or acid and sucked for a time (such as long-lasting boiled sweets, iced lollies).
- Sweetened drinks and beverages (especially if sipped frequently between meals).

Remember:

These liquids all contain sugars which can damage teeth, especially if held in the mouth:

> – fruit juices
> – soft drinks and fruit squashes
> – any sweetened liquid
> – fruit iced lollies.

Remember:

Sugars in any form should be in the mouth for the shortest possible time to minimise risk to teeth, but long enough for effective chewing of the food.

How the frequency of eating and the timing of food intake can influence susceptibility to tooth decay

If sweet, sticky or acidic foods are eaten they should be consumed as part of, or at the end of a main meal. Repeated and frequent consumption of sugar (e.g. between meals) or continuous snacking on sweets results in high levels of acid in the mouth and therefore more chances of decay. Thus high sugar foods if given at all, should be restricted to mealtimes, enabling them to be eaten in one go, and limiting the times acid can be present in the mouth.

Saliva is a natural inhibitor of tooth decay because it both dilutes and chemically helps to neutralise the acid produced by plaque; it also moistens some food particles, helping to rinse some of them from the teeth.

Small snacks produce less saliva than full meals. Meals often contain solid foods which require chewing; this causes an increased salivary flow. Consequently the beneficial effects of saliva are less, and risks of decay from eating between meals are greater. If sugary foods and drinks are taken at these times, the risks are significant.

ALERT
Saliva cannot remove plaque. Plaque can only be removed by thorough brushing.

For caries to develop four factors must be in place:

- Teeth – *to be attacked.*
- Bacteria – *to act on the sugars and produce acid.*
- Simple sugars – *to 'feed' the bacterial reaction.*
- Time – *for the acidic reactions to damage the teeth.*

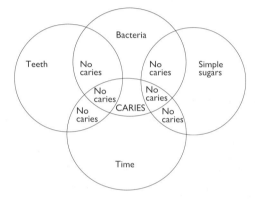

If any one of these four factors is missing, there will be no decay.

How to prevent decay (caries) and encourage healthy teeth

As an early childhood professional you can influence three of the above factors:

Bacteria – is removed when teeth are efficiently brushed. *You can teach this and offer the necessary care to the child.*

Simple sugars – are found in the diet. *Your management and sensible advice can help limit their intake, and ensure if they are provided they are given at the safest possible times to promote dental health.*

Time – the longer the bacteria have to act on the sugars, the more acid is produced in the mouth and the more decay can occur. *Therefore your encouragement and help in cleaning teeth following meals and snacks, and especially morning and night, is very important.*

Cleaning teeth

Teeth need cleaning a least twice a day and preferably shortly after every meal to remove food debris from gaps and crevices, and to clean off and prevent the build up of plaque. Plaque removal should be regular and efficient.

ALERT

After drinking or eating anything with a sugar or acidic content it is important to wait at least 20 minutes before brushing teeth. This gives saliva time to neutralise the acid on the surface of the teeth. When acid is present in the mouth, it makes the tooth enamel weaker and porous. Teeth can be significantly damaged by brushing when in this temporarily delicate state.

Although it is obviously important that from a very early age children begin to enjoy using a toothbrush themselves, babies and **children under seven need to have their teeth cleaned for them.** Children over this age still require close supervision.

It is particularly important that teeth are brushed after any bedtime snack so food particles do not stay on the teeth all night.

■ ■ ■ ■ ■ ■ ■ *Good professional practice* ■ ■ ■ ■ ■ ■

- Teach and enforce effective teeth-cleaning routines and techniques.
- Remember: regular dental check-ups are essential to ensure oral health and to monitor correct growth of teeth. Encourage parents to take children for regular checks. Find opportunities to discuss the positive, interesting and exciting things associated with a trip to the dentist. Invite a dentist to talk to the children at nursery or school and hopefully to let them handle some simple equipment.

ACTIVITY

1. Contact a dentist or hygienist to learn when, how and with what to clean a baby's mouth (a) before teeth appear (b) after the emergence of the first baby teeth, and (c) into early childhood.

2. Learn the correct way to brush young children's teeth and how much toothpaste to use, so you can advise parents and teach children correctly.

3. Obtain a copy of 'Keeping baby teeth healthy: tooth care for 0–2 year olds' or 'Caring for your children's teeth: tooth care for 3–11 year olds', available from the Health Education Authority.

Discouraging tooth decay and damage

HANDY HINTS

- Discourage overuse of dummies.
- Discourage overuse of prolonged bottle drinking.
- Do not allow passive bottle sucking or liquids to be held in the mouth.
- Avoid sugary foods and drinks.
- Take care with and be aware of sticky 'healthy' foods, such as dried fruits and honey.
- Discourage sucking hard, boiled or chewy sweets.
- Discourage sucking highly acidic fruits, or acidic fruit-flavoured sweets.
- Do not give medicines with a high sugar content. Use sugar-free brands wherever possible.

■ – ■ – ■ – ■ – ■ *Good professional practice* ■ – ■ – ■ – ■ – ■

It is also important for early years professionals to know what *positive advice* to give rather than always focusing on the 'Don'ts'.

A positive approach: encouraging the healthy development and condition of teeth

THREE IMPORTANT BENEFITS OF MILK

- Eating calcium-rich foods is vital for the development of bones and strong teeth.
- Milk and milk products in the mouth protect tooth enamel, as the lipids in milk reduce plaque formation.
- Calcium in milk directly helps to replace calcium which has been lost from tooth enamel.

BENEFITS OF CHEESE

- Eating uncooked cheese is particularly effective for protecting teeth from the harmful effects of plaque. It is particularly good for stimulating saliva production.
- Cooked cheese (even adding cheese to cooked dishes) has also been shown to give protection to teeth.
- Cheese contains unique substances which directly inhibit plaque activity.

HANDY HINTS

- Before her first birthday wean the baby from the bottle to a training/lidded feeder cup.
- Encourage chewing by giving appropriate foods (including fibrous foods such as raw vegetables, apples, pears) which also effectively stimulate saliva production.
- Have nutritional, ready-to-eat snacks on hand and give healthy foods as 'treats' (e.g. yoghurt, cheese cubes, milk, carrot sticks, cherry tomatoes, unsweetened and unsalted popcorn, grapes, slices or segments of fresh fruit).
- Read food labels for sugar content. Be alert to the dangers from added 'hidden sugars'.
- Give any sweets or sweet sticky foods during or at the end of meals.
- Encourage eating cheese, especially at the end of meals to allow the residue to remain in the mouth for longer, and include some cheese in cooked dishes.
- Give (chilled) water as children's thirst-quenching drinks between meals.
- Actively promote good teeth cleaning after meals and snacks, remembering to *wait for 20 minutes* between eating and teeth brushing.
- Ensure the child receives regular dental check-ups.

It is important that early childhood professionals teach and enforce good eating patterns and habits. Food treats can be rewarding and exciting without being sweets!

– – – – – – – – – – **–Key point–** – – – – – – – – – – –

You can make the children feel that a tiny bunch of grapes, a slice of apple or a neat cube of cheese are absolutely delicious and special foods. Give a drink of fresh chilled water and talk about its sparkling, thirst quenching qualities. **If you present healthy, nutritious items such as these with real enthusiasm and care the children will learn to appreciate and value them as you do.**

END OF CHAPTER ACTIVITY

In your placement, plan to develop the children's awareness and understanding about healthy eating food choices which also help to promote healthy teeth.

(a) Collect the following resources: a large drawstring bag; a range of items and foods associated with teeth and healthy eating, e.g. toothpaste, toothbrush, empty cheese carton, empty plastic milk carton, empty yoghurt pot, apple, carrot, kiwi fruit, cucumber, small loaf of bread, small bottle of water.

(b) Plan and lead a 'feely' game for a small group, which will allow each child to describe the texture, size, and other material properties of the items. In preparation, list the vocabulary you plan to help the children use during the game. Make plans for children's different abilities and individual needs, ensuring you will both support and challenge everyone's learning.

- Introduce the game by letting all the children see, handle and generally talk about the objects. Discuss who has seen/used/tasted them before.
- Place the objects in the bag. Pass the bag round the group, allowing each child to feel and try to guess an unseen object, pulling it out of the bag when they guess.
- At the end of the round empty out the objects and help the children describe them by appearance, touch, etc. Prompt the use of the vocabulary you planned and note the children's own contributions.
- For the next game, put *your* hand in the bag and give some clues about an object, asking the children to guess what you are feeling. Allow each child to take a turn; before they put their hand into the bag, nominate another child who will try to guess the object they will describe. Give each child a turn at describing and guessing. Offer necessary support for describing and guessing. Help the children to listen, wait and take turns.
- End the session by cutting up the fruits and vegetables with the children. Talk about how they look and smell. Let the children eat them and tell you how they taste.
- Make a note of newly acquired words used by any individuals, and of comments made about foods which 'help me to have strong healthy teeth'.

Quick quiz

Find the answers in the chapter.

1. Why should babies be drinking from a cup by their first birthday?

2. What problems can dummies cause?

3. Why is plaque a danger to maintaining healthy teeth?

4. Why is it important to wait for 20 minutes before brushing teeth after having any sweet or acidic foods or drinks?

5. Name six healthy eating snacks or food treats which are both nutritious and tooth-friendly.

6. What removes plaque from teeth and what are the benefits to teeth of saliva?

7. To help safeguard their teeth, when are the best times for children to eat any sweets, sticky foods or drink fruit juice? Why?

8. What 'food' can help to replace some of the calcium lost from tooth enamel and what food has been shown to give very particular protection to teeth?

9. *Considering dental health*, put the following foods in order from the 'safest' to the potentially most harmful (per 100 grams): real-fruit yoghurt; fruit pastilles with added vitamin C; celery sticks; cheese, honey sandwiches; chewy toffees; natural yoghurt; cheese on toast; tomato ketchup; sugar coated breakfast cereal; sugar coated chocolate 'beans'; raisins.

10. Do the same for these drinks (per 100 mls): full-fat milk; diluted orange squash; diet cola; hot chocolate drink; chilled water; non-diluted apple juice; very diluted apple juice; fizzy orange drink; diluted sugar free orange squash; sugar-free banana milkshake.

Summary

Now you have read this chapter you should understand:

- the importance of caring for the baby's mouth and first teeth
- poor oral and eating habits established in babyhood can affect a child's physical, psychological, linguistic and social development
- how tooth decay is caused and some of the problems it causes
- how to discourage habits which cause decay and encourage those which promote healthy teeth
- some ways of helping parents and children to adopt healthy eating and good dental practices.

12

Children, Food and Education

Aims of the chapter

To enable you to understand:

- why and what children need to know about food, nutrition and healthy eating
- practical approaches to teaching babies and young children about food
- healthy eating, food and nutrition in the curriculum: planning for children's learning in nursery and school.

Although the house was newly decorated, Flossie was determined the baby should experience the full range of early independence skills at meal times.

Why and what children need to know about food, nutrition and healthy eating

National reports on children's understanding of healthy eating and issues concerned with food safety indicate that we need to continue to make improvements in educating children about health, food and eating.

Why?

The British Nutrition Foundation has stated that children are not equipped with the knowledge they need to choose a balanced diet which meets their energy and nutritional needs. It also reports that young peoples' diets are typically too high in fat and sugar, and too low in fibre, iron and calcium. Obesity, heart and circulatory problems, dental decay and diabetes are among the possible outcomes.

In 1999 the Health Education Authority reported that over three million children make their own breakfast each day. The same report raised concern about children's lack of understanding of basic food safety and simple hygiene practices.

As more than 200 people die each year in the UK from food poisoning, it is clear that good hygiene routines and basic facts about food safety need to be taught to all children from an early age.

The main reasons for teaching young children about food, nutrition and healthy eating are:

- to enable them to enjoy food and its related social aspects
- to enrich their learning and self-awareness through sensory stimulation
- to encourage them to take 'risks' (an essential learning behaviour) by experimenting with new real-life experiences in a safe, controlled situation
- to help them develop life skills of selecting, handling and preparing food
- to help ensure their safety, well being and health
- to begin to help them make effective choices which will enable them to develop an understanding about what to buy, cook and eat in later life
- to inform and encourage children to eat a balanced nutritious diet which meets their needs
- to learn about cultural, religious and individual differences and to value these.

Having fun while learning life skills!

What children need to know about healthy eating, food and nutrition

Very young children are choosing and handling food every day, so they need the knowledge and skills to make appropriate choices and follow safe practices.

Children need to develop patterns of eating and attitudes to food which give them a balanced diet. They need actively to experience and learn about different types of food, and to learn that what they eat influences their energy levels, growth and health.

To make informed life choices about what to buy and what to eat, they need to learn where food comes from and what has happened, before it reaches the shops and arrives on the table.

Most importantly, being able to cook, so as to make effective choices about what to eat and being able to prepare and eat food safely, is fundamental to life.

Opportunities for acquiring this knowledge and skill need to be given from a very young age, and to be built on steadily over the years.

Overall, young children need to begin to learn:

- that food is needed for growth and activity
- an adequate, balanced and varied diet is needed to promote health
- where staple foods come from
- how foods are produced and can be used
- what can happens to ingredients and foods during cooking and other processes
- food related health safety and personal hygiene
- how to plan and estimate with a sound degree of practical accuracy
- how to follow a recipe and evaluate the outcome of a practical session
- how to select and safely use a range of equipment and tools
- the importance of food in different cultures and in celebrations
- to gain confidence and enjoyment in preparing food and eating with friends.

Look Anna! A lamb drinks milk too!

The national healthy school standard: a national initiative for promoting children's health

The National Healthy School Standard was established in 1999 as part of the national Healthy Schools Programme. Participating schools receive guidance, training and support to help them work towards achieving accreditation, permitting them to use the national Healthy Schools logo. The leaflet 'What you need to know' outlines the scheme and its eight key areas, which include 'personal, social and educational health' and 'healthy eating'. The scheme emphasises the need to develop a whole-school approach so every aspect of school life consistently follows the main principles of health promotion.

The NHSS guidance gives criteria for assessing schools' quality regarding 'healthy eating':
- 'the school presents consistent informed messages about healthy eating, for example, food on offer in vending machines, tuck shops, and school meals should complement the taught curriculum
- the school provides, promotes and monitors healthier food at lunch and break times and in any breakfast clubs where they are provided
- the school includes education on healthier eating and basic food safety practices in the taught curriculum.'

Some schools already market themselves as a 'healthy eating school'. The National Healthy School Standard seeks to expand these pockets of good practice and develop them to cover every health-related aspect of school provision.

Why have a whole school policy on healthy eating?

A whole-school food policy is vital because it encourages team work so everyone can work well together for the children. A food policy explains exactly what the school believes in; and what it will emphasise, resource and carry out in order to support the children's learning, nutrition and welfare.

A well-run policy will have a positive influence on the pupils, the formal curriculum, all learning in the school and the behaviour and attitudes of everyone working in the school and with the pupils. The same messages and standards taught in lessons are promoted in the school kitchen. Parents are given information about what and how the children will be taught about food and nutrition, and the arrangements for eating at school, which hopefully will positively influence and reflect good practices at home.

To ensure its translation into practice, there must be practical guidelines so every member of staff, catering contractor and parent is clear about their role, responsibilities and specific requirements.

ALERT

Remember: You can teach the children about healthy nutrition in the classroom, but if the food served at lunchtime is not nutritiously balanced, or tuck shops and vending machines sell low-nutrient, high-sugar foods to boost school funds, this gives *very* unhelpful, conflicting and damaging messages.

- - - - - - - *Good professional practice* - - - - - - -

All staff and volunteer helpers who support or have contact with children at mealtimes, including kitchen staff who serve the children, need to know something of their personal learning needs and be aware of the many learning opportunities available at lunchtime. An effective school or nursery will ensure there is regular staff training to keep standards high. If you are concerned about discrepancies in provision, approach the head to organise a staff meeting or training to clarify issues for everyone.

ACTIVITY

In your placement find out what information is made available for parents about food, nutrition and children's eating:

1. Is there a policy about food and children's eating? Does it contain guidance which you find useful?

2. If a meeting is held for new parents, does it include information about food and eating?

3. What help is available for parents concerned about their child's eating behaviours, nutrition and eating?

4. Are there any displays to inform parents about children's nutritional needs?

5. What information is available about school meals and are there any guidelines for packed lunches, drinks and snacks?

The role of the early years professional in teaching children about food

Young children need to learn about themselves and the world around them, which includes food. One of the main aims for early years professionals is to enable children to become confident and self-reliant, skilful in making considered choices and being able to communicate their needs, concerns and opinions. For this to be successful they need to acquire knowledge, skills and understanding.

Planning for children's learning:

- When planning an activity for children you need to be very clear about what learning you are hoping to develop. This will be based on what you and your colleagues know about what your children currently need to learn. The content and pace of the activity must be appropriately matched to these needs.
- Your plans should show how you will:
  - stimulate the most able children
  - enable children with special educational needs to be supported and appropriately challenged
  - try to ensure that *all* pupils make good progress.

As part of your planning make a note of what particular responses and changes you plan to look out for in the children, so you can find out what they have learnt from the activity.

Practical approaches to teaching babies and young children about food

From birth babies need to be talked to constantly, engaged in conversation and develop understanding and skills through feeding routines and adult behaviours. From an early age questions and opinions should be sought and encouraged, so they can take an increasing role in making simple choices ('do you want a drink now?'; 'which piece of banana would you like?'; 'choose a yoghurt for dinner.').

When you or a child is eating, talk about the food's appearance, smell, temperature, texture and taste. Talk about what she is doing, her actions and behaviour, and introduce concepts such as 'more', counting, and order of events. Supplying her with key vocabulary and encouraging her to talk about food, her actions, reactions and feelings will greatly support her learning and development.

Giving her foods of different tastes and consistencies, encouraging chewing and drinking from a cup, develop skills and control which help her to speak, eat efficiently and develop confidence to try other foods. Letting her handle drinks and finger feed herself gives further learning opportunities for physical, language and social and emotional development. In the following weeks, manipulating cutlery, pouring drinks, turning a tap and engaging in cooking or cooking play give her chances to extend, apply and increase the range of her learning.

Helping in the kitchen. Just look at the concentration!

At home and in the nursery young children can be readily involved with shopping, preparing food and mealtimes, serving and feeding themselves, and helping to clear away afterwards.

A shopping trip with a two year old can be made more interesting for her – and less fraught for you – if she feels involved. Show her the empty cereal box, cheese packet or yoghurt pot. Help her to cut a label from a packet or the front off the cereal box. Let her take this shopping so it becomes her first shopping list! Children can also write their own lists, by drawing pictures, sticking cut out labels onto a card or by using emergent writing. Food names can be copied from labels or freely written by older children.

Talk about the foods and the shops you will need to visit. When in the shop talk about the food you are buying. By encouraging her to look out for her item(s) you are helping her to listen and look, to detect size, colour, shape and print, and to predict!

If she helps to set the table, pour drinks, join in cooking and wash up, a great deal of significant learning can take place on a regular and practical basis. These frequent opportunities – for trying out new ideas, practising and refining physical and creative skills, using a great deal of contextual language and early mathematics, and developing confidence and self awareness – are enormously important for a young child.

Children can be involved in many aspects of food preparation if they are carefully supervised and the tasks are appropriate and safe. Moreover by letting her join in the preparation of a meal, she is more likely to eat it.

Children enjoy cooking. They are eager to watch, listen, copy and try new skills. Their natural interest is apparent when you see how many babies like to play with a large bowl, saucepan and some wooden spoons, and how children love to role-play all kinds of cooking and food-related activities. Give a child a chance to join in your cooking and baking and she will be happy and totally involved. Although some extra mess and clearing up will be an inevitable by-product of the worthwhile experience, she can also be included in the washing up, wiping the floor and so on. This may not be exactly helpful to you, but will pay many dividends for her future.

Cooking with children presents excellent opportunities for you to demonstrate good hygiene and safety, to teach children about healthy eating and the need for a balanced diet. Cooking also helps children to acquire many fine motor, linguistic, mathematical and social skills. It is important that the early years professional is fully aware of each child's learning and developmental needs and offers every practical opportunity for meeting these.

A simple event can have a great impact.

A memorable occurrence happened some years ago with a child with significant learning difficulties who had never seen food cooked. Her only understanding of food was based on what was put on her plate. During her first cooking lesson she was given an egg to hold, examine and then crack. As she was helped to fry her egg her face was transformed from curiosity into total amazement, recognition and then pure joy!

Healthy eating, food and nutrition in the curriculum

'Food' is included in the National Curriculum in England and Wales but no longer as an independent subject. In Scotland it still appears in the National Curriculum in its own right. However, aspects of food do feature in different subjects, perhaps most explicitly in design and technology, and in science. However, religious education, history and geography all have significant food related content. There are also secure links for food with English, art, music, physical education, information technology, and personal and social education.

The aim of a food education curriculum policy is to pull everything together across all subjects and areas of the curriculum to give children a coherent view about food which they can apply to their everyday lives. It is important for the children that meaningful links are made.

Offering children learning activities which practically involve food (one of the major daily influences on their lives) is therefore a meaningful, effective way in to many aspects of the curriculum.

A whole school curriculum planning policy gives a framework for what is to be taught and allows us to check for curriculum coverage and to identify any gaps in the food teaching we plan to cover. It also provides a way of ensuring that what we plan to teach effectively builds on what was previously taught, which is often referred to as 'planning for continuity and progression in learning'.

Ensuring safe practice and teaching children about food safety

The responsibility for the safety of the children in your group is yours! Whenever you lead any activity involving food you must prepare carefully and demonstrate good practice yourself.

You must ensure that the children follow and understand instructions and safe, hygienic routines.

According to the children's age, size, and levels of understanding and skill, *carefully choose exactly what activities are suitable for children to do themselves and which you would do for them.* For example, pouring warm or cold liquids gives good practice and confidence to young children, but pouring boiling water must be done by an adult.

▬ ▬ ▬ ▬ ▬ ▬ ▬*Good professional practice*▬ ▬ ▬ ▬ ▬ ▬ ▬

When cooking with young children make sure:

- children are able to see you clearly to follow what you do
- you carefully point out good cookery and food hygiene practices as they arise
- you are aware of food and eating customs which differ from your own
- you are aware of food requirements and limitations set by children's home cultures
- you understand and respect hygiene practices of other cultures; observe these sensitively on behalf of children in your group who have been brought up to adhere to them
- you check foods and planned ingredients against any known food intolerances of your group.

ACTIVITY

1. Obtain a copy of the board game 'Bubble and Slime', which is based on 'Snakes and Ladders' and is aimed at reinforcing teaching about personal hygiene linked with eating and food safety. (The game is part of 'The Adventures of Safe-T and the H Squad' pack available free from The EC Publishing Distribution Centre.)

2. Consider the language used, the complexity and range of information contained and the format of the game itself. For what age groups do you feel 'Bubble and Slime' is appropriate?

3. Decide whether 'Bubble and Slime' is suitable for the children in your placement. Adapt the game *or* create your own game to meet your children's learning needs.

Curriculum links with food and nutrition

Note: Most of the following curriculum links are arranged under subject headings rather than the six areas for learning. This is purely for simplicity of text, to save repetition and to enable fuller discussion of curriculum aspects and food links. All 'subject titled' sections are directly relevant to the early years areas of learning.

Developing personal, health and social education, and much more through cooking and eating together

Daily events such as snack and lunchtimes offer chances for children to cooperate, take turns and help. By offering the children a changing selection of fruit and vegetables, rather than sweet biscuits, experiences of eating these plus discussions about healthy eating can be very valuable.

Handing round a plate of food, taking turns, waiting, asking others what they would like and responding are important aspects of learning. Children can also develop skills and confidence by pouring drinks for themselves.

ALERT
If children's drinks are pre-poured and food given out by staff, a whole range of important learning opportunities are lost.

Looking, listening and taking turns
in the nursery.

Parties also offer many wonderful opportunities for social and personal learning. Looking after others, especially if feeling rather overawed is an important responsibility. Passing food to your friends before helping yourself is a good (if sometimes a hard-to-learn) lesson. Asking politely, saying 'no thank you', being able to choose and to risk trying new foods, all effectively can be learned through eating with others.

Setting out beakers and plates, counting numbers and matching chairs to place settings are all real life mathematical experiences. Estimating the numbers of apples needed to be sliced to give every child two pieces, and making sure there is a chocolate bun for everyone constitutes critical planning for the successful party giver!

Planning party food together and making items for the event are secure means of approaching design and technology, and making social decisions. Cooking is an excellent way to involve children in reading, listening and speaking, mathematics and creativity. Predicting what will happen to jelly cubes stirred into hot water, carefully examining the dishes after refrigeration, working out what has changed and possible reasons why, are all good science!

Party invitations need to be designed and written. A guest list can be drawn up and replies logged and monitored. A menu can be planned and produced. This will involve reading, writing, design, mathematics and the chance to use information technology for publishing and data handling.

Designing and making table and room decorations can be the reason for children to be introduced to different art media, tools and methods of production.

Having thought about all these enriching, relevant and practical ways for children to be actively engaged in a real life and very enjoyable event, you may be tempted to have many more parties in future!

■ ■ ■ ■ ■ ■ ■ ■ *Good professional practice* ■ ■ ■ ■ ■ ■ ■ ■

> Although no one would disagree that healthy food is the best option, it is sensible to accept that when children do eat at birthday parties, a healthy balanced diet may well go by the board! There is no need to produce a 'group five foods only banquet' or a sugar fest. It is not obligatory that parties mean sugary and fatty foods! Party food *can* consist of healthy eating nibbles and snacks, but there is also little point in fretting over the occasional overindulgence as balance in eating needs to be assessed over time. In any case, as young children tend to be so excited at a party they generally eat very little.

Thinking about serving healthy drinks is perhaps more important than planning the food!

Children coping with new experiences: a delight or worry?

Taking part in cooking, handling foods or eating can be fun and exciting, or it can produce anxiety. Encourage children to taste foods but never force, hassle, look disappointed, cajole or insist. Explain the ground rules and stick to them. Tell the children they will be given a chance to try foods *if they wish to*. Give *them* the means to manage the situation and then keep to the agreement. '*If you would like to try some, that is fine. If you don't want to, just say 'no thank you' and I shall give your piece to someone else.*'

If the child does not want to try the food do not question her response, ask her again or suggests she tries 'just a little'. Respect her decision and accept her response. This approach usually works wonders and promotes sound learning! After all a child who refuses is developing self-confidence, becoming more assertive and is learning to say 'no' appropriately. One day she may decide to try a taste because she wants to or because she sees others doing so.

Religious education and personal and social education

To value and appreciate similarities and differences and enjoy the rich diversity of lifestyles, children need to learn about their own and others' cultures and religions. The fact that food is central to all cultures means it can be a useful, meaningful and enjoyable way to access learning, and to help develop understanding and tolerance.

Through food shopping, preparation, serving and eating we can give children 'real' social and personal leaning opportunities, such as sharing, taking turns, problem solving, listening to and helping each other.

Everyone enjoys a celebration! Festivals give opportunities for you to make meaningful links with aspects of food and healthy eating. As many have associated special celebratory foods they allow for substantial learning to take place about significance, types and varieties of food prepared and eaten.

Special foods and religious celebrations can be used as a vehicle to teach many aspects of the Foundation and National Curriculum at Key Stages 1 and 2. Foods and ways of eating in different cultures can be introduced to very young children through role play and story, as well as by cooking and eating.

By finding out about some of the main festivals linked to the cultures of your children, you can provide meaningful experiences. Do not feel concerned if you are not an expert in each one! Ask parents to help you understand the main reasons and features of an event. Ask them for advice about how you could best help the children to become involved in a celebration and what particular foods are required. Give yourself plenty of time especially if you think an occasion may take quite a lot of arranging. Parents may be willing to come in to show the children how to make special foods, use certain cooking ingredients or utensils, or make table decorations. Sharing expertise is an essential aspect of parent partnership. Involving parents builds trust and communication. It benefits everyone, especially the children.

– – – – – – Good professional practice – – – – – –

It is important that children from all cultural and religious persuasions feel included, respected and valued. The backgrounds of the children in your placement will prompt your emphasis but do also try to celebrate events and cultures which are not personally represented to extend their learning even further.

The table below shows some of the religious and cultural events which reflect our multicultural society, and which can have special links with food.

Some Religious and Cultural Festivals and Celebrations

Autumn Term	Spring Term	Summer Term
Harvest festival	New Year	St George's Day
Rosh Hashanah (Jewish New Year)	Rastafarian Christmas	May Day
Sukkot (Jewish harvest festival)	Chinese New Year	Jewish Feast of Weeks
Dusserhra (Hindu festival)	St Valentine's Day	Fathers' Day
Divali (Hindu New Year & festival of light)	St David's Day	American Independence Day
Guy Fawkes (Bonfire night)	Shrove Tuesday (pancake day)	Obon (Japanese festival)
Thanksgiving (USA)	Ash Wednesday (start of Lent)	Wesak (Buddhist Festival)
Shichi-go-san (Japanese festival for girls of 7 & 3, and boys of 5)	Mardi Gras/Latin American/ Caribbean carnival	Festival of Hungry Ghosts (Chinese)
Ramadan (start of Muslim month of fasting)*	Commonwealth Day	Birthday of Haile Selassie
St Andrew's day	St Patrick's Day	Birthday of Muhammed
Birthday of Guru Nanak Dev Ji (Sikh)		World Environment Day
Chanukah (Jewish festival of light)	Holi (Hindu spring festival of colour)	
Start of Advent (leading up to Christmas)	Mothering Sunday	
Id Al Fitr (Muslim festival marking end of Ramadan)	Islamic New Year	
Al Hijrah (Muslim New Year)	Easter: Good Friday	
Christmas Day	Easter Sunday	

Note: *Children under 13 years do not usually fast.

Note: – Dates for many events often change from year to year; they may even be different in the UK from those in the 'home' country. Check dates carefully; ask your parent experts for guidance.
   – Keep a planning diary note of festivals and events which may be celebrated by your children and their families during the year.

ACTIVITY

1. In your placement what coverage and importance do you consider is given to 'food and festivities' through religious education and other curriculum areas?

2. Outline one or two activities that could help nursery children to learn something about foods, styles of eating and food preparation in a culture different from their own home culture.

English: language, literacy and food

There are countless ways that children can talk about and listen to others talking about food. Asking questions, explaining preferences, describing food, listening to stories and presenting factual accounts are all effective ways of linking learning about food and balanced healthy eating with English.

Writing about such things as what happened at the harvest festival, memories of a special party, favourite foods, thank you letters, shopping lists, planning a picnic or writing invitations and menus are all relevant ways of combining teaching children about food with literary composition, writing for a specific purpose, spelling and presentation of work. Children can create their own stories and poems. Sometimes the structure of a favourite story can be used on which to base their own composition. Reading about food can be achieved through following recipes and instructions, and reading lists, labels, poems, stories, lyrics and non-fiction books.

The following well known titles may help to support aspects of learning about food. They can be readily borrowed from children's libraries. Keep a copy of the list in your file and add to it regularly.

- **Traditional tales**

The Little Red Hen	Jack and the Beanstalk
The Gingerbread Boy	Goldilocks and the Three Bears
The Enormous Turnip	Chicken Licken
Stone Soup	The Golden Goose
The Magic Porridge Pot	Hansel and Gretel

- **Stories involving food and food-related activities**

Don't Forget the Bacon	Pat Hutchins
Pumpkin Soup	Helen Cooper
Each Peach Pear Plum	Janet and Alan Alberg
Ice Cream Bear	Jez Alborough
Avocado Baby	John Burningham
The Shopping Basket	John Burningham
The Giant Jam Sandwich	John Vernon Lord
Jam	Margaret Mahy
The Witch in the Cherry Tree	Margaret Mahy
Mr Rabbit and the Lovely Present	Charlotte Zolotow
Pass the Jam, Jim	Umansky & Chamberlain
Meg's Eggs	Nicholl & Pienkowski
The Lighthouse Keeper's Lunch	Ronda & David Armitage
The Very Hungry Caterpillar	Eric Carle
Topsy and Tim Visit the Farm	Jean & Gareth Anderson
Topsy and Tim Visit the Dentist	Jean & Gareth Anderson
The Apple	Dick Bruna
Some of Us	Ljiljana Rylands
The Tiger Who Came to Tea	Judith Kerr
The Bears' Bazaar	Michelle Cartlidge
Eat Your Dinner	Virginia Miller
A Piece of Cake	Jill Murphy

- **Board books**

Things That Grow	A Funfax Book.
Let's Go Shopping	A Funfax Book
First Words: Garden	A Snapshot Book.
First Words: Kitchen	A Snapshot Book.
Babies Eating	Campbell Books.

- **Non-fiction books**

Bees Make Honey	Sarah Allen
Food From the Garden	Sarah Allen
Farming – Our Green World	Sue Hadden
Cooking (Changing Times Series)	(pub. Franklin Watts)
Shopping for Food	(pub. Franklin Watts)
Growing Things	Angela Wilkes

- **Children's cookery books**

Peter Rabbit's Cookery Book	Anne Emerson
Cooking for Beginners	Fiona Watt
Vegetarian Cooking for Beginners	Fiona Watt
Pasta and Pizza for Beginners	Fiona Watt
Cakes and Cookies for Beginners	Fiona Watt
Party Things	Angela Wilkes
Sweet Things	Angela Wilkes
Hot Things	Angela Wilkes

— — — — — — —*Good professional practice*— — — — — — —

For each cookery session provide a suitably written and illustrated laminated recipe card for each child in the group. By making your own you will be able to give more detailed cards to more able children, and cards with simpler instructions and illustrations tailored to meet the needs of children who need more support.

Note: A range of eminently suitable, healthy eating recipes for all ages are contained in *Babies & toddlers good food*. (See 'further reading' list for details.)

Rhymes, games and poems

Finger rhymes, nursery rhymes and other traditional games are good ways of linking learning about food with listening, performing, copying, cooperating, memorising and experiencing word patterns and rhythm.

— — — — — — —*Good professional practice*— — — — — — —

Perhaps parents or grandparents could be asked to visit your nursery or school and show the children some food-related games and rhymes they played as children. Moreover such visits and children learning traditional games and rhymes link well in the early years with developing an understanding of time and personal history!

Both individual and shared (or 'group') writing should be experienced by the children. Composing poems is a valuable and often intense means of challenging children's creativity and thinking. Poems about food and ideas related to food, cooking and eating when based on first hand experiences can be vibrant, sensitive and expressive.

Listening to poetry and rhymes is also important. The following have links with food. Add your own ideas to the lists:

- **Nursery rhymes**

Humpty Dumpty	Sing a song of sixpence
Little Jack Horner	Oranges and lemons
Jack Sprat	Bananas in pyjamas
Five currant buns/	One potato
Five Christmas puddings	Five fat sausages
Simple Simon	Pat-a-cake
Old Mother Hubbard	Jelly on a plate
Tom, Tom the piper's son	Higglety pigglety my black hen
Curly locks	Pop goes the weasel
Peter Piper	Brown potatoes, white potatoes
Dame get up and bake your pies	Handy spandy, Jack-a-dandy
There was an old woman who	Little Miss Muffet
swallowed a fly	Little Tommy Tucker
There was an old woman who	sings for his supper
lived in a shoe	Hot cross buns.

- **Poems**

Today's Recipe – Book Soup	Roger McGough
A Bowl of Fruit	Roger McGough
The Cabbage is a Funny Veg.	Roger McGough
Yellow Poem	Roger McGough
If You're No Good at Cooking	Kit Wright
Say Cheese	Kit Wright
The Tummy Beast	Roald Dahl

- **Poetry Books and Collections**

Poems about Food	compiled by Brian Moses (Wayland)
Tasty Poems	Collected by Jill Bennett (OUP)

Food, mathematics and information technology

Many aspects of mathematics can be addressed through food. For example, children can learn to:

- use appropriate mathematics (e.g. whether to estimate, count, add, subtract, time or measure)
- understand the language of number, shape properties and concepts (such as 'bigger than', 'more', 'less than', 'after' and 'next to')

- organise and check their work (e.g. 'There are five children in my group, have I put out enough plates?)
- recognise patterns and shapes (e.g. The biscuits are star shapes, the sandwiches are triangles; cut the maximum number of small circles from a larger circle of dough)
- ask questions and make predictions (e.g. 'How many pieces will there be if I cut the apple once (and then cut each piece again)?').

Early learning about balance, weights and measures.

Young children not only enjoy eating food, they like talking and thinking about it too.

You can help them to create a simple questionnaire about favourite foods and carry out their own 'market research' by interviewing staff and friends. You can use their natural interest and curiosity about food to teach them about

How many have we made?

handling data, writing for a specific purpose and asking effective questions.

Questionnaires should be easy to read, understand and answer (maybe eliciting just a 'yes' or 'no' response, which can be recorded in writing or by a tick or a cross). Shy children who are reluctant to ask questions can be supported and given confidence by having to do a 'real' task such as this.

Questionnaires designed by more able pupils can be neatly written or word processed. Younger children can use early writing skills, perhaps embellished with drawings, food labels or photographs of products cut from magazines, which will also help them to read the questionnaire sheet independently of adult help.

Children generally enjoy collecting and collating data. Using practical apparatus to enumerate and analyse responses gives relevance to counting, sorting, matching and categorising information gathered by young children. Discussions between you and the children lead to them meaningfully using mathematical language. Results can be recorded and displayed in a range of formats, such as tables, pie charts, bar graphs, or Venn diagrams, using ICT software, collage or drawn illustrations.

ACTIVITY

Plan an activity for children in your placement to develop understanding and use of mathematics and mathematical language, *and* **give practical opportunities to learn about healthy snack foods.**

Science, food and cooking

Cooking is a wonderful way for young children to explore and learn about science. Children can readily experience many different ways of combining and treating ingredients to bring about physical changes. Melting butter, softening margarine by beating, sifting flour, pouring liquids, dissolving crystals, setting jelly, freezing and thawing can all be experienced through cookery and allow the children to investigate changes that occur. Watching a cake in the oven or dough rising are fascinating ways to experience science through food. Handling and manipulating food of different textures is fun and educational.

Seeing and handling food in a raw or unprocessed state can be a revelation for many. Children can examine a sheaf of wheat or handle a corn cob and be helped to understand their part in the origins of a loaf of bread or cornflakes.

Children are fascinated by structures and skeletons. Watching a fish being boned and filleted before cooking is pretty amazing, particularly for children who only previously knew fish as 'ocean stars' or orange-coloured fish fingers.

If you lack confidence in cleaning and boning a fish, perhaps there is a parent keen on fishing or a local fishmonger who could come in to help you. Make sure the children can touch the fish, see each stage clearly and are given explanations about what is happening and why some bits are being discarded. Try to remove the backbone intact, when boiled it can grace an investigation display. For safety ensure all large bones are removed. Finish by cooking it in herb butter adding a squeeze of lemon and offering tastes to the children. Delicious!

Analysing, sorting and classifying foods and their attributes can be an effective means for teaching these aspects of science whilst addressing issues of health and nutrition. Sorting foods into food groups can involve active participation if food packets, containers and real or replica foods, such as fruit and vegetables, are used. A large 'Balance of Good Food' play mat is a useful resource.

Tending plants, feeding pets, or watching a baby being fed can support teaching on the necessity of nutrients and water for growth and health. Gardening is valuable for supporting children's scientific learning. Consider growing plants and vegetables with the children in your placement. Many items such as herbs, cress, salad leaves, spinach, tomatoes and strawberries can be grown in pots or tubs. Growbags allow you to grow a wider range of plants, such as beans, peas and courgettes. If there is not a garden bed suitable for planting root crops perhaps you could enlist some parent gardening experts to help you develop one and who would help the children to sow and tend the growing plants.

Food and geography

Learning where food comes from, where it is grown and produced also links well with geography.

Weather patterns can be studied in relation to the needs of plants grown for eating. If the whole food process from growing simple foods, picking them, through preparing, cooking and eating can be experienced it will be very valuable and meaningful for the children. Arranging visits to markets, local

Learning, during a farm visit, where milk comes from.

shops, market gardens and farms to support school based teaching about food is immensely useful. Involving the children in shopping for ingredients is good, but by letting them see foods being grown and produced, helps them to understand food sources. Pulling a carrot from the earth is akin to magic, especially if you previously believed they originated from plastic bags!

ALERT
When children are involved in gardening or touching any animals or animal enclosures, such as on a farm visit, hygiene safety must be paramount. Closely supervised hand washing is essential before the children eat or drink.

Children can learn about foods grown in this country and in hotter countries; which foods are grown in fields, orchards and greenhouses. Finding out how growing rice differs from growing corn can readily arise from a discussion about favourite breakfast cereals and watching an appropriate video tape, and lead to everyone carefully studying the globe.

Different foods eaten in different cultures and foods eaten in countries children visited on holiday can trigger work on food choices and lead to experiencing particular foods and tastes.

Reading food labels to find the countries of origin can provide an impetus to look at a globe. Parents can be asked to help children play 'The World in my Kitchen', where they look through the food cupboards and refrigerator to find out what countries are to be found represented there. Collections of empty packets and pots can be sorted into continents or countries, and maps embellished with displays showing where particular goods originated.

Mr Gay and Bernard offer a warm welcome to visitors! A successful farm visit depends greatly on finding a friendly and understanding farmer.

History and changes over time: food, eating and cooking

Young children need to have tangible means of experiencing and understanding history. Primarily this will arise from looking both at their own and their family members' history and what differences have occurred over time. Food is an excellent vehicle for developing these concepts. Children can study personal changes such as the drinks and foods they had as a baby, and how and what they eat now. Parents, grandparents and great-grandparents can be asked to share accounts of changes they have seen in food availability and cooking equipment, what their school meals were like and what foods they most enjoyed as children. Make sure you make good use of this valuable resource.

Visits to kitchens in old houses or domestic exhibits in a local museum can give insight into food preparation before the days of stainless steel and electricity. Children can learn about food safety and storage before homes had fridges and freezers. *How did the Victorians make ice cream in summer?*

- - - - - - -*Good professional practice*- - - - - - -

Ask friends, family and children's parents to lend or donate items of old kitchen equipment such as jugs, kettles, pots, bowls, spoons, rolling pins and whisks, so children can examine them and compare them with modern equivalents. Collect pictures which show eating and cooking in past times.

Physical education, healthy eating and nutrition

Children need to develop fine and gross motor skills. Physical activities should give them these opportunities.

Teaching all forms of physical education relate well to healthy eating and eating to give us energy. Health related fitness is now an integral aspect of the physical education curriculum. Young children readily understand the basic concepts of using energy through physical education. Raised heart rates and sweating can be experienced with vigorous activity.

The importance of healthy eating for physical health, fitness, well being and growth can be introduced. Discussions about running faster, throwing further, jumping higher should include appropriate teaching about making healthy food choices and nutrition.

- - - - - - -*Good professional practice*- - - - - - -

Physical education lessons and other physical activities present particularly good opportunities for giving children guidance, encouragement and explanation of the vital importance of frequently drinking plenty of water throughout the day, and especially after exertion.

Dance and drama are valuable media for allowing young children to explore and express moods, attitudes and feelings about food.

- Drama or dance can develop themes of social eating, such as parties and festivals.
- Physical aspects of food consistency, texture and shape can be explored.
- By employing observed movements from a cooking lesson where ingredients were chopped, poured, sifted, beaten, folded, rolled, kneaded, stirred, left to rise, boiled, frozen or melted can result in effective and exciting learning about types and qualities of movement.

Music and food

Children need to be able to sing, play, listen and respond to music, and compose their own works. Learning about food can be approached and supported through these requisite areas of the music curriculum.

For example, tastes, temperatures and textures of foods can be effective stimuli for composing individual or group pieces of music. A composition could reflect the events or moods of a feast, or provide an accompaniment for a special celebratory meal.

Working up a thirst!

Some resource ideas

Many songs and pieces of music illustrate or comment on foods. Libraries, music and record shops can help you find recordings and sheet music of titles. Add your own resources to these lists for future reference.

Songs to sing, listen to or play along with:

• **Nursery rhymes**
See previous list on page 273 as most of these rhymes have melodies.

• **Action songs**
Oats and beans and barley grow
Five fat sausages frying in a pan
Mix a pancake, stir a pancake
Here we go round the mulberry bush

• **Other songs, etc.**

We plough the fields and scatter	Blueberry Hill
All things bright and beautiful	Tea for Two
Cherry Ripe	Don't Sit Under the Apple Tree
Food Glorious Food	Peanut Vendor
Big Rock Candy Mountain	Boiled Beef and Carrots
Brush, Brush, Brush.	Strawberry Fair
(When you clean your teeth.)	Christmas is Coming
I'm a Pink Toothbrush	We Wish You a Merry Christmas

- **Instrumental music**

The Dance of the Sugar Plum Fairy (from Tchaikovsky's *The Nutcracker.*)
Maple Leaf Rag
Honey Rag
Tangerine
Gingerman
Clarinet Marmalade
Cheese and Crackers
Cherry Pink, Apple Blossom White
Jumping Bean
Pineapple Rag
The Wedding of the Gingerbreads
Teatime
Balshaazar's Feast
Ballet for the Unhatched Chicks (Misorgsky's *Pictures from an Exhibition.*)

Food and art: 'investigating and making' and 'knowledge and understanding'.

Children need to be given real objects to observe, examine and handle so they can fully represent their forms and qualities in a variety of media. Food is an excellent and appropriate stimulus. Drawing whole and cut fruits in pencil or pastels, a paper collage of a favourite healthy meal, using acrylics to paint a selection of different breads, or watercolours to paint a shining green pepper are meaningful and challenging tasks for children.

Vegetables and other cut foods can be used for printing. Although many people use potato halves for printmaking, a piece of cut broccoli, the rim outline of an orange skin or a quarter of a pear perhaps give a clearer feeling of the foods' natural forms.

Children can also be helped to make and use simple dyes and paints from foods, such as berries, beetroot, spinach, and onion skins.

Cornflour and icing sugar painting, as well as mixing textured dried foods into paint and glue can give fascinating opportunities both for developing processes of learning (such as problem solving, predicting and estimating), and for producing a rich variety of work.

Some foods and food packing can be used for collage, modelling, sculpture and other three dimensional work. Perhaps, linked to harvest or bread-making, you could show the children some corn dollies, explain their origins and help them to make their own out of treated corn stalks or paper reeds. Dried pasta, seeds and pulses, and food packages, such as card, paper, polystyrene and plastic items are often used in modelling and collage, but are not always sufficiently linked to teaching about healthy eating.

Food has been a popular subject for artists throughout the ages. Aspects of food choice, preference and healthy eating can be reinforced by enabling children to study, interpret and enjoy works of art. When showing children reproductions try to obtain large copies; postcards give insufficient detail and are harder for a group of children to see. Visits to local art galleries or exhibitions are very valuable for allowing children to experience scale and vibrancy of colour, not usually achievable in copies.

The following artists and their work may provide you with stimuli to link art, knowledge and understanding with teaching about food. Add your own references to the resource list below.

Archimboldo	Summer	Chardin	The Cut Melon
Bonnard	End of a Meal in the Garden	Gauguin	Harvest in Brittany
Bonnard	Still Life in Yellow and Red	Gauguin	Still Life with Apples
Cezanne	Still Life with a Basket of Apples	Matisse	Still Life with Oranges
Cezanne	The Kitchen Table	Matisse	Dinner table
Cezanne	Jug and Fruit	O'Keeffe	Plums
Cezanne	Apples and Oranges	O'Keeffe	Grapes on White Dish – Dark Rim
Cezanne	Apples and Biscuits	Pissarro	The Apple Pickers
Chardin	Lady Making Tea	Thiebaud	Various Cakes
Chardin	Basket of Wild Strawberries	Vlaminck	Still Life with Pears and Grapes
Chardin	Glass of Water and Coffee Pot	Vlaminck	Still Life

▬ ▬ ▬ ▬ ▬ ▬ ▬ *Good professional practice* ▬ ▬ ▬ ▬ ▬ ▬

When using these items, entering into discussions with the children about the foods they contained can reinforce teaching about healthy eating choices.

Resources

Many well-planned resources for supporting teaching about food, diet, nutrition and health are available and suitable for use with young children. Some of them are free! Some descriptions and contacts are given in Resources Section at the end of the book.

A final thought about the importance of teaching young children about food and healthy eating

Although it is very important for meaningful 'joined-up' learning that young children are helped to make links and understand relevances in learning a myriad of subjects, **there is no substitute for explicitly teaching children about food and nutrition, about their rights and personal responsibilities to eat food that will promote their growth and development, sustain their energy requirements and keep them healthy and safe.**

To enable children to be able to make appropriate choices and acquire the fundamental life skills needed to eat a healthy balanced diet they need carefully planned early years guidance, care and teaching.

The role of the early years professional is central to ensuring children are nurtured and actively and effectively taught about food, nutrition, diet and healthy living.

END OF CHAPTER ACTIVITY

You are going to plan to make a cheese and vegetable pasta dish and a fruit jelly.

1. With a colleague jot down ingredients and list each task involved in the preparation, making and clearing up.

2. Next to each task indicate if and how you could enable an almost three year old to actively take part, or to be appropriately involved in some way. (Remember that children learn best by doing and not just watching! But safety is critical.)

3. Underline in red any task where you think it would not be appropriate or safe for the child to help. Next to these write a brief

note giving your reason. How would you keep the child interested at these times?

4. What special care, planning and provision is necessary to ensure the child can safely and successfully help with the meal? What do you need to do which would not be necessary if you were cooking the meal by yourself?

5. Share and compare your work with the rest of your group:
(a) Did you all agree on the kinds of tasks where a child could be safely involved?
(b) Is the child as activity involved as possible? Or is she being subjected to your 'cookery demonstration'?
(c) If the child said she did not really like broccoli, carrots and bananas, would you include: none of these in the meal? all of them? one of them?

6. What differences would you make to your planning, organisation, supervision and management of this activity if you were doing it with three children rather than just one?

Quick quiz

Find the answers in the chapter.

1. List four safety features you might choose to promote when cooking with children.

2. What problems might be caused by your insisting a reluctant child tries a taste of a food?

3. Name five nursery rhymes which contain references to food.

4. In which terms are St Patrick's, St Andrew's, St George's and St David's Days? Name a national food from each respective country which children could make and eat to mark the patron saint's day.

5. List five foods which could be used in cooking and science to show physical changes of state.

6. If a child talks about 'more than', 'next', 'beside', 'half' or ' after', what specialist or subject language is she using?

7. During which activities would it be particularly effective to talk to the children about healthy eating and how and why their bodies use energy?

8. Why is it vitally important to teach children about the importance of drinking water?

9. Name three things that children could effectively learn about food by (a) visiting a farm (b) gardening (c) visiting local shops.

10. Why is it good practice to invite parents and grandparents into the nursery or classroom?

Summary

Having studied this chapter you should now understand:

- the importance of teaching children about food, nutrition and healthy eating and what children need to know
- how a whole school policy for food can help to ensure children's entitlement to be taught and to learn about food, nutrition and health
- the place and importance of food in the curriculum and how meaningful links can be made with all areas of the curriculum
- the need for food safety, nutrition and healthy eating to be ensured and explicitly taught to all young children.

Practical Teaching Resources for Early Years Professionals and Parents

Books, booklets and leaflets

The Key to Diabetes
Informs and reassures, gives help on understanding diabetes and its management for children. [Channel 4 Schools; 1998]

The Lunch Bunch
Songs, recipes, experiments. The balanced diet. Food production, food groups, festivals and celebrations. [Channel 4 Schools; 1999]

Food a Fact of Life: Stage 1
Resource kit about food production and nutrition. [British Nutritional Foundation]

Enjoy Fruit and Veg
A leaflet about fruit and vegetables and why they are good for you, how to enjoy eating more of them, and contains recipes. [Health Education Authority]

Smiling for Life
Free pack containing:
Book – *Nutrition and Oral Health: Guidelines for Pre-schools*; a set of 10 activity sheets plus an introduction leaflet;
Booklet – *Smile*; written for parents containing information about nutrition and children's dental and oral health, with some recipes. [Health Education Authority]

Smile
Smile a booklet written for parents to support nutrition and oral health for young children. [National Dairy Council]

Eating Well for Under-5s in Child Care
(Available from PO Box 5, Manchester M60 3GE.)
Provides a set of practical guidelines to help professionals (nannies, childminders, nursery cooks, etc.) working with the under-fives to develop appropriate and nutritional menus which achieve a sound nutritional balance.

Further Reading: Useful Books to Support Practical Activities with Children

The Nursery Food Book
by Whiting, Mary & Lobstein, Tim (1998) Arnold, Hodder Headline Group. (ISBN: 0340 71894 3)
A useful clear comprehensive and practical book. Some chapters contain suggested appropriate activities and ideas for giving children food related experiences in a variety of settings, e.g. gardening, cooking, art and games.

Babies and Toddlers Good Food
by Clark, Pamela (ed.) (1999) The Australian Women's Weekly Cook Books; ACP Publishing Ltd. (ISBN: 1 86936 103 8)
A well illustrated recipe book with a very good range of recipes for every occasion and attractive serving suggestions. Suitable foods aimed at babies, toddlers and young children with recipes grouped in age bands, but dishes will appeal to all ages including adults!

Fun and Food for Playgroups
More Fun and Food for Playgroups
[Available from the Pre-School Learning Alliance, published by West Midlands Pre-School Playgroups Association.]
Practical ideas for activities for young children. The titles say it all!

Healthy Food for Healthy Children
by Duff, Gail (1989) Conran Octopus Ltd. (ISBN: 1 85029 1837)
Contains recipes, practical activities and good commonsense explanations. Ideas also for parties and packed lunches, etc.

Great Grub for Toddlers – Fuss Free Food for Babies and Under 5s
by Clarke, Cas (1998) Hodder Headline Plc. (ISBN 0 74725 6624)
Mainly recipes, ideas for parties, also eating out with young children. Full of practical handy hints.

Equipment, games and materials.

The Replica Food Set and Game
Food identification game, using pictures of single foods and word labels.
[British Nutritional Foundation]

Balance of Good Health Play Mat
Large plastic mat marked with plate model, suitable for sorting, classifying, choosing favourites, etc. to teach balance of good health. [Newcastle Nutrition]

The Plate Game
Game to help children make choices, reflect on and understand foods they eat. [Newcastle Nutrition]

The Adventures of Safe-T and the H Squad
Free food hygiene teaching pack aimed at 7–10-year-olds but contains useful information, posters, activities and ideas, including children's board game 'Bubble & Slime', which can be adapted and used with younger children. Also could part form displays to inform parents. Order code: X1001. [EC Publications]

Happy Heart 1 and *Happy Heart's Playground Games Pack*
Resources for 4–7-year-olds promoting links between heart health and physical activity.
Covers national Curriculum Key Stage 1. [Health Education Authority]

Posters:

Gorilla – Fruit and Veg, Polar Bear – Fruit and Veg, Pack a Healthy Lunch and *Strike a Healthy Balance*
Examples of range promoting wide variety of information and topics about food suitable for young children. [Health Education Authority]

Now wash your hands
Fun poster for encouraging personal hygiene in young children. [Health Education Authority]

Balance of Good Health Plate Model
Cartoon type, zany interpretation of conventional model. [East Surrey Health Promotion]

Addresses for Resources and Information

Milk is Cool Educational Project
Resources
Freepost NH4190
Northampton NN17 4WN

The National Dairy Council.
5–7 John Princes Street
London W1M 0AP
www.milk.co.uk

The Health Development Agency
Trevelyan House
30 Great Peter Street
London SW1P 2HW
www.hda.online.org.uk

The Health Education Customer
Services
Marston Book Services
PO Box 269
Abingdon
Oxon OX14 4YN

East Surrey Health Promotion
West Park Road
Horton Lane
Epsom
Surrey KT19 8PH

The EC Publishing Distribution
Centre
European Commission
SR House
Blackhorse Road
London SE8 3 JR
Tel: 020 7463 8177

Channel 4 Schools
PO Box 100
Warwick
CV34 6TZ

The Sugar Bureau
Duncan House
Dolphin Square
London SW1W 3PW

British Potato Council
Public Relations Manager
4300 Nash Court
John Smith Drive
Oxford OX4 2RT

British Fluoridation Society
Fourth Floor
University of Liverpool School of
Dentistry
Liverpool L69 3BX

Oral B Laboratories
Educational Project Resources
Freepost NH4190
Corby
Northants NN17 4WN
www.oralb.com

Del Monte Foods (UK)
Del Monte House
London Road
Staines
Middlesex TW18 4JD

The Food & Farming Education
Service
National Agricultural Centre
Stoneleigh Park
Warwickshire CV8 2LZ

Food Sense Booklets (MAFF)
Admail 6000
London SW1A 2XX

EC Publishing Distribution Centre
020 7463 8177

National Health Service
Health Development Agency
Trevelyan House
30 Great Peter Street
London SW1P 2HW

Newcastle Nutrition
Royal Victoria Infirmary
Queen Victoria Road
Newcastle-upon-Tyne NE1 4LP

DfEE Publications
PO Box 5050
Annesley
Nottingham NG15 0DJ
www.wiredforhealth.gov.uk

Qualifications and Curriculum
Authority Publications
Tel: 01787 884444
Fax: 01787 312950
www.qca.org.uk/

The Stationery Office
Publications Centre
PO Box 276
London SW8 5DT
Tel: 0870 600 5522
Fax: 0870 600 5533
www.tso-online.co.uk

Food and Nutrition Contact Addresses

The Food Commission
3rd Floor
Viking House
5–11 Worship Street
London EC2A 2BH

The Soil Association
Organic Food and Farming Centre
86 Colston Street
Bristol BS1 5BB

Ministry of Agriculture (MAFF)
Consumer Helpline: 00345 573012
Food Safety Information Bulletin:
0171 238 6335
Foodsense Booklets: 0645 556000

The Health Education Authority
Trevelyan House
30 Great Portland Street
London SW1P 2HW
www.quick.org.uk

The Vegetarian Society
Parkdale
Dunham Road
Altrincham
Cheshire WA14 4QG
www.veg.org/veg/Orgs/VegSocUK/
(*produces guides on nutrition for
pregnant women and children*)

The Vegan Society
7 Battle Road
St Leonards-on-Sea
East Sussex TN37 7AA

SAFE (Sustainable Agriculture, Food
and Environment) Alliance
94 White Lion Street
London N1 9PF

The Pesticides Trust
Eurolink Centre
49 Effra Road
London SW2 1BZ
www.gn.apc.org/pesticidestrust

United Kingdom Register of
Organic Food Standards
Room G43/44
Nobel House
17 Smith Square
London SW1P 3JR

Organic Food Federation
The Tithe House
Peaseland Green
Elsing
East Dereham
Norfolk NR20 3DY

The British Nutrition Foundation
High Holborn House
52–58 High Holborn
London WC1V 6RQ

Contacts for Information on Pregnancy and Babies

National Childbirth Trust
Alexandra House
Oldham Terrace
London W3 6NH

Association of Breastfeeding
Mothers
Sydenham Green Health Centre
26 Holnshaw Close
London SE26 4TH

La Leche League
PO Box BM 3424
London WC1N 3XX

Sainsbury's/Wellbeing Eating for
Pregnancy Helpline
Centre for Pregnancy Nutrition
University of Sheffield
Department of Obstetrics and
Gynaecology
Northern General Hospital
Herries Road
Sheffield S5 7AU

Department of Health
PO Box 410
Wetherby
LS23 7LN

Baby Milk Action
23 St Andrew's Street
Cambridge
CB2 3AX

Organisations giving Specialist Information and Support for Special Needs

The Anaphylaxis Campaign
PO Box 149
Fleet
Hampshire GU13 9 XU

Action Against Allergy
PO Box 278
Twickenham
Middlesex TW1 4QQ

Association for Spina Bifida and
Hydrocephalus (ASBAH)
ASBAH House
42 Park Road
Peterborough PE1 2UQ

British Diabetic Association
10 Queen Anne Street
London W1M 0BD

British Dietetic Association
7th Floor
Elizabeth House
22 Suffolk Street
Queensway
Birmingham B1 1LS

Cleft Lip and Palate Association (CLAPA)
134 Buckingham Palace Road
London SW1A 9SA
0171 824 8110

Crohn's in Childhood Research Association
Parkgate House
356 West Barnes Road
Motspur Park
Surrey KT3 6NB

CRY-SIS (Crying Babies)
0171 404 5011

The Disabled Living Foundation
380–384 Harrow Road
London W9 2HU
0870 603 9177

Eating Disorders Association
1st Floor Wensum House
103 Prince of Wales Road
Norwich NR1 1DW
01603 621414

Hyperactive Children's Support Group
71 Whyke Lane
Chichester
West Sussex PO19 2LD

Makaton Vocabulary Development Project
31 Firwood Drive
Camberley
Surrey GU15 3QD

National Portage Association
127 Monks Dale
Yeovil
Somerset BA21 3JE

Play Matters (*information on play and special needs*)
68 Churchway
London NW1 1LT

Sense (*for deaf-blind/rubella support*)
11–13 Clifton Terrace
London N4 3SR

Twins and Multiple Births Association
PO Box 30 Little Sutton
South Wirral
Liverpool L661TH

REFERENCES

Brand Miller, Prof. Jennie (1998). *G.I. Index*. Hodder & Stoughton: London.

Stanton, Marion (1997) *The Cerebral Palsy Handbook: A Practical Guide for Parents and Carers* 2nd edition. Vermillion: London. (NB Chapter 4)

Lawrence, Ann (1998) *Understanding Food Additives*. CIEC: University of York, England.

Greenberg, Karen B. (1993) *The Complete Guide to Children's Dental Care from Pre-natal through Teens*. Health Monitor Press: Southampton, N.Y.

Kidd, Edwina A. M. & Joyston-Bechal, Sally (1997). *Essentials of Dental Caries*. Oxford Medical Publications.

Hudson, Philippa & Symonds, Catherine (1996) *Nutrition and Food Hygiene*. Hodder & Stoughton: London.

Harvey, Joe & Passmore, Sandra (1994). *A New Policy For Managing Food and Nutrition in Schools*. Birmingham Health Education Unit.

Lowe, C. F. et al (1997) *The Psychological Determinants of Children's Food Preferences*. University of Wales: Bangor.

Lowe, Dowey, Fleming & Horne (1995) *An Effective Procedure for Changing Food Preferences in 5–7 year old Children*. University of Wales: Bangor.

Murcroft, Anne (ed.) (1998) *The Nation's Diet: The Social Science of Food Choice*. Economic & Social Research Council. Addison Wesley Longman Ltd: London.

Dietary Reference Values for Food and Nutrients for the United Kingdom, Report on Health and Social Subjects, No. 41 (1991) HMSO: London.

Weaning and the Weaning Diet (1994) Committee on Medical Aspects of Food Policy. HMSO: London.

Good Nutrition for Infants and Pre-school Children: A Practical Interpretation of the DH Report 'Weaning & the Weaning Diet' (1996) The National Dairy Council: London.

Child Support Handbook 1999/2000, 7th Edition. (June 1999) Child Poverty Action Group UK.

Poor Kids: Trends in Childhood Poverty in Britain 1968–96 (1999) Institute of Fiscal Studies: London.

Health Survey of Children and Young People (1998/0587) Department of Health. HMSO: London.

School Meals: Public Provision and Children's Health (1999) East Midlands Unison.

School Meals: First Report of Education & Employment Committee (1999) The Stationery Office: London.

What are Today's Children Eating? The Gardner Merchant School Meals Survey (1998) Gardner Merchant UK.

Ingredients for Success (1998) DfEE Consultation Paper.

Eating Well for Under-5s in Child Care (1998) Caroline Walker Trust.

Nutritional Guidelines for School Meals Caroline Walker Trust.

Diets of British School Children (1989) Department of Health. The Stationery Office: London.

National Healthy School Standard Guidance (1999) Department of Education and Employment Publications: Nottingham.

The 1992 National Food Survey (1993) Ministry of Agriculture, Foods and Fisheries (MAFF).

The National Food Survey (1997) Ministry of Agriculture, Fisheries and Food. The Stationery Office: London

How Green Are Our Apples? Report of the Sustainable Agriculture, Food and Environment Alliance.

The Pear Essentials. Report of the Sustainable Agriculture, Food and Environment Alliance.

Food Sense: Series of Booklets. Guides from the Ministry of Agriculture, Fisheries and Food.

Drinking Water in Schools (1999) Department of Public Health Medicine, Leeds Health Authority.

Improving Children's Diets (1997) School of Psychology: University of Wales, Bangor.

Voluntary Labelling Guidelines to Benefit the Consumer (1998) Institute of Grocery Distribution.

Dietary Sugars and Human Disease (1989) Committee on Medical Aspects of Food Policy. HMSO: London.

Bunting, Grace & Freeman, Ruth (2000) 'The Influence of socio-demographic factors upon children's breaktime food consumption in North and West Belfast'. *Health Education Journal*, Volume 58, Number 4.

Dowler, E. A. (1998) 'Food poverty and food policy' *IDS Bulletin 29*, 58–65.

Dowler, E. A. & Pryer, J. 'Socio-economic status: relationship with diet and nutritional status' in Sadler, M. J. (ed.) *Encyclopaedia of Human Nutrition* (1998) Academic Press: London.

Watt, R. G. (2000) 'A national survey of infant feeding in Asian families: summary of findings relevant to oral health' *British Dental Journal*, Volume 188, Number 1.

Moynihan, P. J., Ferrier, S. & Jenkins, G. N. (1999) 'The cariostatic potential of cheese: cooked cheese-containing meals increase plaque calcium concentration' *British Dental Journal*, Volume 187, Number 12.

Levine, R. S. (1999) 'Briefing paper: oral aspects of dummy and digit sucking' *British Dental Journal*, Volume 186.

Bender, A. E. & Bender, D. A. *Food Tables* (reprinted 1995) Oxford.

Food and Nutrition; Guidance on Food and Nutrition in Primary Teacher Training (1998) Department of Health: London.

The National Curriculum – Handbook for Primary Teachers in England (1999) DfEE. The Stationery Office: London.

Curriculum Guidance for the Foundation Stage (2000) DfEE. Ref. QCA/00/587. QCA Publications.

Index

absorption, of food 25, 27, 28
acids, food additives 233
activity, and energy needs 72
advertising, and choice 60, 176–7
alcohol, DOH guidelines 6
allergic reactions *see* food allergies;
    food intolerance
alpha-linolenic acid 44–5
amino acids 27, 28, 39, 41–2, 192
anaemia 196
anaphylactic shock 199
anti-caking agents 234
antibacterial cleaning agents 224
antioxidants 59, 233
art, and food 281–2
attitudes to food *see* eating habits

babies
    energy needs 71, 104, 130
    feeding 88–109, 134
    growth rates 88
    iron 114, 122
    milk products 79
    nutritional needs 87
    protein requirement 44
    teeth 238–9
    weaning 113–36
    see also children; newborn babies;
        young children
bacteria *see* food bacteria
Balance of Good Health model 73–81
'best before' dates 213
bonding, through feeding 88, 97
bones, poor growth 196
bottle feeding 100–9
    giving a bottle 108–9
    making up formula 103
bottled food, 'use by' date 223
bread 49, 76–7, 162, 192
    storage 222
breakfast clubs 172–3
breast feeding 90, 91–9
    frequency and duration 95
    medication and 99
    nutrition for 93
    position of baby 94, 99
    problems 98–9
    shape of nipples 93
breast milk
    composition 96–7, 98
    food hygiene 99, 106–7

calories 19, 68, 71, 85
    see also energy
carbohydrates 15, 16, 31, 37–9, 40
    in Group 1 foods 76–7
    served with fats 16
caries *see* tooth decay
cereal 49, 76–7, 162, 192
cheese, in protecting teeth 250
child development, and food 125,
    142, 261, 262, 265

children
    amino acid requirement 41
    with disabilities, eating 185–90
    fat requirement 47
    healthy eating 70–1
    influences on eating habits 2–3,
        10–11, 143–6, 171
    learning about nutrition 25–7,
        263, 265–83
    need for milk 79
    need for minerals 51
    need for vitamins 59
    obesity and overweight 47, 68
    see also babies; young children
choking, causes 126, 140, 188
cleanliness 131, 223, 277
coeliac disease 200–1
colic 134
colon 27
colostum (breast milk) 96
COMA (Committee on Medical
    Aspects of Food Policy)
    recommendations
    on labelling 212
    on weaning 113
commercial baby foods 131–2
complete proteins 41–2
complex carbohydrates 38, 40
conflict, management of 149–51
constipation 134, 196
contamination, of food 215
convalescence, nutrition in 205–7
cooked food, for eating later 227
cooking, to destroy bacteria 225
cow's milk 101, 204
cultural differences
    in food choices 24, 181–2
    influences on eating habits 144
    professional response 185
    in weaning 116
cultures, food in festivals 267–9
curriculum, and food 263, 265–82
customs, and diet 181–3
cystic fibrosis 201

daily servings 77–81, 128
dairy products 78–9, 162, 192
dance, exploring food 279
dehydration 27, 62
dental disease *see* tooth decay
dental health 238, 248, 249–50
Department of Health, guidelines
    on healthy eating 6–7
diabetes 202–3
diarrhoea 27, 135, 197, 207
diet 24
diet drinks 17
dietary fibre 6, 27, 32, 48–50
    effect of excess in children 33
dietary problems
    resulting from poverty 160
    vegetarian diets 191–4

dietary problems (*continued*)
    young children 195–7
dietetics 23
diets
    for diabetes 203
    exclusion 197, 199, 201, 202,
        204–5
    'food combining' 15
    gluten free 201
    lactose free 204
    low fat, in children 47
    for PKU 202
    in pregnancy 85–87
    therapeutic 197
    vegetarian/vegan 16, 191–5
    weight loss, drawbacks 4, 67–8
digestion 25–7, 28, 43
disabled children
    equipment 187, 189–90
    food preparation 187
    independence 189
    management of eating 185–90
    oral hygiene 242
disaccharides 38
drama, exploring food 279, 280
drinks
    effects on teeth 244, 246
    in illness 206
duodenum 26

E numbers 234
eating habits 72
    establishing 150
    influences on 2–3, 10, 11, 143–6,
        171
    see also healthy eating
eggs
    cooking 226
    digestion of 15
    food intolerance 204
    storage 222
    in weaning 123
    see also dairy products
emulsifiers 233
energy
    body's storage mechanism 67
    nutrients for 30–2
    sources 69
    see also calories
energy needs 29, 67, 72
    babies 71, 104, 130
    children 38, 70, 73
    frequency of meals 145
    individual differences 140–1, 142
    in pregnancy 85
    three to four year olds 142–3
english, learning about food 270–3
enjoyment, of food 7, 133, 141
environmental health officers 219
enzymes, in digestion 26
equipment, for disabled child 187,
    189–90

essential nutrients 28, 31–2, 234
  balance in weaning 120
  in food groups 73–4
  in pregnancy 85
exclusion diets 197, 199, 201, 202,
    204–5
excretion 28
extrinsic sugars 39
  effect on teeth 244

family foods *see* home cooked meals
fast food 16–17
fat
  consumption 19
  DOH guidelines 6
fat soluble vitamins 55
fat stores 19, 67
fat-rich foods 31, 40, 45, 80–1,
    162, 193
fats 26, 31, 32, 44
  in group 3 foods 78
  served with carbohydrates 16
fatty acids 26, 27, 44–6
fibre *see* dietary fibre
finger foods 124–5
first class protein 41–2
fish 79–80
flavour enhancers 234
flavourings 233
flour improvers 234
fluids, in illness 206
folic acid, in pregnancy 59, 86
food
  enjoyment 7, 133, 141
  purchase
    on a budget 162–3
    safety 220–1
  see also shopping
food additives 233–5
food allergies 134, 197–9, 200, 204
food bacteria 28, 215, 217–18, 225
  risk in pregnancy 85
  see also food poisoning
food choices
  factors determining 24, 60, 176–7
  effect of variety 145
'food combining' diet 15
food education *see* learning
    opportunities; teaching about
    food
food groups 73–81
  cheaper healthy options 162–3
food hygiene 28, 233
  in bottle feeding 104, 105–7
  expressed breast milk 99, 106–7
food intolerances 197, 204
food labelling 212–14
  additives 232, 235
  checking for allergies 205
  GM foods 232
  instructions for storage 222
  sugar content 245
food myths 12–19
food poisoning 85, 214–19
  prevention 219
  see also food bacteria

food preparation 78
  cleanliness 223
  for disabled child 187
  and minerals 56–8
  participation 152, 261–2
  preserving vitamins 56–8
food products 24
food refusal 147, 153–4, 197
food safety 131, 219–30
  buying food 220–1
  key points 229–30
  in teaching children 263–4
  in weaning 131
Food Safety Act (1990) 219–20
food storage 212, 221–2
  formula/breast milk 106–7
  vitamin rich foods 56–8
foods
  harmful in pregnancy 85–6
  introduction of 119, 122, 140
  for weaning 120–1, 122–3, 128
foremilk 97
formula feeding *see* bottle feeding
free school meals 165–6, 171–2
frequency of food
  and energy needs 145
  and tooth decay 246
frozen food 19, 223
fructose 26, 27
fruit 32, 40, 45, 49, 77–8, 162, 192
  in weaning 120–1, 122
fruit juice 17, 246

gardening, and food 277
gelling agents 233
genetically modified (GM) food 231–2
geography, origins of food 276–8
glucose 26, 27, 28, 38
glycogen 38
'good' and 'bad' foods 6, 13, 17
Group foods 76–81, 162–3
growth 11–12, 196
  and energy needs 72
growth rates, babies 88
gum disease 243

harmful foods
  babies 119, 120 128, 129
  in pregnancy 85–6
  for teeth 39, 245–6
HBV proteins 41–2
health 1–2
  and poverty 160
health disorders 200–5
healthy eating 5–7, 70–1, 75
  DoH guidelines 6–7
  key points 81
  on limited budget 161, 162–3
  principles for development 153
  social factors affecting 159
  teaching principles 255–6, 283
hindmilk 98
history, researching food 278
home cooked meals 123, 124, 132
hyperglycaemic attacks 203
hypoglycaemic (hypo) attacks 203

IDF (insoluble dietary fibre) 48–50
incomplete proteins 41–2
independence
  for disabled child 189
  in eating 139
  in weaning 125, 133
  young child 141, 142
individual differences 140–1, 142,
    181, 186
information technology, and food
    273–5
intrinsic sugars 39
  effect on teeth 243–4
iron
  for babies 98, 114, 122
  children's requirement 51
  deficiency 196
  in pregnancy 51, 59
  in vegetarian diet 192, 194

kidneys, function 28

lactose intolerance 204
LBV proteins 41–2
learning opportunities, in
    curriculum 263, 265–82
lifestyle
  and culture/religion 181–3
  effect on family meals 144
linoleic acid 44
literature about food 270–1
liver 27
  role in protein digestion 43
'low fat' foods 14–15
low income
  healthy diet on a budget 161,
    162–3
  effect on healthy eating 159

mathematics, and food 273–5
meat, lean 17
meat and meat alternatives 31–2,
    40–1, 45, 79–80, 162, 192–3
meat products, introduction 122
medication
  in breast feeding 99
  and sugar content 245
metabolism 23
metabolites 23, 26, 27
milk
  avoidance, in illness 206
  composition of types 18
  for under fives 140
milk production, breast feeding 93
milk products 78–9, 162, 192
  for healthy teeth 238, 244,
    249–50
  infant formulas 101
  introduction in weaning 122
milk sugars, effect on teeth 244
minerals 6, 32, 51–4, 56–8, 59
  in Group 2 foods 77
misconceptions, about food 12–19
monosaccharides 38
monounsaturates 45–6
music, exploring food 281

National Healthy School Standard
(1999) 257–8
'new' foods *see* protein rich foods
newborn babies, feeding 87–9
nursery school meals, standards 168
nutrients *see* essential nutrients

obesity 19, 80, 196
in children 47, 68
oral habits, effects on teeth 239
oral hygiene *see* dental health
organic food 230–1
overfeeding 135
overweight 47, 68, 120

packed lunches 228
parents *see supporting parents*
participation, in food preparation
152, 261–2
pepsin 26
peristalsis 26, 27
personal hygiene 223
physical education and healthy
eating 279
PKU (phenylketonuria) 202
plaque 242, 247
poly-unsaturates 45–6
polysaccharides 26, 38
portions, recommendations 76–81
possetting 135
potatoes 76–7, 162, 192
poultry 17–18
poverty, and healthy eating 159
pregnancy
good nutrition in 85–7
need for minerals 51, 59
preservatives 233
primary school meals, nutritional
standards 169
proportions, of food 74, 75, 81
protein 15, 192
body's requirement for 43–4
digestion of 26, 43
protein rich foods, commercial
development 43
proteins 31, 39, 41–3
in Group 3 foods 78–9
pureed food, in weaning 119, 121

raising agents 234
recommended daily totals 9
'reduced fat' foods 14–15
reheating cooked food 227
religion
effect on diet 181–3
food and festivals 267–9
reluctance to eat 147, 149–51,
153–4, 197
see also conflict management
roughage *see* dietary fibre

saccharides 37–9
safety
of children preparing food 152,
263–4

safety (*continued*)
food handling 131, 219–30
saliva 26, 207, 246, 248
salt, harmful for babies 119
saturated fats 45–6
school meals 11, 165–76
social importance 170
storage of packed lunches 228
'School Meals' DoEE report 167
schools, whole school policy and
healthy eating 258
science, and cooking 275–6
SDF (insoluble dietary fibre) 49–50
second class proteins 41–2
'sell by' dates 213
shopping
taking food home 221
with young children 261
see also food, purchase
simple carbohydrates 38, 40
snacks, for babies 130
solids, introduction of 119–27
songs, about food 280
sore throat, suitable foods 207
soya 204
spoons, for weaning 116, 119
stabilisers 23
starches 38
state benefits
free school meals 165–6, 171–2
for low income families 160–1
sterilisation 99, 105–6, 131
stomach, function 26
sugar-rich foods 6, 31, 40, 45,
80–1, 162, 193
sugars 38, 39
in Group 3 foods 78
supervision, of babies 126, 131
supporting parents
babies' feeding 90–2, 100
of disabled children 188
discussing concerns 150
on low incomes 164
managing conflict 150
placement information 144
weaning 118, 134
sweeteners 233

'TAKE 5' 6, 78
TB, increase in children 166
teaching about food 256–7, 260–1,
262, 263, 265–82, 283
teeth *see* dental health; tooth decay
textured foods, in weaning 122–3
tinned food 222–3
toddlers *see* young children
tooth decay 17, 63, 80, 135, 196,
242–4
in babies 241
causes 239
damaging foods 39, 245–6
frequency of food 246
prevention 247, 249, 250
see also dental health
'tooth friendly' sweets and drinks 244

trainer cups 123, 240–1
treats, nutritious 250
tuberculosis, in children 166

underfeeding 135
underweight 196
unsaturated fats 45–6
'use by' dates 213

vegan diets 191
vegetables 32, 40, 41, 45, 49, 77–8,
162, 192
fresh and frozen 19
in weaning 120–1, 123
vegetarian diets 43, 191–5
problems and deficiencies 191,
192–3, 194
vitamins 6, 18, 32, 55–8
drops 124, 140
in Group 2 foods 77
in pregnancy 86
preserving in food preparation 78
supplements 59–60

waste products 28
water 32, 60–2, 206, 207
absorption 27, 28
after physical activity 279
daily requirements 60, 61
water soluble vitamins 55
weaning
4–6 months 118–21, 128
6–9 months 121–4, 128
9–12 months 124–7, 128
appropriate time 113–15
feeding plan 128–9
food safety 131
learning process 117
role of professional 115–16, 118,
134
supervision of baby 126, 140
weight loss diets 4, 67–8

'yo-yo' diets 4, 67–8
young children
conflict over food 148–51
dietary problems 195–7
eating habits, influences 143–6
food poisoning 216
healthy diet guidelines 75
independence 141, 142
learning about food 255–7,
265–83
nutritional needs 139–40
school meals, standards 167–8
see also babies; children; newborn
babies